THE VERY BEST OF
STEVE CHANDLER

THE VERY BEST OF

STEVE CHANDLER

MAURICE BASSETT

To Kathy

Contents

Wealth | 65

Relationships | 115

Mind | 175

Choices | 245

Mind | 175

Presence | 293

Recovery | 341

Creativity | 385

Courage | 447

THE VERY BEST OF

STEVE
CHANDLER

The keys to the kingdom

A re you a cake person?

When one of Steve Chandler's coaching clients explained that she was, and that this was why she couldn't resist a piece of cake, it took Steve by surprise:

> Her words hit me like a ton of bricks . . . I'd never heard it described that way . . . *I'm a cake person!* Up until that very moment I didn't know I could *be* a cake person. I thought it was always about the eating of the cake. . . about bad choices in the moment. Choices that lead to my plump stomach. But what if? What if I'm a cake person? Then when someone points out that I'm violating my paleo diet commitment by eating cake, I can simply let them know that the choice is not mine. Why? I'm a cake person.

Anyone who's read more than a few pages of Steve Chandler's remarkable body of work—more than thirty books on subjects as diverse as business, fundraising, creativity, time management, mindfulness, recovery and coaching—knows that this is just the beginning of the story.

In fact it's the beginning of everyone's story. As we grow up and the innocence and joy of childhood slip away, we gradually

xvi | *The Very Best of Steve Chandler*

accumulate labels (beliefs, ideas, and so on) that we come to accept as definitions of who we are. Maybe we wear them loosely at first, but eventually they become straightjackets. "I'm a procrastinator, I'm lazy, I'm an introvert, I'm just an anxious person, I can't stop drinking, I'm nobody, I'm a liberal, I'm a conservative, I'm bad at math, I'm a cake person . . ." And we add more generalized beliefs to the list: "Life is hard, money is evil, you always lose, there's no point in doing anything."

As Steve writes,

> We slap labels of permanence and frozen characteristics onto what was formerly unlimited joyful energy . . . We pin ourselves down. We chain ourselves up . . . We now struggle and strain against life . . . but we are really just struggling and straining against the way we have labeled ourselves.

In moments of profound contentment or joy or creativity or concentrated action, those labels slip off all by themselves and we get glimpses of who we are at our essence—and of how we could be all the time if we lost the labels.

But how do we do *that*?

This book is a great place to start.

It has gradually dawned on me that what Steve Chandler offers in his writing is nothing short of the keys to the kingdom. Said another way, Steve's work invites you to break the ice of who you think you are and rejoin the flow of life. Most of our problems arise from feelings of being stuck, and most of those feelings of being stuck arise from our limited notions of who we are. Steve shows us that our limits are largely self-created.

He also shows us how to free ourselves from the prison of our beliefs. The British philosopher Colin Wilson, an author both Steve and I admire, devoted his life to elucidating what he called the "mechanisms of consciousness" that allow us to express our limitless creative potential. Steve does the same thing, in his own inimitable way. His work explores our fundamental freedom to *create who we want to be in the world.* From here, the possibilities are endless.

Steve's writing is an invigorating combination of the utterly practical and the utterly profound. He draws inspiration and ideas from music, poetry, literature, sports, business, coaching, and his own rich and occasionally tumultuous life. Reading Steve often feels like having a relaxed conversation with a good friend. He's so approachable, in fact, that at first it's easy to miss the wisdom packed into every paragraph. On one page he's talking about eating cake, and on the next you realize you've just glimpsed the fundamental problem of human experience and what to do about it.

If there were any need to justify *The Very Best of Steve Chandler*, this would be it. Most of us who've read Steve have also *re*-read Steve to our benefit. Not just because we missed something the first time around, but because as we grow, we catch up with what he's sharing. With each read, we see his wisdom— and ourselves—in a new light. In Steve's school for coaches, *Advanced Client Systems*, there was an adage that went: "Read once for information, twice for transformation." One could read Steve three, four, five times, and the transformations would continue; his work is a gift that keeps on giving.

Although this book weighs in at a hefty five-hundred or so pages, it could have easily been much longer. It is a daunting task to select the "best" of a writer with so prolific and diverse a body of work. One guiding light was that Steve wanted to create a book that would appeal to everyone, regardless of their profession. Accordingly, we set some parameters, the most noticeable of which is that we have not included selections from his seminal books on coaching, such as *The Prosperous Coach* (with Rich Litvin) and *How to Get Clients*. Also left off the "greatest hits" playlist, for example, is material from his excellent novel (*The Woman Who Attracted Money*), his informal and playful literary commentary (e.g., *Two Guys Read Jane Austen*, with Terrence Hill) and anything more than snippets from his days making a living as a songwriter (with Fred Knipe).

What you *will* find in these pages is quintessential Steve Chandler: stories, ideas, humor, insights, compassion and love, buoyed on the undercurrent of an almost painfully poignant and joyous recognition of life's beauty. *The Very Best of Steve Chandler* can serve as a compass that guides you home. Steve shares:

> I used to wander the earth wondering what I "should" do and how I should do it. I'd look outside myself for all the answers. But the answers were inside me all along. I always knew much more than I thought I knew. I always had all the resources I ever needed to solve my problems in life. And so do all the people I know today. They've got all they need. There is a creative spirit inside each one of them, ready to self-express and find the next action.

Here, as in all of his writing, Steve invites us to explore the undiscovered country of ourselves, and to share what we find with the world.

Chris Nelson
Seattle, Washington
June 2022

Introduction

Change is great unless you think about it

I was the shadow of the waxwing slain
By the false azure in the windowpane;
I was the smudge of ashen fluff—and I
Lived on, flew on, in the reflected sky.

~ Vladimir Nabokov
Pale Fire

As my talented editor, Chris Nelson, and I were selecting these short pieces of writing, it was like choosing chips of tiles for a mosaic, and it occurred to me that they all reflected a common theme.

There was an answer to the question, "And your point is?"

And that answer is: People can change.

Back in the late 1970s, when I was learning to change from being an alcoholic to being a person, I started my lifelong obsession with how people change. (In fact, it began earlier than that, if I'm honest, when I was a weakling of a boy, around age ten, seeing an advertisement on the back of a comic book selling a Charles Atlas course in "Dynamic Tension" [isometrics, it turned out to be] that said it would change you into a muscular marvel that bullies would no longer torment. I sent away for the course and used it. I began to look and feel different. I discovered that a person could change . . . at least physically.)

In the 1980s, as I learned that one could live sober, my brain became restored to clarity and I pounced on books about psychology, like Allen Wheelis's *How People Change* and Nathaniel Branden's *Six Pillars of Self-Esteem.*

As brilliant and as helpful as those books were, I still marveled at the superior rapidity and thoroughness of changes I saw happening in me and my fellow participants in the 12-step meetings I was attending. I asked my sponsor why he thought that was, and he said, "Because we go places psychology isn't reaching. We focus on the spiritual."

That wasn't easy for me to understand back then. Like most people, I associated spirituality with religion, and I'd joined the clique of literati, psychologists, and contemporary Western philosophers who either quietly dismissed, or openly made mock of religion and its attendant "myths" about supernatural beings needing to be worshipped. I had studied literature and poetry in college and developed an exaggerated and misguided picture of myself as an atheistic intellectual.

Alcohol brought that inflated picture to its knees. The recovery process punctured that ego like a bad balloon. And so I became desperate to make the spiritual part of recovery make sense, and have it become something I could really make useful. I lucked out when a kind and compassionate friend changed everything by giving me his copy of Yogananda's *Autobiography of a Yogi.* From that moment life would never be the same.

Spirituality made sense. Later on, as I grew more open to

reality, I saw the value in what religions were doing, and how valid their own path to spiritual awakening could be.

But for me, Yogananda's book was what did it.

Maybe I'm amazed

Isn't it amazing what the right books can do? I finally understood what Franz Kafka meant when he said, "A book must be the axe for the frozen sea inside us."

However, I never dreamed I'd end up writing books myself. The first time I even thought about it was when I'd written a hand-out for a course I was teaching that I called "25 Ways to Motivate Yourself." I gave the hand-out to my boss at the corporate training company I was in, telling him that I thought there might be a book in it if I expanded it, and he said, after a day or two of reading it, "No, I don't think so. There's nothing original here, and I can't imagine anyone buying it."

I was heartbroken and depressed by that and decided that he was probably right, given that he knew the subject better than I did. Fortunately, I knew a person in that company named Steve Hardison who came to my psyche's rescue. He told me not to listen to the boss.

Not long after that I expanded the handout into a full manuscript, and not long after that *100 Ways to Motivate Yourself* became an international bestseller. Who could have guessed? Certainly not me.

That book was about change, from being under-motivated to motivated, and how possible it was. My next book, *Reinventing Yourself,* took an even deeper cut into how people change, and it was even more popular than the first.

Here I was in my early fifties and I was just beginning to write?

My father used to call me a "late bloomer" which was his hopeful term for someone who had become a longstanding disappointment but who might just be turning things around.

My early boss had been right about one thing. There was nothing "original" in my book, and nor would there be anything very original in any of the thirty-plus books that followed. Much of what I wrote was about how other people had helped change me, especially how Steve Hardison—who became my coach after we'd both left the company we were in—changed me.

Hardison was a master at connecting me (and all his clients) to the divine creativity that lives inside us . . . all of us. Any time he led me to the brink of another major change in who I was being in the world and I shared my fears, he would point to his head and say, "It looks harder up here than it really is out there."

In other words, we get scared by what we think, not by what we do. Hardison taught me to create change at a deep level of being, and then the doing would take care of itself. I'd always fantasized that I'd write a book all about him called *Meet My Mentor the Mad Motivator*. But every time I'd start on it, I realized I'd already put each story of his work on me into one of the already-published books. (Fortunately, a book about his work, called *The Ultimate Coach*, has just been published, and it exceeds anything I could have written. If you are reading this, you probably have that book by now, and if you don't have it, please read it. It's the best book yet on how people change.)

Meanwhile, this book is a way for readers to learn about my own unoriginal (but no less joyful) experience of how people change. The short segments strung together show exactly how the changes in me happened and how my work as a coach has been a way for me to pass it along to others.

Reinvention

1

Remove your ball and chain

It helps to have a picture . . .

In order for us to learn to be owners of the human spirit, it helps if we know what being an owner looks and feels like. It helps to have a picture.

I remember a time some years ago when I gave two of my daughters a picture.

Margie and Stephanie were both rehearsing for school singing assignments. Margie was in sixth grade singing a school choir solo of a song from *Beauty and the Beast,* and Stephanie was rehearsing for the junior high school talent show, in which she was singing a Mariah Carey song called "Hero."

Both girls asked me to listen to their rehearsals, and I did, and I told them that they sounded good enough musically. Both girls had good voices and were hitting the notes, but something was missing: the spirit—the vital principle—the animating force.

I told them it was okay to let loose a little. To really get into it. I recommended that they start to over-rehearse. To rehearse enough times to reach a state of *ownership* of the song. To get that feeling that the song was all theirs. Flowing out of them naturally, powerfully.

Margie pinned a piece of paper to the wall of her bedroom and made a mark on it every time she sang her song. She sang it over, and over, and over.

Stephanie also rehearsed more and more, and still her song was coming out tentative and prissy, held way back.

But they both pushed on.

Finally, Margie's concert came and she was great. She stood out when her solo came because she sang with fire and force, whereas the other girls and boys that night were like little cautious robots. The extra rehearsals had given Margie ownership.

Next up was Stephanie's talent show, and things still weren't right with her song. Her rehearsals still weren't taking it anywhere.

So I got an idea. I went to a video store and found a used copy of a musical documentary of Janis Joplin's life. It contained a concert performance that I had been lucky enough to be present at personally—her performance at the Monterey Pop Festival with her band Big Brother and the Holding Company.

At the time of the concert I was stationed at the Presidio of Monterey in the U.S. Army. I was there that late afternoon sitting by myself in a fourth row seat when Janis blew a hole in the music world with her performance of "Ball and Chain." The moment is also captured in the film *Monterey Pop* as Mama Cass Elliot is seen in the same audience in a reaction shot to Janis Joplin, her mouth gaping in awe.

Janis Joplin was on fire that day. I never saw anything like it. None of today's feisty, angry female rockers quite have the exact spirit, because Janis wasn't as angry as she was, well, on fire.

I put the videotape in for Stephanie and Margie to watch, and I'd cued it up to the performance of "Ball and Chain." We watched together, and as usual, I got goose bumps and tears in my eyes when I watched it.

I got that same feeling I always get when I see the ownership spirit. I got it when I saw the early, young Elvis. I used to get it watching a lyrically insane football player named Chuck Cecil play football. I've gotten it watching Michael Jordan play basketball with the flu and still outplay the whole court. Or watching Alvin Lee and Ten Years After at Woodstock. I've gotten it watching Pavarotti sing "Nessum Dorma" and almost explode with the joy and volume of the song. I've gotten it watching Marlon Brando in *One-Eyed Jacks* and Jack Nicholson in *A Few Good Men*. I've gotten it hearing Buffy Sainte-Marie sing "God Is Alive, Magic Is Afoot" from Leonard Cohen's *Beautiful Losers*. When you're in the presence of an owner of the spirit, you know the feeling.

Owners of the spirit *are* beautiful losers. They risk all. They are losers because they have lost all fear of embarrassment. They have lost all inhibition. They have lost all concern for what other people might think.

Stephanie's eyes grew a little wider as Janis Joplin sang on. The passion and abandon and power in that one small woman was something that only a corpse would be unmoved by. When the song was over, the video showed Mama Cass mouthing the word "wow" just as Stephanie was saying, "Wow."

And a hero comes along

While I was putting the tape away, I told Stephanie, "There are times in life when you know you have a chance to really go for it. You are a great singer, so I know you're going to sing your song very well in the show. You have to decide for yourself how much you're going to go for it. You are never who you think you are. You can be anyone you want. When you're singing, you might remember Janis Joplin."

The night of the talent show was fun and lighthearted. I had all but forgotten about my Janis Joplin lecture with Stephanie, and

I was just there to enjoy the show and see her sing.

After a few acts in which the performers showed varying degrees of talent and self-consciousness, it was Stephanie's turn. She had a compact disc of the background music and background vocals to the song "Hero," and she stepped out on stage in a black dress and began the song as her friends in the audience in the gym cheered and clapped to encourage her.

Her voice was a little weak and nervous at the start, although right on pitch as she softly sang through the first verse, looking out at the crowd and occasionally smiling with self-consciousness. As her song continued to build, I saw something start to change in Stephanie. She stomped her high-heeled shoe forward as the song took the turn into the last verse and she was no longer smiling. Her voice grew louder and louder and you could tell that the audience no longer existed for her. It was just the song. I began to get tears in my eyes and I could feel my heart race and my throat tighten, and I remember thinking, "She's going for it, she's going for it."

Stephanie rounded the corner into the last chorus in full possession of the song, sending it through her spirit and out into the auditorium in a way that I'd never heard her sing before. The kids in the audience jumped to their feet and raised their hands and started screaming, but Stephanie's voice soared beyond them, above it all, living only for itself as the song came to an end among the loudest sustained cheers of the evening.

Even grownups were on their feet at the end, knowing that they had seen a moment they themselves may not have lived in a long while—a moment of the human spirit on fire.

I turned to my friends and family and said, "Wow." I was inspired. I'd shown Stephanie Janis Joplin, and then Stephanie showed me Stephanie.

The trick is to pass it on.

The song of the hero is in you

Oliver Wendell Holmes observed, "Most people go to their graves with their music still in them." He was right, most people do. But that's because they've never heard that music. They simply don't know it's there.

There was nothing in the circumstance itself that caused Stephanie to find her spirit. The whole point of watching the Janis Joplin video was to show her that it can be invented.

You can tap into the spirit in yourself. Any time you want. It's always there. Stephanie doesn't have anything that you don't have. Janis Joplin didn't have anything that Stephanie didn't have.

The next time you see the spirit in someone else, don't just admire it; think of how to do your own version of it. Don't envy it; duplicate it.

Talk to yourself. Start thinking about it. Practice saying, "I can do that!" every time you see someone do something great. Most people say, "Wow, I could never do that."

They've built a deep neural pathway with that negative affirmation. By saying, "I could never do that," they deepen the illusion that they are stuck in something mediocre, that they are stuck in *someone* mediocre.

You can set yourself free by how you talk to yourself about your capabilities. The greatness you see in others is in you. I promise you that you can find it inside you, no matter who you are.

No matter who you've invented yourself to be.

Stephanie saw herself in Janis. You will see yourself in Stephanie. Someday I will see myself in you. The trick is to pass it on. *~ Reinventing Yourself*

Time

2

What in the world is non-linear time management?

What is non-linear time management?

Non-linear time management is a commitment to action in the present moment. It's looking at a task and choosing NOW or "not now." If it's not now, it's got to be NEVER, or placed in a time capsule that has a spot on the calendar and therefore out of the mind.

The mind must remain clear and empty of all future considerations.

In non-linear time management there is no line extending from my mind into the future. No tapeworm of unfinished business coming out of my body.

Non-linear time management is best expressed by Elvis Presley when he sings, "It's now or never, come hold me tight."

The old-fashioned time management programs had a huge, burdensome focus on the future. The line of tasks stretched out forever into the future. It was fear-based and it was overwhelming to have so much of a future to carry around with you.

It resulted in massive, pathological procrastination. Everything got put off in the name of perfectionism. Nothing was bold or reckless anymore. Therefore there wasn't much astonishing success happening for the world-weary practitioner.

But when I teach people to go non-linear, a strange thing

happens. New life and energy come in. When they open their emails they don't get to save them for later. They have to deal with them if they open them. Like little attackers in a computer game, there is no longer anywhere to hide. Life becomes a great game and everything is handled right now on the spot.

All fear comes from picturing the future. Putting things off increases that fear. Soon we are nothing but heavy minds weighing down on weary brains. Too much future will do that.

Only a warrior's approach will solve this.

A warrior takes his sword to the future. A warrior also takes his sword to all circumstances that don't allow him to fully focus.

I am a coach by profession, and when I work with a client who is "overwhelmed" with too much to do and not enough time to do it I will often ask them to give me an example of one of the things they are burdened by every time they think about it. The client will give me an example and we will do that thing right now. The client is amazed. The only thing missing in this client's life was a bias for action.

Most people think too much. Then they compound that problem by studying the feelings that come up for them as a result of that thinking.

All this time that they spend thinking and feeling they could have been taking action. In a non-linear way.

Linear time starts with your birth and ends (at the end of the line) with your death. Along that long linear line it's just one damn thing after another. Then the lights go out. What was the point?

Non-linear time management stops all that weary nonsensical treading on the road to one's destiny.

Rather than inching along horizontally you must simply rise up. Your life can now become vertical. Now you don't postpone challenges, you rise to them. You become a warrior. And it works.

~ *Time Warrior*

3

Why not do something with your time?

Bruce Lee identified the warrior as an average person with laser-like focus.

But what if the average person has no focus, laser-like or otherwise?

We average people are usually too diffuse to connect with anything. We scatter our forces. We try to please. We unconsciously change ourselves every day while desperately trying not to. We try to cling to the foolish consistency known as a permanent personality, but it never holds. One foul mood sweeps in and no one recognizes us.

Or a buoyant mood overcomes us and we get our hopes up. Then the mood fades and we become someone else again.

Who are we? Buoyant or foul-tempered? We fight to regain control and come in somewhere in the middle. We don't want people to be afraid of us, but neither do we want them to expect too much. All our personalities, therefore, are crafted from the most hair-raising mediocrity. It's the middle way. Team Mediocre.

All the energy it takes to try to hold this mediocre personality—this one consistent person—together could have been used to create something.

But who knew? I mean really, when you were growing up, who told you that?

You had a hard enough time dealing with Santa not being real. How were you to handle *yourself* being a total fabrication?

~ *Time Warrior*

4

"Violence" is sometimes quite good

The "violence" in the words "time warrior" was intended. For although the work you do can be slow and easy, you must pull out your sword ahead of time to carve out periods of space and silence.

Devoted time.

It's your war against interruption and distraction. Because if you can bring gentle, sustained focus to a task, you'll never regret the results.

As my friend and colleague Dusan Djukich says in his marvelous book, *Straight-Line Leadership*, we stop. We start something and then we stop. When Dusan coaches his clients his recommendation is this: stop stopping.

The more space we open up for ourselves the more problems we solve. The faster we achieve our goals. The great philosopher Voltaire observed, "No problem can withstand the assault of sustained thinking."

The key word in Voltaire's observation is "sustained." We don't sustain. We don't take long, thoughtful, sustained walks. We don't sit quietly in space and solitude until a problem disappears (which it would) because we are too busy.

Or, we think we are. Same thing.

We think we're busy, especially today, with the way our

"phones" hook us up to the whole nagging planet. We are so connected now! We never have to be alone again!

This is good?

In most ways, it is. It's fun and exciting when I sit in my Arizona office and get an urgent text from a client in Scotland. The phone beeps and I grab it and check it.

But what happens when I do that? I interrupt my meditative train of thought and it might have been a train that was taking me to a HUGE breakthrough solution to a major challenge. Beep, beep, beep! And I stop. I am *on to* something beautiful if only I would continue, but I stop.

Are you a good piano player? No? But you took lessons, once, didn't you? Yes? What happened?

"I stopped."

Have you ever looked back on your life and wondered what would have happened if you hadn't stopped? Piano, a foreign language, studying a certain subject, a distant love, *anything*.

Management and efficiency studies in the workplace tell us that one hour of uninterrupted time is worth three hours of time that is constantly interrupted.

Or, as the old saying says, winners focus, losers spray.

So the warrior element in how you relate to time is how "violent" a swordsman you are going to be before your day begins. How much uninterrupted time will you carve out for yourself? Will you be a true time warrior? Because if you will, you'll love your timeless time. You'll be amazed at what you can create when time is not an issue.

I travel differently now than I used to. When I go on a speaking trip I build extra time and space into my journey. In the past, it was different. I raced around like most everyone else, booking flights that left right after my speech was over. Running through airports, chattering on my phone in taxicabs, coaching people on the fly! It was a chaotic storm of a life. It was frantic and even unfulfilling, always unfinished and incomplete. I was *racing against time*, trying to get ahead of myself, trying to break the sound barrier so that I could get into my own future.

Do you know people who live that way? They try to live faster than the speed of sound. And then they wonder why they never hear anybody.

What couldn't they hear? They were going so fast they couldn't hear the universe whispering to them. What was the universe saying? The universe was saying "yes" to whatever they might ask for.

Joyce Carol Oates wrote a fascinating book on boxing that she was creative enough to call *On Boxing*. She is a prolific and accomplished novelist who has always had a fascination with the sweet science of boxing. In her book she studies the undefeated heavyweight champion of the world, Rocky Marciano. Marciano was a rather extreme example of what happens when you become enough of a time warrior to place sustained, relentless, uninterrupted focus on one single thing you are seeking to accomplish. Here's what Ms. Oates wrote:

"Marciano was willing to exclude himself from the world, including his wife and family, for as long as three months before a fight. Apart from the grueling physical ordeal of this period and the obsessive preoccupation with diet and weight and muscle tone, Marciano concentrated on one thing: The upcoming fight. Every minute of his life was defined in terms of the opening second of the fight. In his training camp the opponent's name was never mentioned in Marciano's hearing, nor was boxing as a subject discussed. In the final month Marciano would not write a letter since a letter related to the outside world. During the last ten days before a fight he would see no mail, take no telephone calls, meet no new acquaintances. During the week before the fight he would not shake hands. Or go for a ride in a car, however brief. No new foods! No dreaming of the morning after the fight! For all that was not *the fight* had to be excluded from consciousness. When Marciano worked out with a punching bag he saw his opponent before him, when he jogged he saw his opponent close beside him, no doubt when he slept he 'saw' his opponent constantly—as the cloistered monk or nun chooses by an act of fanatical will to 'see' only God."

Sportswriters studied Marciano's style in the ring for years, trying to analyze his amazing success. No one ever defeated him. But what they didn't study was what a warrior he was *in preparation*. To exclude everything that was not the fight from consciousness was where the real fight was won.

A warrior of time is like Rocky Marciano. He is also a spiritual seeker in that he is willing to begin his life over each morning. And that secret is to truly begin all of life all over again each day. Instead of thinking in long-term, linear patterns, the warrior tears the fabric of time wide open.

Yes this is spiritual.

St. Francis de Sales wrote: "I am glad you make a fresh beginning daily; there is no better means of attaining . . . than by continually beginning again."

~ Time Warrior

5

Situations don't cause feelings

Sometimes people think radical, innovative time management is something they are going to have to get into later. Right now, they are dealing with a difficult situation. And they are feeling overwhelmed.

They don't realize something important.

Situations—even "dramatic" situations like bankruptcy, divorce, death and economic recession—cannot directly cause a feeling of any kind until the brain interprets and creates a story about said situation.

Sadness, depression, frustration, upset, and anxiety can only be produced by seeing a situation and then producing an interpretation of it and then believing that interpretation. So, therefore, you and I can only be overwhelmed by our thoughts about something, never the thing itself.

I keep daydreaming a scene I'd like to put in a book or movie. A mad man (Me? Why not?) lives in a mental ward. (Me? It fits.) Each day they let this man into the recreation room. He's in his pajamas. He sits down at the circular table. The attendant gives him a big blank pad of paper and a box of crayons. He takes out the crayons and draws the head of a monster. He stares at the monster, screams, and runs out of the room.

The whole thing looks funny to the attendant. It looks, shall we say it . . . insane. The poor mad man is scaring himself to death!

And crazy as that looks, we ourselves do that each day. We use our crayons (our imagination) to scare ourselves instead of to create.

One person sees rain and gets sad because of their story about rain that they are believing. ("It's gloomy. It means I'll be cooped up.") Another person sees rain and gets happy because of their story about the rain. ("It's refreshing. It's romantic. It grows my garden.") It's the same rain in both cases. Rain has no meaning until we add it.

Each person believes the rain is causing the feeling, but in neither case is the rain causing the feeling. In both cases it is the thought believed that is causing the feeling. We add the meaning ourselves. Something happens, and we add the meaning of it. Circumstance carries no meaning by itself.

Rain has no meaning. That's the beauty of the rain.

~ Time Warrior

6

A laughable absurdity

*We possess such immense resources of power
that pessimism is a laughable absurdity.*

~ Colin Wilson
Poetry and Mysticism

But where are those immense resources today? They cannot be accessed because today I am nursing my resentments.

Did I put it on the top of my "to do" list to nurture my smallest resentments? Do I consider going out, purchasing gauze and dressings for my psychic wounds—wounded pride, wounded ego, and all of that? Can't I see that these are all the things that shut me down? All the things that hide who I really am?

When I'm shut down like that I am out of action and my life is getting worse. Because I am out of action. But now there's a crisis. And in a crisis? In a true emergency? I rise up and you see me at my best!

So the overriding question of life is: Who will produce the crisis? Fate or me? How will I now live? Waiting for outside emergencies and challenges to wake me up?

Or living another way? The way of the warrior.

~ Time Warrior

7

Why am I not sticking with my goals?

L ooking back on my own dysfunctional life, I remember I would always set goals and then worry about them.

Then I realized everything was distended, out into the future. No wonder it was hard for the mind to hold on to.

So I made my goals shorter. Short-term "process goals" that I always finished and felt good about. I no longer thought about long-term goals. Therefore I never had to worry about "sticking with" something.

I wrote on my wall: Be brief. Be swift. Be effective.

Process goals encouraged me to enjoy the present moment. They are brief and achievable. I set up process goals and fun tasks and projects so that I never had to worry about future "outcome" goals.

The best futures get created in the present moment.

The worst thing is to be so worried about your future that you miss *creating it* right now—right here in the present moment. The only place it can ever be created. (Worth repeating, obviously.)

Process goals should be very precise. Two miles. Twenty-one pushups. Thirty minutes writing the new book. Five sales calls. $23,000 in sales proposals this week.

But . . . isn't that reducing life to the mundane? "Mundane" is a story that we add to very interesting and exciting small challenges. Adding a negative word like "mundane" to a colorful task is like painting a wildflower with black paint.

Only you yourself can fire you up. Challenge yourself more. Get creative.

Create projects and small adventures that lead you to the grand vision you want. None of this has to be experienced as pressure. Ever. The great quarterback Fran Tarkenton used to say, "If it's not fun you're not doing it right."

8

Let's all get drunk on information

We live in an embarrassment of information. We are connected to everything. It's all here. A few keystrokes away.

And the only downside is the intoxication of it. Because we can become drunk with options. Games, blogs, chats, videos, social media, gossip updates; there is no end to where we can go. Oh the places.

Two hours later we step back from the screen wondering where the two hours went. Sure, we took a lot in, but what went out?

That's why the warrior of time must keep his sword sharp and at the ready.

To carve out and cut away the clutter. To open up a clear space for creation. For it is active creation that will produce wealth and well-being. Not information.

Even though we understand the value of self-education, we know intuitively that we must, sooner or later, provide service to others. We must create something of value with our time.

Therefore, more than ever before, focus is vital. Uninterrupted time is the portal through which we now succeed. Not the flurry of multitasking and chaos.

And the addictive seduction of information is huge. It calls us.

We may be alone, in silence and solitude, creating something powerful and new . . . and then: little dings and beeps and clicks from our devices call to us, like little tiny bartenders asking, "Can I pour you another?"

It's so easy to feel important and busy as we scurry like insects along linear time. One hour after another gets strung along. We are strung along and then we back away feeling strung out.

Our only hope is non-linear. It's certainly not in the old-fashioned time management tools. It's not the route of anally retentive linear organizing of task lists. But rather a rising up. A better use of this moment now, this eternal moment.

Pull something out of your future, and do it now.

~ Time Warrior

9

Time to change the world

It's what you do with your time that frees up more time and draws life into your world.

Are you doing what you're doing right now better than you have ever done it? Be truthful. Or is it just "as good as" or "good enough"? The "good enough" stuff we do is **not good enough** for the time warrior.

My favorite American philosopher is Ralph Waldo Emerson, who once observed, "If you write a better book, or preach a better sermon, or build a better mousetrap than your neighbor, the world will make a beaten path to your door."

Do you want to succeed at something? Good work *right now* will help you do that. Most people want to start by improving how they "market" their services. Maybe a new website, or a better network of affiliates. But most of the time that's not where the answer lies.

The answer is in the work itself.

Let's slow down. Let's write a better book, preach a better sermon or build a better mousetrap, because that's where the magic is. That's where your secret leverage lies.

But how do you master mastery by slowing down? How do you master time that way? Don't you fall behind?

No, because slowing down gets you in harmony. You're not

out of tune any longer.

Without slowing down, you get way out ahead of life itself. I'm only asking you to slow down to the speed of life. You want to dance *with* life, not race out ahead of life.

People who race out ahead of life are falling down on the dance floor. They are living in their own future, which is where fear lives. But when you slow down to master this present moment, life gets fearless.

For example, I was coaching a man I will call Ben. Ben was excited because a large company had hired him to come in to give them a sixty-minute talk. Ben couldn't wait. The talk was on his calendar for a month from now and he knew exactly what he was going to present. It was a talk he had given many times before and he knew it would be a big hit.

So now that it was all set and on his calendar, Ben was onto other things. Ben was spending his days racing around mentally and physically trying to get other new business. He was answering every call, checking email thirty times a day and living in a whirlwind of chaos. Ben was always in his own future, so Ben was always anxiety ridden (as all anxiety is about the future).

My job as Ben's coach was simply to *slow him down*. Down to the speed of life itself. Because life was on Ben's side; he just couldn't see it. He saw life as a giant opponent. Something that needed to be won over.

Once Ben relaxed and let himself take some deep breaths, I asked him to go back to the client who had hired him for a talk.

"What if someone passed a law," I said to Ben, "that said you could only have one client for the rest of your life and you would have to make all your income from this one client, and this was your client, Ben. What would you do?"

Ben was silent. I could see he was thinking.

I asked Ben to spend the rest of our coaching session thinking about this one client. To slow everything down, as if this client were the only thing that existed in his world.

I was teaching Ben to go non-linear . . . to be a time warrior. The time warrior slows time to a standstill. Now there is no time. Ultimate victory. There is only timeless, eternal presence. Or "now."

Ben and I began to list the many other ways he would *love* to serve that company. He wrote a list of people in the company he wanted to go visit prior to his talk, to gather research on the many problems and challenges Ben could help them with. Two weeks later Ben had converted a $3,000 one-time speaking contract into a full year's program with more than twenty times that income.

Just by slowing down and applying what Bruce Lee talked about in the first quotation in this book: laser-like focus. That's the only difference between the average man and the warrior. The warrior has focus.

Remember that such focus cannot be frantic. It has to be relaxed and slowed down.

Notice when you're out on a boat and someone points out something on the shoreline for you to look at. If you strain your eyes, trying to force your focus, you won't see it. Only when you relax and let the image come to you do you now see it clearly.

~ *Time Warrior*

10

Failure is the ultimate success

I've missed more than 9,000 shots in my career. I've lost more than 300 games. Twenty-six times I've been trusted to take the game-winning shot, and missed. I've failed over and over and over again in my life . . . and that's why I succeed.

~ Michael Jordan

It really isn't fear of failure that stops us from trying exciting things. It's fear of the appearance of failure. It's the fear of looking like a failure.

Because if we fail in private, with no one knowing, it doesn't matter. If I try to write a poem in the privacy of my room and fail, who cares? If I try to do something that no one knows I tried to do, and I fail to do it, I don't mind that at all.

So the problem isn't really fear of failure, is it? It's fear of appearing to be a failure. So it's back to living my whole life for the sake of appearances, for the sake of other people liking me and approving of me.

Time warriors drop all of that. In fact, it's the FIRST THING they drop forever. They don't live for the approval of others. They live for the service project they are committed to.

~ Time Warrior

11

Warm up to what you're doing

Worry produces the opposite of action. It produces a chilly block of Jell-O where a human heart used to be. Trembling.

Therefore, worry is the ultimate in dysfunction. It's a misuse of the imagination. It chills the body.

But if you're a warrior, you want the body to be hot. Or at least warm. Warm and friendly until you catch even more enthusiasm for your task (which happens by doing it) and soon you are on fire.

Why keep doing the default into worry when it keeps you mentally spinning in your own worst-case future when you could have been taking action in the present moment? Notice again: Worry chills the body.

Action warms the body into fire.

The biggest fallacy about making good use of one's time is that you *have to feel like doing something* before you can do it. That you have to know how to *motivate yourself* prior to your action.

Try this: Have the action happen first. You can work up a sweat with wild action just by doing it. Then a funny thing happens. The motivation shows up. It was there all along.

The feel-like-it feeling was always there after all!

Plato was a philosopher, so most people just talk about his thoughts and theories as mental concepts. But Plato also said, "Lack of activity destroys the good condition of every human being, while movement and methodical physical exercise save it and preserve it."

~ Time Warrior

12

Creating your future

The best way to predict the future is to create it.

~ Peter Drucker

People without creative mindsets lapse into the victim position without even realizing it.

Just like a garden does. Without nurturing care, a garden lapses into weeds and dying plants. Faded yellows and browns. The mind does that, too. Without nurturing, it lapses.

It goes to default mode of faded brown and yellow, ominous stories. It becomes a victim of circumstance.

And then the fear creeps in. On insect's feet. When you've lapsed into victim, fear creeps into every part of your life. Even the formerly beautiful parts that you used to feel so grateful for: Your family, friends and children. Fresh fears creep in about them. A person mentions your child's name and your heart stops. That once beautiful gift of a child is now something that causes your system to crash at the very thought of him.

Soon you look at family and friends and feel bad for what *might happen.* (See what the future does to you?) You fear for them and you fear for yourself should anything ever "happen."

The story of you is no longer inspiring. It's no longer a story you'd ever read a child at bedtime. If you wanted them to sleep peacefully.

And the fear doesn't stop there. Because you also fear poor health. And you fear your money will run out.

No wonder there is no more creativity available to you. There is no more love of life! To a victim mindset, love of life is now just a childhood memory.

But warriors clap their hands and turn that all around. Clap their hands and bring the light. They can get up *into* the light and dance and laugh and sing and feel action again. Any one of us can do that.

The great warrior who invented aikido said this:

> *In the art of peace a single cut of the sword*
> *links past, present and future; it absorbs the universe.*
> *Time and space disappear.*

~ Morihei Ueshiba

13

Serving is the opposite of pleasing

The most efficient use of your time is to serve with it. Serving is always effective. It always has an amazing (though sometimes delayed) return on investment of energy.

The least efficient use of your time is to please people with it. To try to win approval. To impress someone.

Most people who feel stuck are devoting their days to trying to figure out what other people could be thinking of them. It's an endless, fruitless, hopeless task of rolling a "pander" stone up a hill, fighting to win the acceptance and love of others.

Besides that, even successful pleasing never lasts. (Small, annoying detail.)

Because you wake up the next morning in a cold sweat, trusting no one to remember how you won them over. So it has to start all over.

Ineffective people think they need more and more love from others. They go to their counselors, mentors, coaches, therapists, religious guides and they ask, HOW DO I GET MORE LOVE COMING MY WAY?

Here is what they never ask: "How can I love more than I am now loving?"

If that were their inquiry, time, love and money would not be a problem.

~ Time Warrior

14

Creator vs. reactor

I gave a seminar recently that identified two kinds of people in the world: creators and reactors.

I love doing these either/or kinds of teachings because people remember the contrasts forever. If you make a clear either/or distinction, people can immediately access that and see life from one side or the other.

They can also choose to quickly jump over the divide from one to the other.

If seminars simply give out lots of information, they will not be transformative. I've learned that from experience. In fact an "informative" seminar will bog people down with a lot of things to try to remember.

One top leader called me once and asked what kind of information was in my creators/reactors talks. I said there was none.

"No information?" he said.

"No, just a single distinction that gets repeated and illustrated throughout the seminar so people can use it and never forget it."

He said, "I'd have to have you give me a list of bullet points of the information in your talk before I could get my company to hire you for our keynote this fall."

"There aren't any bullet points," I said.

"I don't know how you expect to be hired," he said, "Or how you expect to be booked."

"I don't expect anything," I said. ". . . in any area of my life."

"Then how do you make your living?"

"By speaking to groups unlike yours who are led by people unlike you."

He later decided to hire me. Even though it was clear I had a significant personality problem. (I've never denied that.)

Creators create their day based on a compelling, irresistible future. Reactors are reacting to the opinions of others all day.

Creators are always to be found in the middle of another bold creative move while reactors are on the phone reporting another travesty or injustice they have just suffered.

Creators create their futures by what they do today. Reactors are obsessed with talking about the immediate unfortunate past. The best future a reactor ever produced was simply a bandaged-up version of the past. For them, a fresh, new future is never created. Therefore, for them, life is always unfair.

I was one of them. A reactor. Big time. I was sick, ruined, bankrupt, addicted to drugs and alcohol, lying to everyone I knew, especially the ones closest to me. A life of fear and more fear. The best I could ever feel, on my best day, was just worried. I was often okay with being worried. It was better than being flat-out terrified. But the terror would always return. And the pink cloud period of constant worry never lasted.

My life was saved by a recovery program.

Then, from there, I had the stunning privilege of learning to live freely. I never knew how before. Now I found teachers. I found new books. I found friends who were learning the same thing. I found a mentor.

I found creativity.

I work with people now who are learning to create their own futures. I coach them. People call it life coaching, and that's just a handy term. Who knows what really happens when two people work with each other to create a good, prosperous life?

If I was born in the image of my Creator then I know what my job is: to create. It's that simple.

If, on the other hand, I was born in the image of my Destroyer, then my job is to react. To figure out how to please people and react to everything they say to me. To worry constantly about how to win their approval.

Until the worrying finally, totally, destroys *me*.

That's when I want to talk to my Destroyer. "Why," I ask him desperately, "are you leading me down this obsequious path of constant people-flattering? Why am I on this quest for total approval? Because the more approval I try to win, the worse I feel."

What I got in my spiritual recovery was that winning the approval of other people is a descent into cowardice as a man. It's the act of going pathetic in the face of circumstance. Surrendering my own power to the judgment of my superiors, who would be just about everybody. Such activity had me despising myself and resenting others.

So how can winning friends and influencing people be the good mission everybody says it is?

~ *Time Warrior*

15

How do I make her perfect?

The paradox of change in others is this. People change faster when they don't need to. People change faster when they're already perfect the way they are.

So if I'm sitting with you and in my eyes and in my heart you're just perfect the way you are, you now feel more freedom to change. You now have a sense of safety and peace and openness.

If your wife walks in and says, "I think I'm going to go on a diet," and you say, "Thank goodness!" that's not very supportive, even though you think it is. It's not supportive because she is embarrassed by your urgent agreement that she "needs" to change.

The best thing you can say when she says she's going on a diet is, "Why?"

"Well, don't you think I should lose some weight?"

"No, I think you're perfect the way you are. I don't have any opinion on that. That's your business, your world, it's your life. I'm fine with you. You're the perfect you for me."

"Well, OK. But don't you think I should lose weight?"

"Not if you don't want to."

"Well, I do want to."

"I want what you want."

"Will you support me? Will you help me? Will you help me fix the meals I'm going to be eating on this program?"

"Of course."

"Because you think I should lose weight, don't you?"

"No. It's just the project you're on. If you love it, I'm into it."

"All right then."

If someone is perfect the way they are, they have freedom now to create a new path without feeling judged or feeling they *need to.*

Without feeling they have to. Without feeling they "should." Because all those negative beliefs of obligation will have it not happen.

That's the basic rebellion of a free human being.

Thinking you are obligated or thinking you *have to* will have you resist it and fight against it. But thinking it would be cool, and thinking it would be fun and thinking you would love it— now you are talking. Now you're really moving.

I want to *live* the optimism that tells me my loved ones are perfect the way they are. Because that saves me huge amounts of time. Can you even estimate the amount of time we waste judging others and worrying about them? What if that time were returned to us?

And when I say I want to *live* this optimism about others, I am differentiating that from preaching it. So many people make that mistake. "I try to tell my children . . . I've always tried to teach them how to . . . I try to get them to be more . . ."

Wait a minute. Let them *see it* for themselves.

~ Time Warrior

16

We know what we need to know

*All of us know much more than we think we know. We may not
know everything, but all of us have the chief resources
we need to solve our problems.*

~ Nathaniel Branden

The great author and psychologist Nathaniel Branden has helped countless people find the resources they have inside themselves to solve their problems. Fortunately, back in the late 1980s, I was a client of his and benefited greatly from his psychotherapy sessions.

Was I crazy enough back then to need psychotherapy? Oh my. Why did I wait so long? That was the real question.

Dr. Branden taught me to ask myself questions. Is the act I'm about to do going to raise or lower my self-esteem? Is the day I am planning out going to end up raising my self-esteem or lowering it? It's a valuable guideline, and Dr. Branden's books are the best on this subject.

I used to wander the earth wondering what I "should" do and how I should do it. I'd look outside myself for all the answers.

But the answers were inside me all along. I always knew much more than I thought I knew. I always had all the resources I ever needed to solve my problems in life.

And so do all the people I know today. They've got all they

need. There is a creative spirit inside each one of them, ready to self-express and find the next action.

~ Time Warrior

17

Do you fear death or commitment?

*When you say you fear death you are really saying
that you fear you have not lived your true life.
This fear cloaks the world in silent suffering.*

~ David Viscott

The breakdown of language foretells the breakdown of results. Always.

For example, when I say I was committed to doing X but I only did Y, I have misused the word commitment, and language no longer means anything.

So now anything I say is just noise that conveys no power at all.

My language can no longer make anything happen. It can still be descriptive (it can tell you how I feel, it can describe the past) but it can no longer be generative (it can't make things happen).

First of all, a commitment is something you keep, no matter what. It's not something that feels optional to you. For example, you have a commitment that your kids won't go hungry. No matter what happens, you lose your job, whatever, and you still keep that commitment. Because your kids are important to you? No. Because it's a commitment.

I had a friend who kept breaking promises and then saying he was sorry and it was not what he was committed to doing. I finally told him that he misunderstood commitment, because commitments, by definition, are kept. He said, "Ontologically speaking I've related to commitments as who I am and not something I have."

That's exactly where he checked out of the game. Commitments are not something ontological or theoretical. They are creations. You make them up. Then you keep them. You have total control of them.

He had said to me in many communications that things he was "committed to" simply didn't happen. I said to him, 'Please realize (for your own sake so life is not such a frightening "mess' as you call it) that those were not commitments at all. They were intentions. Hoped-for outcomes, but certainly not anything you were committed to."

Some human beings have no commitments at all, and some have very few beyond the commitment to stay alive and out of jail. You can choose and make your commitments very carefully because you know that if they are commitments, you will keep them.

My same friend asked me, "Couldn't there be competing commitments in our committed place and commitments that are hidden from our view inside there? Like I may be committed to watching TV instead of committed to spending time with my family?"

How could you think of watching TV as a commitment? It could be an intention, or a choice for an activity. But a commitment is a really big deal. Maybe you promised your client you would watch her being interviewed on TV at 10 p.m. THAT is a commitment. But just to watch TV at the end of the day? There's no commitment in that.

What about "competing commitments"?

Don't make them. Why would I commit to finishing a work project and taking my kids to the zoo on the same Saturday if the commitments compete? I would not do that.

Commitments are things you keep no matter what happens to make them difficult to keep. Commitments are powerful. So be very selective when using them.

Just like a flame-thrower is a powerful weapon. It's not necessary to own one, but it makes an intruder think twice before proceeding further into your home when you show him what it can do.

Commitments are like that.

~ Time Warrior

18

Your problem is not time management

When you say "I'm having a real problem with time management," my first objective is not to come up with some kind of better tips or techniques for you because that's really not what's at play.

What I want to find out is what's *beneath* the time management problem.

Because if you had a clear objective—let's say your objective was to go to the airport and fly to New York City—you would have no problem managing time.

You're on your way out the door to the car to drive to the airport and somebody says to you, "Hey, do you have a minute? I've got a couple of things I want to discuss." You simply say, "No, I don't. I don't have time right now, I'm on my way to the airport."

You are a warrior in that moment of time. You can say no.

Purpose makes you that way.

And you would get into your car and you would go to the airport, and maybe make an appointment to talk with that person later.

You wouldn't have any problem whatsoever managing your time! The reason for that is you have a specific mission. You have a commitment. People who have that don't have problems with time management because they always know what to say yes to and what to say no to.

I am always committed to getting to the airport on time to catch my plane. If a call comes in for me and somebody says "Maurice is on the line," I say "Tell him I'll call him from New York." And if somebody else says, "Do you have a minute? I'd love to talk to you," I say "I don't, I'm sorry, I'm on my way to the airport."

So with a clear mission driving me, time management is never a problem. Even if my car breaks down, I grab a cab real fast so I can still get to the airport. Nothing gets in the way of me going to New York.

Now what if I could live each day that way!

I truly would not have any time management problems ever because I would be so on purpose and so focused that I'd always know when to say "no" and when to say "yes."

The problem comes when someone gets up in the morning, gets out of bed, and sleepily walks into the never-ending "demands" of their day with no sense of purpose or mission. There's no New York that day.

These people have nothing that they're up to and no primary goal. So when someone pokes their head in the office and says, "You got a minute?" the answer is always yes. Why would they say no? That wouldn't be very pleasing.

So I say yes to that, like I say yes to everyone, I open every email, I take every call. Pretty soon I'm falling behind with what I know I have to do and I then believe at the end of the day that I have a time management problem when I don't. I have a mission problem.

Soon I'll go around telling people "I have more to do than I have time to do it in!" Even though that's not really true. The truth is I have no direction.

With the people that I work with who have "time management problems," the first thing we create to counter it is boldness.

What's always missing is boldness—an ability to be brave and strong in staying on mission. We are on our way to New York.

~ Time Warrior

19

What are the steps I should take to overcome procrastination?

Do the things you're procrastinating on. Those are the steps I would take.

List three things you've procrastinated on. Do those three things. Those three things will be your first *three steps*. If you really want real steps that will always work in a guaranteed way.

Why didn't you do these things before now? Why do you care? I don't care if it was fear, laziness, or because your father never showed you how to do it. I don't care if it's a DNA imbalance on the right side of your spiral nebula.

I don't care about anything like that.

If procrastination is occurring, *do* the things you are procrastinating on. It's a very simple cure and it's the last thing people really want to do because they don't really want to cure procrastination. They want to find some mysterious psychotic fault line in themselves that *causes* them to procrastinate and then try to examine that fault line (even if it takes years) rather than do the thing.

Emerson has written many wonderful essays on this and one of the things he said is "Do the thing and you shall have the power." That's the opposite of what most people think. They think, "I don't seem to have the power to do the thing! That's my problem. I don't really have the willpower or the energy to DO THE THING!"

Well, OK, if you're a procrastinator on mowing the lawn or shoveling the walk, go do it. Then do it again, and do it again, and I promise you the procrastination will go away.

In his very poetic autobiography, *Speak, Memory,* Vladimir Nabokov wrote about his experience of life. He realized that true spiritual enlightenment came not in a passive dreamy state, but rather during the most intense action. People believe somehow that passivity and repose are the sources of vision. But Nabokov said no, "It is certainly not then—not in dreams—but when one is wide awake, at moments of robust joy and achievement, on the highest terrace of consciousness, that mortality has a chance to peer beyond its own limits."

~ Time Warrior

20

Willpower, or the choosing to begin it?

Begin—to begin is half the work, let half still remain;
again begin this, and thou wilt have finished.

~ Marcus Aurelius

I've never seen anyone without any willpower. People have all the willpower they would ever want or need. It's sitting there inside of them ready to be called upon at all times. Even children have almost limitless willpower.

So what's actually missing is a choice. The choice to do it.

Let's say I have a bunch of drudgery and legal work that I've promised myself I'll do by tomorrow and I notice I'm not doing it.

That's not because of lack of willpower.

That's only because I have not chosen to start it yet.

I haven't started the game called doing it! So I haven't set up the circumstance and talked to myself so that it would get started. The minute I tell myself, "I'm doing this," (followed by simultaneous *action* of some sort, any sort) I've got all the willpower I would ever need.

Willpower was never missing.

What was missing was my *move* to get it started. A simple choice to jump in and start this. That was missing.

Willpower is merely the force you can call on anytime you need to get something done—once you've chosen to start doing it. So when I decide to start walking to the store, nothing else matters. I can be tired, but that won't matter. Maybe I haven't slept in two nights, but that won't matter. The circumstance can be anything in the world, but the minute I choose to walk to the store, I walk to the store, because I automatically utilize my willpower to do it. I've got a limitless amount of willpower following any clear choice.

The real issue in life is the choices I am making.

So what's this desire I have to want it to be about willpower? Why do I want my lack of action to be about a "thing" inside me I don't have? The answer is this: I would rather find and identify some defect in myself than take that first step. Isn't that the easier, softer way to live? Identifying flaws and defects all day?

Many people have adopted a very popular story: "I'm a procrastinator who doesn't have much willpower." Well, the game's over then. You're out of luck. You'll never get what you want in life. You'll never succeed. Because you believe you don't have the basic qualities you need to do it.

That's the easiest way out, but it's all a mind game. Why do you want out of this game? Why not win this game?

Whatever it is you are not doing, notice that you are *choosing* not to do it. There's no defect in you! There's the opposite of a defect. There is, instead, a power. A power to choose. Choose to, choose not to, same power. Always power. There's nothing wrong with you. There's no weakness. There's no lack of willpower. There's no gene for procrastination. It's always a conscious choice.

Let's say I decide to walk to the store and it's two miles away. Once I choose to walk to the store I put my shoes on and head out the door. Getting to the store? No problem. Starting toward the store? The only problem there could ever be.   *~ Time Warrior*

21

The future consumes time and energy

*Never let anyone come to you without coming
away better and happier.*

~ Mother Teresa

She said that work without love is slavery. She said, repeatedly, that it is not what we *do*, but how much love we put into doing it. She said preoccupation with the future is always a mistake.

She said future worries "take the love out of everything."

I love reading about the long and eventful life of Mother Teresa, a woman who kept insisting that joy in this present moment *is* strength. And worrying about the future is the very definition of weakness.

And, as business efficiency expert Kerry Gleeson has noted, "The constant, unproductive preoccupation with all the things we have to do in the future, is the single largest consumer of time and energy."

Slow down. Focus. And love what you are doing.

~ Time Warrior

22

Stop forcing things to happen

The individual human mind is like a computer terminal connected to a giant database. The database is human consciousness itself, of which our own consciousness is merely an individual expression, but with its roots in the common consciousness of all mankind. This database is the realm of genius; because to be human is to participate in the database, everyone by virtue of his birth has access to genius.

~ David R. Hawkins
Power Vs. Force

I love Hawkins' book because he makes such a great case for finding the inner power in you that was there all along. For using the genius you already have instead of trying to force the outside world to conform to your longings (wants and wishes) . . . Longings caused by deficits of inner peace.

True creative power always comes from within.

And power is so much more, well . . . *powerful* than force.

We have extreme time management problems when we are forcing things into our schedule and trying to do too much at once. Soon we're just playing around on the computer, visiting strange, alluring blog sites and off-mission entirely. This caving in to distraction comes from forcing.

The samurai uses a sword. The warrior carves out devoted time. Uninterrupted time that's reserved for a certain project or activity in a very devoted way. (The principle of devoted time is worth repeating as many times as necessary.) Time carved out and devoted. That's the best time to do anything important. That's when true, pure power emerges: inside devoted time.

~ Time Warrior

23

Looking for the perfect lover

We waste time looking for the perfect lover,
instead of creating the perfect love.

~ Tom Robbins

This observation of Mr. Robbins, who wrote *Even Cowgirls Get the Blues,* is precise and true in my experience.

We waste time looking for the perfect lover instead of creating. We waste time looking for happiness instead of making someone else happy. We waste time looking for purpose when it's right here in front of us. We fall in love with stories instead of people. We fall in love with a story called wealth instead of life's wealth.

And then, as if to wake us up, wealth and love stop coming in. So we switch lovers. We seek new employers. Always looking down the long linear road for a better future.

If you want this to end, it's time to go non-linear; to carve out a sacred *now* and stay inside it until you create the perfect love, the perfect life.

~ Time Warrior

24

Passion to transform your world

*Contained within the human heart is an inextinguishable drive to
make greater sense of our world while also cultivating the
freedom, passion and capacities to transform it.*

~ Ken Wilber

Most linear time management systems cancel out the
possibilities of freedom and passion.

They leave out everything the great contemporary philosopher
Ken Wilber teaches about. Here he is talking further: "I'm sure
you have noticed that while living integrally starts as something
you know, it proceeds to something you do, and ends as
something you embody. It is embodiment, this final step, that we
all seek—the 'on-board capacities' to grow anywhere we want to;
to live completely, deeply in touch with our unique gifts and
vision. Not merely as something we know, but also as something
we are."

This is it exactly. The primary question! Is our transformation
something we *know* or is it something we *are*?

When I went into recovery from alcohol and addiction I found
something in my life I'll just call spirit. I didn't find it in the long,
linear future, but rather in a brand new understanding of this thing
we all call "today."

"You mean I can never drink again?" I asked.

"Nothing says that," they said.

"But to be clean and sober must mean that. Never again! Not even on New Year's Eve? Not even if someone dies or I win the lottery or on Elvis's birthday?"

"No, we're not asking that."

"Well, what are you asking?"

"Just for *today*."

"What do you mean by that?"

"Could you stay clean and sober just for today?"

"Yes, of course."

"That's all we ask."

"What about tomorrow and the next day?"

"They aren't here yet. They don't exist. Do they? Or are we missing something?"

And so it began: a transformation. A journey of more than thirty wonderful years of having gone to clear, clean and sober living. A life transformed. Devoted. It was transformed within the warm confines of a single non-linear day. Today.

~ Time Warrior

25

I'm worried about growing old

Not ever growing old would be one way to try to manage time.

But is it really a good thing to not grow old? Is it worthwhile to even think about these things when we could be living instead? Why contemplate approaching old age? Fear comes from contemplating the future.

Love, on the other hand, comes from present-moment active service. If you are swept up in pure, creative service you won't know what age you are. You won't care.

Practice everything you want to be good at no matter what age you think you are. Whether things go "according to plan" is far less important than *who you become* in the process. Practice taking on "problems" as intriguing and amusing challenges that fire you up.

Practice.

Have your life be your piano. Or your martial art lesson.

How do you get good at playing your life? Practice now. Not in the future. It's really the answer. It eliminates the whole growing old issue. You're too swept up to worry about some number that our social convention of "aging" tries to attach to your life.

~ Time Warrior

26

What if I don't have a life purpose?

Help some people! Get into action. Get involved. Your life's purpose can't always be "figured out" in advance. In fact, trying so hard to figure it out and figure out what purpose label fits you will often keep you from your life's purpose.

Purpose, in my experience, gets discovered in the heart while you're on the wing, when the heart is pumping and you are soaring. You don't see it ahead of time; you look back over your shoulder and there it is . . . trying to catch up with you! So fly.

And be flexible as you fly. Swing and expand. Limber up as you rise up. Dance through the clouds, sing and have some fun. Let success *find you* based on your incredible energy for serving. Don't chase *it*. It will always run from you. If you catch yourself chasing, turn around and fly in the other direction. Watch it try to catch *you*.

~ Time Warrior

27

How do I deal with my ego?

If you have a healthy ego—designed by you for successful interaction with society and other egos—you can use it consciously to achieve goals and keep commitments. You can also preserve your spirit and soul in the process, being *in* this world but not *of* it.

Healthy egos are built with healthy self-esteem. To not keep a commitment to yourself lowers your self-esteem and self-trust. So practice keeping them. All it takes is practice.

People often struggle with their self-esteem. If you struggle, it is not useful to believe you lack some good quality. Like an inability to focus for a long time or an undisciplined personality.

It's not discipline that you struggle with, because you have as much as any of us do. It's your story about yourself that has you struggle. I wrote *The Story of You* to share accounts of how people can see that it's the story—not reality—that's in your way.

People have a story that says they have very little influence over the results they get in life. Not a true story. Your life is created. It's not delivered to you.

You can *create* the future—through process-goal-setting and achievement—without *living* in the future. Just like studying a map before you go somewhere. Or looking at a menu before the meal. You don't walk on the map. You don't eat the menu. Once

you've created your goal and project you set the future aside. You don't live there or even give it another thought. Just enjoy the present moment fully. That's a warrior's way with non-linear time.

If I want to play guitar like Clapton, I can start learning some chords today and realize that Clapton did this very thing, struggled to form these very first chords. So my vision of being Clapton is already happening *right now.*

Anything that has you stop or quit or get discouraged is always just a thought. Capture each negative thought or image on paper and work it. Challenge it. Go to war with it.

Challenging your own beliefs is very hard to do and takes more unflinching courage than anything I know of on this planet, but it also yields more immediate, amazing, beautiful-feeling rewards than anything I've experienced. The unexamined life is not worth living because our dreams are never realized in such a life.

My clients try to tell me (their story) that they are uniquely and personally not good at following through with things. I remind them that we are all imperfect at following through because we are human. No one is unique this way. So drop that story—it doesn't serve you—and look closely enough and you'll see a lot of examples in your life when it's not even true.

Process goals are impossible to fail at when executed and they require no follow-through. If one of your process goals is to walk two miles today, get out there and walk the miles. End of story. No more follow-through necessary.

Still have ego problems? Problems make you better, stronger, wiser and more creative. If we had a pill for that we'd all be addicted. Yet we demonize problems, run from them, and think they are awful and shouldn't be happening. We have a story of a future perfect world and it's a story that ruins the even better world right in front of us. It's the story that has you desiring something other than the opportunity in front of you. That desire is what keeps you from being a time warrior.

Don't use desire that way. Don't use it for longing and wishing. Use it for instant energy.

We don't always know how to desire effectively but we once did. Kids, especially the really young ones, really know how to desire. So it's in you. You were born with it. Then you added the negative stories. All those stories are untrue, but you believe they keep you safe.

They don't.

Here's how success happens: You create the project and you create the power. It's always down to you and back to you. And you can also choose *not* to create, and that's fine too if that's what you want. There will be no ego in any of that because pure action leaves the ego behind.

With no ego nagging you, you now get to make it all up. Now it's all made up, rather than being driven by your identity. There are no projects that are "right" for you until you say they are. And you can change your mind.

Now you're having fun creating new habits through practice. Playing the game differently. If your deadline is Friday, you might play a game called "I'll do it by Thursday." It's all games anyway, so why not make up some that serve you instead of all the games you *imagine* are out there that scare you?

28

How do I learn to trust that there will be abundance?

Why do you need to learn to trust? If you want to make scrambled eggs, do you need to first trust that the eggs will scramble?

You just make the eggs.

You don't walk around trying to trust the scrambling process first.

We add way too much to our minds. We burden ourselves in the mind.

While life waits.

You *could* just wake up and make the eggs. Very efficient. You can do the same with the economy. Just make money. Perform the service. Receive the money. And of course you can budget and save. That's a fun thing. They aren't mutually exclusive.

I wouldn't waste any further time trying to "trust the abundance of the universe." I would, instead, *test* it with action. Test whether it's abundant or not by serving people to such a degree that you finally know. (Spoiler alert: it is.)

Abundance! Everyone I know who really tests it, finds it. Much better than trying to believe in it.

Your mind and your intentions are there to serve you, not scare you. Learn to use your mind (more powerful than a thousand computers, plus it has imagination, insight and intuition) in a way that keeps you in action.   *~ Time Warrior*

29

Stop lying to yourself

People want their lives to be different. People want success instead of failure. But then people begin sentences with "I don't know how to . . ." and right then they are down the rabbit hole. They have become victims. The primary thought of a victim is "I don't know how to." And it's always a lie.

People tell me, "I want to be a coach, but I don't know how to . . ." Whatever. And why would I want to help a liar like that? My book about the 17 lies was about that whole false approach to life. A toxic mind swamp of self-deceiving. (I only know it because I did it myself . . . but only for forty years.)

If you want to be a coach, coach. If you want to be a singer, sing. If you want to be a writer, write. If you want some money, go ASK for it and serve someone. Notice the common thread here. And I repeat this quote again by Aristotle: "Whatever we learn to do, we learn by actually doing it. People come to be builders, for instance, by building, and harp players by playing the harp. In the same way, by doing just acts we come to be just. By doing self-controlled acts, we come to be self-controlled, and by doing brave acts we become brave."

A warrior doesn't have to "know" what to do. A warrior doesn't have to "know how to" do something. A warrior simply *chooses* to do it.

~ *Time Warrior*

Wealth

30

Now I'll work hard to get my thinking clean (and sober)

That's been one of my mantras—focus and simplicity. Simple can be harder than complex: You have to work hard to get your thinking clean to make it simple. But it's worth it in the end because once you get there, you can move mountains.

~ Steve Jobs

My recovery changed my life.

The world through the eyes of a clean and sober force was a new world.

I went to meetings and learned and cried and laughed—and prayed I'd never drink or use drugs again. There was a sign on one of the walls in a meeting room that said, "YOUR BEST THINKING GOT YOU HERE."

That was dark humor indeed. All the best thinking I had ever done landed me in a room full of hopeless alcoholics whose lives were basically ruined.

So much for clever thinking. So much for the supremacy of thought.

That's where I began to see that there was more to life than the thoughts that flew into my head like Hitchcock's birds.

In my past, the darker my thoughts, the more I believed them. Each thought was a freshly-caught bird—each thought I believed.

And those caged birds (thoughts believed) were *who I was.*

Except they weren't.

In fact they were just thoughts flying into my head.

Another sign on the wall of another recovery meeting hall said, "JUST FOR TODAY."

That sign never left me.

I later built my whole time warrior training and coaching around that sign. It's the most counterintuitive sign ever put up in any room anywhere.

Why? Because it eliminates the future. In fact it eliminates the hypnosis of linear time altogether, and linear thinking as well (always, in the past, a dreary cocktail mix of paranoia and regret).

What did "JUST FOR TODAY" really mean?

When I got into those recovery meetings my biggest worry was that I was now going to have to go *the rest of my life* without a drink. Impossible to conceive or believe. But they told me I wouldn't have to do that.

"Í don't have to quit drinking forever?"

"No, of course not."

"Well, does that mean you'll teach me how to drink sensibly? Like other social drinkers?"

"No, we've never seen that work for people like us."

"Then what do you mean?"

"Just for today, don't drink."

I was stunned. That seemed so doable. But wasn't that just a trick? A way of putting blinders on a horse?

They told me, "Today is all you have. It's part of your spiritual progress to see that."

That took a lot off my mind.

I was really worried about this sobriety idea. Because not only did I believe I was missing a work-ethic gene, I also thought I lacked a "follow-through" gene. I would start things and not follow them through to completion. In my mind I was *absolutely incapable* of following through. It wasn't just that I wasn't good at it.

So the "JUST FOR TODAY" sign in the meeting hall gave me my first taste of freedom and my first flirtation with this wonderful thing I call the "higher self." (You can give it any name you want.)

Many years later I would admire the achievements of UCLA basketball coach John Wooden. He won more national titles than any coach before or after him. And his method was to eliminate the future.

He called it, "Make each day your masterpiece."

And when he got his whole team to devote all their skills and attention to today's Wednesday afternoon practice (instead of the upcoming "big game"), they became the Zen Masters of college basketball. Linear thinkers could not beat them. Because Wooden's boys were always in the moment they were in.

There is no reference to the future in this good phrase:

Give us *this day* our daily bread.

~ Wealth Warrior

31

My work-ethic gene theory begins to fall apart like a bad game of Angry Birds

I am the one who loves changing from nothing to one.

~ Leonard Cohen

I was sober now. The monkey was off my back.

But the circus was still in town.

All those negative beliefs were still there. Yet the stressful beliefs I had about myself and my life were beginning to look like nothing more than fleeting thoughts.

Birds flying in.

Birds flying out.

What used to be a web of beliefs, thoughts and the absolute "truth about life" had now become merely birds-in-birds-out.

I no longer had to cage them or believe them.

Maybe *now* I could create from zero.

I could start from nothing. With nothing to lose.

Was it really true that I might recover completely from this seemingly hopeless condition? That I could leave behind my disease? (Disease? What is this "disease" called? It's called "Being drunk all the time." It's called destroying the gift of life. It's called a willful pollution of consciousness.)

Yes, it was happening, but it presented me with some new

challenges—the main one being: "How do I make money?"

This was a frightening question to a person with no previous sustained work experience. But my newfound freedom and sobriety, and my newly-restored full head of consciousness, was open to anything.

If I could stop my drinking I could do anything.

So I decided to learn how other people made money.

I knew my father made a lot of money but I never knew how. He didn't know how to teach me. He was never home anyway, flying around the world tending to his many businesses. He once took me to a movie called *The Carpetbaggers*. It starred George Peppard as Jonas Cord. He told me that the movie was a pretty good illustration of his own life. The hero was a heavy-drinking, brilliant, power-hungry, womanizing business genius who destroyed himself in his quest for continued achievements. Wow! Thanks, Dad! I'll see if I can do that, too.

I wanted to learn to do it differently.

One day at a time.

But I was confused until a good friend noticed my confusion and gave me a book by Napoleon Hill called *The Master Key to Riches*.

The book blew my mind. One of those book experiences where you say, "And the rest is history."

Well . . . Maybe it didn't happen that quickly, but it was a great start.

I was on the path now. One book would lead to another. Those eight wasted years of college were being made up for. I was now reading day and night.

I became a college of one.

And the best part was that what I was reading was not just good information. It triggered new and unprecedented *action*.

~ *Wealth Warrior*

32

How to stop trying to save the world from the outside in, and start saving ourselves from the inside out

When we talk about settling the world's problems, we're barking up the wrong tree. The world is perfect. It's a mess. It has always been a mess. We are not going to change it. Our job is to straighten out our own lives.

~ Joseph Campbell

S erve the world with what you love to do.

What would you do with your time if money were no issue and you didn't have to "work"?

And I don't mean, "How would you passively entertain yourself."

That only lasts three days.

Having all the pleasures and material dreams you ever dreamed of?

Three days.

All that stuff up there on your law of attraction treasure map on the wall?

Three days. Three days of that glut and then you feel bored, bloated, vaguely nauseous and guilty.

The path is where you want to be.

For pure joy.

What active, moving, action-oriented *path* would you take with your life if you did not need money?

That's a great fantasy/inquiry because it helps you know your own strengths. We don't want to have you playing out of position. If you're a true quarterback, why are you playing tight end?

If you *are* playing tight end—"stuck" in a job you don't like— be great at that job as you plan for a different one. The bad (job— or anything else) is the source of the good.

If Viktor Frankl (*Man's Search for Meaning*) can make a concentration camp work for him—if he can find joy inside that sorrow—surely you can make your job work.

Create a side job, Plan B. Call it a money-making hobby if you like.

Soon you'll transition to it. Then, once you've transitioned and are enjoying your new work, create another Plan B.

Produce something and sell it on the internet.

Serve people on the side. For fun and profit.

What do you love to do?

Monetize it.

What fires you up?

Light that fire, then monetize the fire.

~ Wealth Warrior

33

When the student is ready there are teachers showing up every day

Ron Hulnick is the president of the University of Santa Monica. He is also one of the teachers, authors and founders of the whole spiritual psychology movement in the world today. I've known him as a friend, and we've worked on various projects together for many years.

What I love most about Ron is how cheerfully relentless he is in spreading the good word about his work.

Every time I see him, and I mean literally *every* time, he lights up and tells me the latest good news about what his school is doing in the world.

"You won't believe some of the things that are happening right now!" he says as soon as we see each other. Then he tells me about the latest USM prison project. Or the new German and Portuguese translations of the latest book by him and his wife, Mary. Or the man who just donated a million dollars to help USM go online. Every time I see him he is brimming with good news.

"Well, lucky him!" one might say. "I'd be Mr. Positive too if someone gave *me* a million dollars."

But maybe one would have it backwards.

Ron is not in a positive, good-news-spreading mood *because* someone gave him a million dollars. Someone gave him a million dollars because he is a positive, good-news-spreading person. (Emerson says life is a perpetual teaching of cause and effect. True cause and effect.)

Ron Hulnick *creates* good fortune by who he *is* each and every day. And who he is is created by internal and external language.

Both verbal and non-verbal. Ron is good news itself—at the level of soul. (St. Francis of Assisi said, "Preach the gospel at all times and when necessary use words.")

Ron Hulnick doesn't wait to see if his teaching will make any money. He had been a psychologist, a university president, a coach, a seminar leader and an inspirational writer long before the wealth flowed back into him and his school. He gave before he got. And he still does.

But here is the point (and he makes this point, too): Anyone (including you) can do this.

We all have good news to spread. Whether we want to admit it or not.

Why wouldn't we want to admit it?

Because maybe it doesn't fit our story.

I was the worst at this. Mine was a story of martyrdom. I was always the ultimate victim of circumstance. So I told everyone my victim stories. I was Ron Hulnick's evil twin brother. He shared good news, I shared bad.

This always bought me some sympathy. It had people feel for me, which was my hidden motive. Feel for me, will you?

One day I took a seminar on success (since I had none) and there was a questionnaire for me to fill in at the beginning. One question in particular woke me up:

"Would you rather be a) envied or b) pitied?"

I circled "pitied" then dropped the pen on the table in surprise and disgust. I pushed back my chair and picked up the paper again and stared at the word I had circled. PITIED! Are you serious? How sickening was that? All of a sudden I had air sickness. I wanted a vomit bag. Could this be true? How dysfunctional would a human being have to be to answer the question that way?

That was right around the time I discovered Nathaniel Branden and his powerfully clear books on self-esteem. That's when a major component of reinventing myself began.

Soon I started to do phone therapy sessions with Dr. Branden, and I later flew to California to meet with him at his house in Beverly Hills to work with him further. We did his sentence-completion exercises until I finally grasped his final and deepest teaching:

NO ONE IS COMING!

I put it up on my wall. At first it was frightening. No one is coming? Who's going to bail me out? But soon it was liberating—no one was coming to live my life *for* me. No one was coming to earn money *for* me.

The power to do all that was now back in my court.

Game on.

~ Wealth Warrior

34

Create relationships like you would a painting, one bright dab of color at a time

The next big thing I learned about wealth creation came from meeting someone.

(And when a book is truly life-changing, like Hill's books were for me, how is that different from meeting someone? A book is just a way of meeting and talking to someone you don't know—like I am talking to you right now.)

I met someone who changed my life dramatically.

He was a young assistant track coach at the University of Arizona named Mike Bassoff. He had just been through a very traumatic time. He had walked into the office of the head track coach Willie Williams one day and found him dead. An apparent suicide.

Williams had been a colorful, charismatic mentor to Mike, and Mike was in shock.

When the offer came to leave coaching and join the development office, Mike jumped on it. He welcomed the change of scenery. He didn't know anything about fundraising other than what he had learned staging a successful benefit run for the athletic department. But he was willing to learn more.

The University wanted to see if it could raise money and build a cancer center on campus for research and treatment, and they put Mike in charge of the project.

Mike's greatest skill coaching track had been in the area of recruiting. He'd created a way of communicating with athletes' families so that they were reassured that the University of Arizona would be a wonderful place for a young person to begin an adult life, not just in sports, but in personal education and skill-building.

"I somehow knew that recruiting was all about relationships," Mike said. "We out-recruited other schools because of the relationships we created."

Mike saw his job as one of simply creating relationships—not just recruiting athletes. And through the strength of those relationships, athletes chose his school over others.

This is what Mike taught me.

Success is all about creating relationships, and relationships are all about giving. You give your time, your love and your attention, and you create a relationship.

This was different from what the world outside was saying about relationships. The world seemed to say that a relationship was something that happened to you when the chemistry was right, when two people understood each other, felt a bond, and experienced an almost serendipitous connection.

Mike Bassoff said otherwise.

A relationship is yours to create.

You build it.

Like a house, one brick at a time.

You create it. Like a painting. One dab of glorious color at a time.

When Mike hired me to help him (I owned an advertising and PR firm at the time, and he'd admired a political campaign I'd run for a congressman) he said he didn't know anything about fundraising, but if it was anything like sports recruiting it would be all about relationships.

I nodded as if I knew what he was talking about.

It turned out that what I learned from him about *giving before you get* would change my life forever.

35

Yet I was going bankrupt at the time

Now let's pause for a moment to note that I was the owner of an ad agency and PR firm.

True. But I was also going bankrupt.

My family life was in turmoil because of the medical challenges faced by my children's mother, and because of my own inability to be strong with money. I was barely keeping my company afloat. I had some skills for writing and creating, so clients came to me, but I had no talent for creating wealth, and my debts were nightmarish.

That's when I got the relationship piece, and Mike's key to it all: giving.

Giving? But wasn't fundraising about *taking*? Don't you learn in fundraising to make the big ASK?

Not in Mike's world.

"The way we're going to build this cancer center is by creating relationships," he said, "and the way we are going to have those relationships grow is by giving. Small donors will turn into major donors. That is, unless I've got this all wrong."

Mike laughed and so did I.

He might have it all wrong.

We really had no idea if the two of us would succeed in raising any money. But we were excited about trying. (Spoiler alert: the

University of Arizona Cancer Center is now one of the largest, best-funded and most prestigious cancer research centers in the world.)

* * *

Some people call it the universe. Some people call it God. We called it the Giver, and our mantra became, "You can't outgive the Giver."

Turns out money was not about getting. It was about giving. If you gave all day and stopped focusing on getting, you would create wealth.

That's what Mike taught me.

No matter how small a donation someone made to the Cancer Center (which back then was just an idea without a building or anything), Mike and I would give *more* back to the donor.

We made a creative game out of it. All our meetings were about what we could give people who contacted us.

The meetings were never about what we could get.

I was starting to learn: A life based on giving becomes a life that produces wealth. A life based on *getting* is a life of anxiety and money problems.

We gave small donors talks by research doctors. We gave long letters reporting breakthroughs in cancer research. Mike gave his time and effort to each donor. If a donor had a sister with cancer in Iowa, Mike would have one of the Arizona doctors make phone calls to have that sister cared for by the best people.

Even if that donor had only given $100!

Mike explained it to me. He had a miner's scale he had bought to make his point. (You've seen those scales, with two brass plates on a chain? When a miner would put a gold nugget in one plate the scale would tip up until he put another nugget in the other to balance it.)

Mike would tip the scale one way and say, "She gives us $100 and now our challenge is to tip the scale back in our favor."

He then pantomimed putting nuggets in the other side.

"We make calls, we help her sister, we give her time and attention, we send her a letter..." And the miner's scale would tip back in our favor.

"Never let the donor outgive you," said Mike. "That's our game, and that's our job."

Soon the money was pouring in to the cancer center. People made it their pet cause. They could really *see* the effect their donation was having because Mike stayed in such close contact with them after their gift, reporting everything, thanking them repeatedly, and getting other people to thank them, too.

Giving and giving all day long.

It made the work worth doing.

And no matter how much we gave, we couldn't keep up. We couldn't *outgive the Giver*, try as we might.

While participating with Mike in this amazing success—this huge illustration to me of how wealth is created—I was also continuously reading my Napoleon Hill books and noticing that he was urging his readers to always go the extra mile. He said, always do *more* than what you are paid for, and soon they won't be able to pay you enough.

The book was giving me the philosophy of success, while Mike's work and mine were becoming real-life verification.

I love it when that happens. When an exciting philosophy turns out to be exactly how the world works.

~ Wealth Warrior

36

Stupid question: Do I need a college degree to make good money in today's world?

Credentials were vital in the old world—the world of my father and mother.

You'd apply for a job and people would say, "Where did you get your degree?" or "What's your degree in?"

In my own life, as the years went on, things changed.

No longer were people all that interested in what college you attended. Yet they still felt like they had to ask.

Many companies would ask me: What are *your* credentials?

"Alcoholism," I would say. "Bankruptcy and divorce."

And you know what? They didn't care. Oh, they weren't exactly *happy* with my credentials. But they moved quickly to the next question—the question they *really* wanted to ask:

"Can you help us?"

"Yes, I think so, so let's do a pilot seminar, a trial workshop, and *find out*."

I ended up training more than twenty Fortune 500 companies and a couple hundred smaller businesses, schools and organizations that way.

Not because of my credentials. But because it turned out that I could help.

That's good news for all of us today. It's no longer who you know or what your credentials are. Now it's WHAT YOU CAN DO!

This allows you to build your skills and deepen your professional strengths *any way you like.*

Knowledge?

It's all online now.

What do you want to learn how to do?

It's all right there.

It's not that colleges aren't good. Of course they are, for so many different things. It's just that they no longer contain the master key to riches.

Not long ago an older man told me in subdued, breathy tones (the kind of voice reserved for the most sacred stories of suffering and victimization), "I am sad that I was never given the education that I should have had. Not being given that educational advantage, my ability to get a high-paying job has been limited."

And I could hear the hushed reverence in his voice as he described the tenets of his victim religion. It was deeply personal for him, and the fact that he was "sharing" his weakness with me was an example of how "authentic" he had learned to be.

Except for one little thing.

One flaw in the presentation:

It was all nonsense.

He could have learned anything any time, including that very moment. That very minute, that very day. He could learn *anything.*

People hire you today because of *what you can do.* Your past history might be somewhat interesting, but your skills and (personally developed) talent are really what they want.

It's not whether they are impressed.

It's whether you can help.   *~ Wealth Warrior*

37

If I just slow down, life will show me where money comes from

Life is a perpetual instruction in cause and effect.

~ Ralph Waldo Emerson

If we sit and reflect (or stand and reflect, or even better, take a good slow walk and reflect) on Emerson's words we realize that we see cause and effect everywhere.

This came to me abruptly and joyfully once at the end of an extremely powerful coaching session with my coach, who spent our entire two hours together getting me to see that I was *CAUSE* in all the matters I thought I was EFFECT in.

Especially with money.

What *causes* me to increase my flow of wealth?

Increased service. Increased creativity. Increased focus on a single path. Increased awareness of opportunity and potential relationships. Increased awareness of (and discipline around) life's greatest time-waster, pleasing people instead of serving them.

And another very vital cause: play.

It is vital because an overly serious person is not all that fun to hang out with.

To increase your flow of wealth you need other people communicating with you.

I don't want to be overly serious about money or even service. I want to play games.

Sincere? Yes.

Committed? Yes.

Serious? Why?

Once I was facing a salary negotiation with a boss who was an insecure, vicious miser, someone for whom money was more serious than God (and I don't mean that description to sound negative or judgmental, because, after all, I did understand that he was, technically speaking, a human being).

But my victim mind thought I was getting paid about one-fiftieth of my true value to his parasitic system. I had a friend at the time named Forbes who said he would help me negotiate a fair wage by coaching me for an hour ahead of time.

I was an ignoramus at that time in my life, which is to say that I had no idea about the causative role of my own thoughts. I thought feelings were produced by external events and annoying people. So I was upset about my life (and wage) situation.

Forbes could see I was serious.

He also knew, fortunately, something I did *not* know, and that was this: a serious person is a wealth-repellent.

"We're going to have some fun today!" he shouted across the parking lot as he saw me slowly getting out of my car, the weight of the world on my shoulders. At the time I was both a martyr and a victim, a single father with full custody of four active children, trying to make ends meet at home while laboring for a fool's wage during the day.

Fun? This guy Forbes is not like other people. Does he not get the seriousness of my situation?

No. He doesn't take seriousness seriously.

He never sees seriousness as a profitable, productive operating principle for wealth-generation. Sincerity, yes. Commitment? Most important! Seriousness? Counter-productive!

By the time we were inside the conference room and he was standing at the white board, he could see that we were not on the same emotional wavelength.

To me, money was a life and death matter.

To him?

A field of play.

"Hey," he said, "you look really down. Tell me what's going on with you. Can't you see this is *only money* we're talking about?"

"Easy for you to say," I said (or maybe I just thought it). "You're financially successful. I'm not."

"Okay," he said. "Let's find out why that is, and let's get you an agreement you like with your employer."

Then we began to play. He did role-playing exercises with me and I was laughing by the end of our time together.

At this point he said, "You cause the money to come into your life and you also cause it to stay out. If there's any way you can trick—or program—yourself into remembering this, it would be valuable for you. I recommend getting a license plate that says CAUSE on it."

That was one of the most fun encounters of my life.

And the only reason I made up the name "Forbes" for my friend was to protect his privacy and identity because I do not have his permission to tell this story. But many of you will guess who "Forbes" is.

Yes, I got a very fair wage after that session, and my tormentor-boss turned out to be a great guy who could laugh and smile along with me throughout our contract talks.

Then came my second shock.

It was my second wake-up call on the value of spirited play

when it came to money (versus grim, greed-based reaping).

I had started my career as a seminar leader, and although I was capable enough, I wasn't putting my best self forward in my work.

That very same coach took me aside and encouraged me to lighten up, to just be me and tell the funny stories I told in private about being a father, and about all the failure I'd experienced in my life.

"Stop trying to look so successful," he said. "Just be you. Stop trying to look like you've got your act together. People aren't buying it anyway. Just be you. Stop teaching—just share your experience. Have fun. Fly."

Fly? Me?

I remembered a quote I loved from Chesterton: "Angels can fly because *they take themselves lightly.*"

38

Put your helmet on, strap in, and buckle up: get ready to experience Cosmic Habitforce

H abits are the answer to anything we want to change in life. They control what we do. And, eventually, they make what we do easy and automatic.

They feel like they control us, but when we are clear we see that we also create and control them. So it is a kind of paradox.

They control us, but we control them.

This force is so powerful that Napoleon Hill called it "Cosmic Habitforce."

Wow.

That's like a gamer's phrase.

They say Hill is too old-fashioned to have an impact in today's world. And in a way this might be true. If you give a young person *The Master Key to Riches* or *Think and Grow Rich* they might be immediately turned off by his antiquated language and sexist diminishing of women and references to industrial heroes young people never heard of.

But what a loss to miss his principles. Especially the role of habit in creating wealth.

First we form our habits, then our habits form us.

We almost never realize that habits are under our control,

because changing them always has to occur outside our comfort zone.

Habits *are* our comfort zone.

It may be one person's habit to walk three miles every morning and another's to have three doughnuts and a Coke. Those habits were formed. They didn't just show up.

But they are not comfortable to change. What's your relationship to discomfort? Are you ready to change that relationship?

Are you ready to experiment with it?

MAYBE START HERE: Which of your various habits produce income for you and which do not?

If Napoleon Hill is too old school for you to relate to, then I recommend Tim Ferriss, a young dancer, martial artist, man of the world who wrote a brilliant book called *The 4-Hour Workweek*. Notice the genius of his book's title. It calls to the world's laziest people and the world's most ambitious people simultaneously!

But Ferriss delivers inside his book. Especially his section on the 80/20 rule. Hardly a new concept, but he gives it new life. 80 percent of your results come from 20 percent of your efforts. If you can grasp that and apply it, you can transform your wealth creation immediately.

Especially if you have your own business or professional practice. You can go back through your daily calendars and see that 80 percent of your activities are *not* wealth-producing. (They are usually people-pleasing activities, or habitual internet and email surfing to see if anyone "likes" you or your ideas.)

By identifying the 20 percent that produces wealth, you can expand it to 30 and 40 and now 50 percent of your day, and your income will more than double.

Just theory?

No. It actually works.

When my clients—who are consultants, coaches, and sole practitioners of any kind (lawyers, accountants, personal trainers, etc.)—look at their calendars and they can see that the one activity that brings them business and money (a sales conversation, maybe) is being shoved down to 20 percent or less of their time, they discover the master key to increased riches.

So I want habituation to serve me, not hold me back.

If my 80/20 keeps happening out of habit, I want to step outside my comfort zone every day and take a look!

I want my habits to be power sources created by *me* to insure I become as productive as I can be with my time.

~ Wealth Warrior

39

How to get rid of all your problems

You never suffer from a money problem,
you always suffer from an idea problem.

~ **Robert H. Schuller**

Even the word "problem" is a problem, because just thinking about it brings me down.

When I am down, I am not creative. I am not innovative. I am not entrepreneurial in my thinking. Opportunity knocks but I can't hear it, because this problem is the noise in my head.

So how to shift?

How to see the problem but then immediately convert it into a creative *project* full of fresh ideas and a plan of action?

Simply by asking that question!

Given this problem, what's a good plan of action?

Ask, and the mind will open.

The problem is now a project.

~ Wealth Warrior

40

Okay, then, how do I motivate myself?

Author and business consultant Ron Wilder co-facilitates a coaching school with me.

The other day he told our group about how he solved the problem of motivating himself to write every morning while writing his latest book, a political thriller called *The 100-Watt War*.

He would sit down at his computer keyboard and place the morning newspaper next to him. If the words to his novel weren't coming to him he would just type in whatever was on the front page of the newspaper.

Soon enough the words to his novel would begin to flow into his mind and he could set the newspaper aside.

No more jump-start needed. No more matches for the fire, it was now burning.

This is an example of overcoming the fallacious myth of *prior motivation*.

Most underachievers believe this myth. (I know I did, but only for forty-seven years.)

The myth says you have to be motivated to do something before you do it. You can't do anything you don't *feel like* doing ahead of time.

That's a profound misunderstanding of motivation.

Motivation and action ultimately arise mutually. They work together. But motivation does not have to come first.

So if the one is not ready, the other can start. But they must eventually arise together. They are like two wings on a single angel.

And soon you'll see that the angel is you.

If I don't feel motivated I can start to write anyway. Soon the motivation *catches up* with the action and we have lift off.

If I don't feel like swimming I can just dive into the deep end of the pool *anyway*, and believe me I will then start swimming!

This mutual arising, once it's understood, is such a transformation—such a breakthrough for underachievers.

Once underachievers begin to practice this they realize that they knew it all along. That wisdom was already there. (Because children utilize it often until advertising and society lure them into a world of attempted comfort and perpetual worry.)

That's why Nike's slogan, "Just do it!" has been so popular and inspiring.

We all knew that it was *the master key to motivation* all along. Just do it. Just let the games begin.

But . . . you've got to prime the pump.

You've got to blow on the embers.

You've got to jump-start the vehicle.

The world is nothing but metaphors for how to go from underachieving to super achievement.

~ Wealth Warrior

41

How I became a conspiracy nut

It's a castrating, emasculating culture –
Now, why did I say that? I already regret it.

Now I'm going to get up from my desk and walk funny for the rest of the day.

Did I mean that?

Or did I just mean what the great Emerson said: "Society is a conspiracy against the manhood of each of its members."

But even that's still too sexist to make real sense in today's world.

Let's translate it into what Emerson might have said today. Society is a conspiracy (entered into by all of us) against the courageous, independent individual in each of us.

Man or woman.

See it for what it is.

Detoxing from culture and society—notes for my course outline:

1. Creators vs. Reactors

CREATORS create their *own* community
- create their own media resource list
- create a lot of silence zones
- create periods of solitude

My perfect seminar would be all people all day in silence with a pen and a legal pad.

REACTORS turn on the so-called news and REACT to it
- go to every new movie no matter how violent, frightening or gross, and react to it
- react to whatever gets posted that day in social media
- react to job postings "available" if they are out of work (Whereas creators create action plans for finding work and developing relationships.)

2. Choosing/books, blogs and movies

- Wealth creators choose their own culture
- They choose their own society
- They find the internet sites that give them ideas and lift them up
- They read inspirational and thought-generating ideas from optimistic writers who love being alive in the global free market
- They rent movies that inspire them and cheer them up
- They read the books that give them new ideas about their profession
- They read books that get them excited about life
- They choose the elements of society and the culture that strengthen them and give them more inner resources
- All day long they choose

3. Reactors react to what is randomly thrown at them

- They do not develop the strength to choose
- They watch whatever movie comes out

- They read whatever anyone sends them
- They allow society and the culture to pollute and infect their systems at random
- Like going to a pharmacy and taking the first four pill bottles on the shelf no matter which drug is in them
- So their lives and financial resources are not deliberately created, but rather accidentally formed by chance

* * *

But it's worse than chance.

Because the media and entertainment companies they allow to wash polluted material into their brains each day are actually *trying* to come up with the most negative, shocking and alarming stories they can find to provoke fresh curiosity, and to seem postmodern, progressive and edgy.

The reactor takes it all in without resistance and truly REACTS negatively—he or she shudders at the gross-out or gasps at the tragedy and then shuts down or simply seeks survival-level comfort.

The creator is a warrior in matters of physical, mental, material and spiritual wealth. Solitude and silence are valued treasures—to be carved out of a random culture with a terrible, swift sword.

A long walk. A meditation. A time for solitary swimming. An hour playing a musical instrument. A half-day in a room quietly doodling with a legal pad allowing ideas to rise up and present themselves.

The mind is programmed one way or the other—creator (warrior) or reactor (worrier)—your choice. What do you let in to your life?

At the end of today, the information I expose myself to will have gorged on my attention. It was not some meaningless passive flow washing over me. It washed into me. Ripped my cities to the ground.

It can pollute like toxic water.

But if I choose it wisely, it cleans, refreshes and inspires.

~ Wealth Warrior

42

The key to productivity
is creative subtraction

It seems like adding would be the answer.

Right? What's missing? What do I need to ADD to my life? Adding!

Adding activities, adding projects, adding contacts, adding toys, adding networks to join, adding friends, adding investors, adding knowledge, adding new dreams.

But subtraction is the real key—because subtraction leads to simplicity and power.

Bruce Lee said he did not fear the opponent who knew (and had added an additional) 10,000 kicks. He feared the opponent who practiced one kick 10,000 times.

My time management seminars and *Time Warrior* book infuriate some people and liberate others. The infuriated don't want to simplify, they want to add.

They want to add tricks and schemes and tools and rules and apps and information.

(Steve Martin once said he wanted his business card to say, "Master of All Space, Time and Dimension.")

But taking away, or subtraction, is the key to mastering time.

Subtraction the way Michelangelo subtracted.

He subtracted *creatively*. He stood in front of a huge slab of marble with hammer and chisel and began taking away what was not necessary to the statue, the beautiful angel in the stone.

Utilizing the non-linear time warrior system to make your professional work more profitable is a matter of being able to take away, to eliminate and say "no" to all the things that keep you so busy all day *not* making money.

What makes you money?

Do that.

What do you fill your days with to give yourself the *feeling* of being busy?

Take that away.

Like a dieter takes away carbs and sugar from the body to reveal an angel in the stone.

Is it easy being simple?

No it is not. But no pain no gain applies here.

Creative subtraction is a microscope that shows you your work life at a cellular level, that lets you see with clarity all the busy little cells swimming around with unnecessary hyperactivity. Those are the ones you want to take away.

A warrior takes those away.

Sometimes when a struggling business asks me to coach them back to prosperity I ask them to put their last twenty customers' or clients' names up on the white board.

We then go through each name and determine how that person came to the business. We make a list of the activities that led to those customers coming in. Now we have our high-return activities identified.

We now do more of that and less of the other stuff.

Success comes to those who are willing to eliminate the other stuff.

Fear is often a new problem when you dedicate yourself to

subtraction. Because the low-return activity was not done completely out of ignorance. Sometimes the high-return activity is much harder to do, scarier to enter into, than the easy, low-return busyness.

But you must go there anyway.

Talk to the people you are afraid of. That's where the money is, because *you* become more resourceful each time you do it.

The two ways I know of to eliminate fear are 1) to challenge the thought that produces the fear, and 2) to do the thing you are afraid of doing whether you feel scared or not.

Both ways work.

And when you are willing to *do both with regularity*, money no longer becomes a problem.

Consciousness is raised.

To master anything, consciousness must be raised.

And the good news is that it feels good to raise consciousness. It's the ultimate "high." So much you can see from way up there! (And you think to yourself: what a wonderful world.)

~ Wealth Warrior

43

Your lizard is not going to make you any money

Without deliberately practicing the warrior mindset, my life was dominated and governed by imaginary threats.

I saw a bad driver in traffic as a threat to my future well-being. I yelled and flipped him off.

When somebody didn't answer my email, I saw it as a threat to my financial life or a threat to my career or a threat to my need to be loved and approved of.

Without the warrior mindset I was obsessed with worry about money and love!

I thought about them all day long. Instead of taking repeated glorious actions that lead to them, I thought about them! I brooded upon them. I worried a lot.

Most of us imagine that money and love come from outside of us. But they absolutely do *not*. They come from inner wisdom and strength. Getting this wrong can cost us an entire life of happiness.

Most people get this wrong.

As Colin Wilson so eloquently writes in *Poetry and Mysticism*, we form our habits of social safekeeping and turn them over to the robot. (Our habituated social selves.)

The robot drives our car, and does most everything else somewhat automatically. However, a robot cannot and will not dream. This is why dreams now only occur at night when we are asleep. Lawrence of Arabia said we ought to be aware of someone who dreams during the day, while fully awake. That person will achieve great things.

Most of the time our robot sees threats where there are no threats.

So, let's say some poor innocent guy is trying to drive his pregnant wife to the hospital and I see him as a total jerk who's jeopardizing my safety on the highway, and I'm flipping him off and honking and yelling obscenities. I am dysfunctional in my anger.

This trapped angry ego is what Seth Godin sometimes calls the "lizard brain," a phrase that comes from Robert Bly's wonderful book, *Leaping Poetry*. The lizard brain is just the amygdala, the survival part of the brain.

It will always be a part of my biology, but I don't have to *live* there all day.

The lizard cannot dream. Or plan. Or create. Or serve.

If I recognize that the lizard brain is where my current threat-based thoughts are coming from, and if I can be awake to this fact, I won't get caught up in all these bursts of anger. I can relax and stay on the path to my financial goal.

Anger is dysfunctional, but it can be converted into service if one is awake to what it is. My friend Sam Beckford (my co-author on *100 Ways to Create Wealth*) used to flash with anger about conditions in Africa. Some of the drinking water was unfit for humans. Now he has evolved and become enlightened about how his brain works. (It's there to serve him and others.) He now puts all that formerly wasted angry time and energy into creating money. Then he donates the money to groups that build wells in Africa.

Anger is a war you declare on yourself.

That warrior instinct is better turned toward productivity.

I call it being a wealth warrior, but you can call it being a charitable donor and a philanthropist if certain words don't work for you.

People feel flashes of anger because they're coming from the lizard brain, and because they are so obsessed with being "consistent" and *approved of* they'll add a lot of mental energy to justifying their anger. To really building a case for why they *should* be angry.

Meanwhile they have money problems. Which makes them even angrier about life.

The first step is to notice that you don't have to take every little flash of anger and spend the rest of your life justifying it.

That's where people really go wrong. That's where they make themselves dysfunctional and reduce their potential for developing inner strength.

It's in that ongoing justification: like the family members who call and say, "Can you believe that Josh didn't even show up at Thanksgiving?" Now all of us are on the phone talking about it. And what this is is an attempt to justify and get support for an uncomfortable feeling of anger.

But when I see it, and I can identify the flash as a passing biological blip from the lizard brain, I am all of a sudden using my larger, fuller brain, including the right side of my brain, the most creative part of me. I can now see that my justifications were just a misuse of my imagination in an effort to explain what the lower brain felt.

And this was absolute madness.

Because that bigger part of the brain, the creative imagination, could have been creating the wealth and health I wanted.

But instead it was caught up in justifying the anger that I felt.

Once we can see this, we've got a new sense of freedom.

And freedom comes first. Then prosperity.   ~ *Wealth Warrior*

44

One good way to wreck our bodies and our minds

You and I are standing this very second at the meeting place of two eternities: The vast past that has endured forever, and the future that is plunging on to the last syllable of recorded time. We can't possibly live in either of those two eternities—no, not even for one split second. But, by trying to do so, we can wreck both our bodies and our minds.

~ Dale Carnegie

Gentlemen songsters off on a spree, doomed from here to eternity.

"The Whiffenpoof Song" by Yale's Whiffenpoofs. Based on the poem by Rudyard Kipling, *Gentlemen-Rankers*

The gentlemen in the song are *doomed* because they regret the past and fear the future.

Peter Diamandis and Steven Kotler wrote an exciting book called *Abundance.*

It is not about channeling your spirit guide and picturing expensive things. It's not about the law of attraction.

It's full of research and discoveries about the positive developments that are happening globally. Now. In the now. This now.

The media won't enjoy reporting the kind of material the book offers: breakthroughs in world peace, improvements in the world's water supply, and the prospect of future prosperity. Because ratings go *down* when the news is good and *up* when the media sounds the alarm. And ratings are the only way the media brings in any money. Unless they borrow it, like *The New York Times* did from billionaire Carlos Slim of Mexico.

Seth Godin writes in a blog post about the media, "In a relentless search for clicks, profit-focused media companies are racing to the bottom as fast as they can get there."

Should we care about this?

Godin says yes, "We should care about an influential industry (media) that creates and amplifies fear, on deadline, distracts us, and festers, like a fast-growing tumor diminishing the healthy tissue around it."

We are drawn to alarming things and the media makes money off of that attraction of ours. We get hooked on worst case scenarios. Soon we are living all day long in our own negative imaginary future. And pharmaceutical companies are more than ready to step in and help with that.

There is no healthy way to live in that future.

There's no *now* there.

This was the whole maddening (to some) point of the time warrior program I delivered on non-linear time management as the only way to get your life back on track.

To bring your life back to the joyful, creative place where it was when you were young.

When you were young IT WAS ALWAYS NOW.

But it maddens adult people to think in non-linear terms. They make a fist and pound the table when they hear about it. Bang! Sometimes they throw the book at a wall. After a lifetime of linear thinking ("Time heals all wounds . . . It takes time.") they find their brains scrambled by the non-linear option. After a lifetime of thinking in segments, plodding along, one damn thing after another, they are asked to now think like a starburst, and it is not easy.

The only good use of *any* future is artistic.

You paint a picture of your *positive* imaginary future on your whiteboard. Then you PULL THAT PICTURE—WITH EVERY OUNCE OF STRENGTH YOU HAVE—into the present moment.

45

How would you like to be a mad scientist and an inventor when it comes to who you really are?

*We must be willing to get rid of the life we've planned,
so as to have the life that is waiting for us.*

~ Joseph Campbell

I was not a time warrior.

And I was certainly not a wealth warrior.

Until I was.

So what happened?

I reinvented myself.

I most certainly did. (With a lot of help from my friends. Friends who didn't think anything when I sang out of tune. Friends who did not get up and walk out on me.)

The really deep reason that I wanted to reinvent myself was my realization (and realization for me means *making real* for me) that reinvention was all there was anyway.

In other words, I invented my "self" (my presenting egoic personality) to begin with. And when I could see that my whole personality—who I thought I was—was an invention, freedom arose.

My previous identity was all made up!

And it was made up during childhood of various responses to things that scared me.

People accused me, or people frightened me, or people threatened me, and what I came back with was a *way of being* that countered that and made me feel somewhat safe.

Personalities: People who have come up with different *ways of being* that make them feel safe.

Some people invented a really boisterous, bossy, controlling way of being, and when it was refined later in life it looked more like just being a leader—aah, he's a real leader!—but actually it was invented to counter something.

Other people are shy and reclusive as they shrink away—they never say much in meetings—but that part of them was invented too.

It's not as if it is in their DNA to be shy.

It was an invention to cope with or respond to something—or to have a safe way of being, a way that wouldn't embarrass them further.

We invent these safety masks along the way in early childhood and we create a few more reinventions around the junior high school and high school era, so that the huge fear of being embarrassed by our peers gets countered.

So, do I want to continue to be the "ME" that a five-year-old and a fifteen-year-old, and an eighteen-year-old made up?

Do I want to live with that forever?

Are they the best me?

Are they the wisest me?

Do I really want to live from a five-year-old's perspective of how scary the world was?

Do I really want to live from a fifteen-year-old's perspective of how scary other fifteen-year-olds were? How scary relationships were?

That would be a nightmare, but it's a very familiar nightmare to most people.

The great companies in this world see the value of reinvention.

They reinvent themselves almost every day.

You never know who they are going to be next, or what they are going to offer you.

Who knew I could buy groceries on Amazon? Or watch my son sing a song by looking at my "phone"?

You can do that kind of reinvention too. With your "self" and your career. I mean, you're inventing yourself anyway. Why not *re*invent yourself consciously and creatively?

~ Wealth Warrior

46

Now here's a secret insider's trick that can make you some real money

The best and most effective way to build your career is to do such a GREAT job with your existing clients that they renew, expand and refer others to you.

That actually happens.

When our service is an 11 on a scale of 1 to 10, we never have problems acquiring clients and building a practice.

Ralph Waldo Emerson had the perfect formula for this:

"Make yourself necessary to somebody."

Then: Stay on the service path you are on.

Don't let family and social "obligations" pull you from your path or you will end up resenting your family and friends and failing professionally as well.

Be a warrior about carving out devoted time for client service.

If you stay on the service path it doesn't matter how slowly you walk the path—*you will get to where you want to be.* The only people not getting to where they want to be are the ones leaving the path.

We went to the funeral service of a good friend recently and I still can't forget the words of a song by Brad Warren that was sung in memoriam:

You can spend your whole life
building something from nothing
One storm can come and
blow it all away . . .
Build it anyway.

Why did the song say "build it anyway"?

Because it isn't the something you built that is important, it is the Having Built It inside you that is important.

That's what will never leave you.

~ Wealth Warrior

47

Talk to real people—ask for what you want

Basic human contact—the meeting of eyes, the exchanging of words—is to the psyche what oxygen is to the brain. If you're feeling abandoned by the world, interact with anyone you can.

~ Martha Beck

Often our wealth-creation projects involve staying at home, or being in front of a computer.

A lonely place to be.

Yet abundance comes from serving others. So any time you are feeling down, or under-motivated, reach out and communicate.

Wealth through service is a relationship game, and relationships are created by contributing to the lives of others, sometimes with just a simple, helpful conversation.

I was in a seminar led by Byron Katie once when she said, "You could have anything in the world you wanted if you were willing to ask 1,000 people for it."

So far no one has disproven that.

Because people tend to quit before they reach 1,000. Before they reach 100?

Before they reach 10.

~ Wealth Warrior

Relationships

48

Use the element of surprise

Experiments never fail.

~ Dale Dauten

I'll never forget the one Saturday morning my college roommate was rustling around and I woke up to see him putting on a tuxedo.

"Are you going somewhere special?" I asked him while rising up on one elbow in my bunk bed.

"Not really. Just over to Heather's apartment."

"Well, would I be out of line to ask you why that would require a tuxedo?"

"It's her birthday today."

"Okay. Fine. Are you taking her someplace really special?"

"No. I don't even have a date with her. We've sort of been having problems. We have kind of been split up for a while. I just wanted to take her a rose and a card and wish her a happy birthday."

"So you're wearing a tuxedo for that?"

"Right."

"Why are you doing that?"

"I want her to know that she's still means a lot to me, and I honor the day she was born. That's what I'm going to tell her, and then I'll give her the rose and the card and leave. Because we're not really together right now."

I went back to sleep thinking he was insane and I didn't give it another thought until a couple months later when I asked him how he and Heather were doing and he told me they were engaged to be married.

49

The tomb of personality

I can spend my life trying to control my reputation—trying to control what other people think of me—but the problem is that when I turn my control to what other people think, I, myself, go *out* of control. Living my life this way is, in the novelist Richard Brautigan's words, "Like trying to shovel mercury with a pitchfork." Or like trying to nail Jell-O to the wall.

And so we face the inevitable paradox of good relationships: less is always more. The less I try to get you to like me, the more you like me. If I focus instead on my own small acts of difference-making, then my reputation will take care of itself. It won't be my anxious concern; it will be my pleasant surprise.

50

Break someone up

If I had no sense of humor,
I should long ago have committed suicide.

~ Mahatma Gandhi

When two people are laughing together, they don't need any systems for how to create a relationship. The relationship is already, in that brief moment, as good as a relationship can get.

When Victor Borge said, "The shortest distance between two people is a laugh," he was describing an instant relationship.

Humor is something we often forget about as we go through the day communicating with other people. In fact, many of us have a belief that work has to be separate from fun. Work has to be grim and serious. So we white-knuckle it through our daily existence. We're hoping, I suppose, that maybe in the hereafter we will be able to lighten up a little. Fly around and share a laugh.

So we miss the opportunity that is always there to lighten up and fly around right now. To experience a little bit of heaven right here on earth.

As the great NFL quarterback Fran Tarkenton used to say, "Whatever you're doing, if it isn't fun, you're not doing it right."

This is especially true of creating relationships. If creating them isn't fun, they can always be created differently.

There is an elderly man that I see at the local post office almost every day. He looks to be in his eighties. And either he and I have similar schedules, or he hangs out at the post office all the time, because I almost always see him when I go there. The most remarkable thing about this man is that he *always* tells me a joke. As I'm walking to my car, he asks me if I've heard why "six is afraid of seven?" "No," I always say to his questions, so he can tell me the answer: "because seven ate nine."

At first I used to dread seeing him coming at me. I knew a new joke would be presented to me, and I would have to force my first smile of the day, whether I felt like it or not. But soon his jokes, all of which were so innocent and corny, began to have their effect on me, and now I can't even see him without starting to laugh. I actually look forward to seeing him when I go to the post office. One day recently as I was driving through town I saw him walking rapidly across an empty lot with a huge sack over his back. Is he homeless? I wondered. But as I saw how fast he was walking, with obvious purpose to get somewhere important, I began laughing in my car. All his jokes came back to me at once, and I couldn't stop laughing. It suddenly occurred to me that this absurd old man, this man who may have nothing at all, just might be the biggest difference-maker on the planet.

~ 50 Ways to Create Relationships

51

Give the gift of silence

The single most important principle I have learned in the field of interpersonal relations is: seek first to understand, then to be understood.

~ Stephen R. Covey

There is a gift that I can give others that almost never occurs to me to give: the gift of silence.

This was taught to me by Steve Hardison. He is a personal coach who has coached professional athletes and business leaders, and, fortunately for my life, he has coached me.

Steve Hardison is as good a listener as I have ever been with. Half of his effectiveness in coaching comes from his ability to really tune in to what people are saying. When I am with him I sometimes feel my entire mind light up, like a big city at night.

Steve coaches his clients to respect silence. He recommends that you have certain meetings with important people when all you do is bring silence. Let *them* do the talking. Let them do the thinking. Let them really open up and say what they always wanted to say but were too intimidated by another's clever words to say.

Steve Hardison describes it this way: "When I am silent, the purity of self speaks to me, guides me, nudges me. When I am silent, I hear the purity of another's self. It also speaks to me, guides me, and nudges me. Through silence, I am learning and being taught things I never heard before. In essence, I am discovering that silence is a symphony of selves."

If I am on my way home from work and I know Margery, my teenage daughter, is going to be there, I don't have to have any special agenda in my mind. My intention can be silence. I can decide that I will not fix her, teach her, correct her, shame her, improve her, or advise her tonight.

Tonight, I will be silent. She can talk and talk, and I will be happy in my silence. I will ask questions and I will give affirmations of what she says, but other than that, I will be silent. Silence is a gift we rarely remember to bring.

52

Rise above yourself

*When you told me you didn't need me anymore well, you know I
nearly broke down and died.*

~ John Lennon & Paul McCartney

Whenever I talk to someone who is having a tough time in a relationship on the job, I get a funny impression that I am listening to the words of country music.

You know those country song sentiments I'm talking about: "I've been hurt so many times, I'm never going to reach out again," or "I've had my heart broken over and over and over," "I don't trust women anymore," or "I just don't trust men." Songs with titles like, "Is It Cold In Here Or Is It You?" or, "My Wife Ran Away With My Best Friend And I Miss Him."

Country music in and of itself can be fun to listen to, and the really sad songs—the ones that express the poetry of lost love—are beautiful in their own way. But their basic philosophy does not offer us an effective way to build the relationships we want.

We've already looked at the relationship trouble that comes to people who live their lives reacting emotionally to the behavior of other people. These people truly are miserable. They react all day long. They wake up in the morning and begin their day reacting to all the bad news on the radio or on the television, all the crime, all the injustice, all the evidence that they can't trust people. Then they react to other people in traffic, flipping people off, getting flipped off, honking as they weave their way to work. Then at the job, the reacting continues. A harsh word, an implied reprimand, a cold email from management, and blood pressure goes up. Breath becomes short, the throat constricts, and there is an unpleasant fluttering in the stomach. Soon the heart races and headaches form behind the eyes, all in the name of reacting. This is the toll taken by the daily habit of reacting. No wonder we end up resenting other people—no wonder we can't trust anyone. We hold them responsible for all these unpleasant bodily feelings.

What lifts us up when we're in the depths of reacting is a gentle shift; not a huge *change*, not a transformation, but a shift. Just like the gentle shift of gears in a finely tuned car. We need to shift up from reacting to creating. And one sure way to shift is to ask ourselves a simple question.

It's a question first asked by Ralph Waldo Emerson many years ago: "Why should my happiness depend on the thoughts in someone else's head?"

53

Learn to do Picasso's trick

All children are artists; the trick is to remain an artist.

~ Picasso

The reason all children are artists is because children instinctively use their imaginations to create. It's a use of the imagination that unfortunately falls out of favor as the years roll along.

In a television interview on NBC that took place shortly before his death, the spiritual teacher Abraham Heschel was asked what message he would leave for young people. He replied,

> I would say: Let them remember that there is a meaning beyond absurdity. Let them be sure that every little deed counts, that every word has power, and that we can—everyone—do our share to redeem the world in spite of all absurdities and all frustrations and all disappointments. And, above all, remember that the meaning of life is to build a life as if it were a work of art.

Not long ago, I was invited into an elementary school to give a short talk on goals. I noticed that the kids in the class were just finishing putting their art work away. (They were all doing watercolors.) So, impulsively, I asked the kids, "How many of you are good artists?"

And they *all* raised their hands!

"I am! I am! I am! I am! I am!" they said.

Then they started holding up their paintings saying, "See?!"

Now, I wonder if I had asked a group of grown-ups the same question, would I get the same answer?

I doubt it. In fact, I doubt if *anyone* in a class of adults would raise a hand in response to that question.

Can you picture the adults? Some of them would be looking down, some would be looking at each other, maybe one would point to someone else and say, "She is," with the other person looking shy, saying, "Would you stop it?"

We're good artists as children but we're not as adults. Why is that? What happens to us?

Something happens.

Something very definite happens to grown-ups that causes them to lose that creative belief about themselves. And the more you study human performance, the more clearly you see that children use their imaginations to create with, and grown-ups use their imaginations for something else entirely—grown-ups use their imaginations to *worry* with.

But what most grown-ups don't always see or understand is that worry is a misuse of the imagination. Especially when it comes to relationship-building.

Albert Einstein used to insist that imagination was more important than knowledge. He didn't say that knowledge wasn't important—he knew it was. But his point was that imagination is even more important. Because of how powerless a thinker becomes without it.

Most adults have forgotten how to use their imaginations to their own advantage. In fact, they now use their imaginations to their own *disadvantage*. They imagine a future that frightens them, and in the very imagining they hold themselves back from life and love.

Children simply don't do that.

~ 50 Ways to Create Relationships

54

Bring it with you when you come

To love is to be happy with.

~ Barry Neil Kaufman

The best way to build strong relationships is to bring your happiness with you. Have it on you when you arrive. Get caught holding it when you pass through customs.

The more common practice, however, is to arrive without it and then try to borrow it from every person you meet. Sometimes even to demand it. And then, when you don't get it, to complain.

One of the many problems that comes from having your happiness come from someone else is that you can't trust it to stay with you. Because you had no hand in creating it, you feel alienated from it.

I can't tell you how many times people have said to me (and to you!), "If only my manager would start doing this, then I would be happy." "If only my husband would not do that." "If only my wife would . . ." "If only my company would start . . ." "If only my daughter would respect my . . ."

If my happiness depends on other people, I have *no* way of controlling my experience of happiness, because I've put myself in a powerless position. Let's say that I think I'm unhappy because my wife has a habit I don't like. "If she'll just quit that,

I'll be happy."

I now enter the folly of changing other people: Even if she quits, I'm still not happy. In fact, I might even be less happy if she quits, because now the nervous part of me that made that habit "wrong" has just found something else to fasten on. What's wrong with others comes from the nerves inside of us, not from anything inside of them.

A woman wanted to talk to me during a seminar break. When she was sure no one else could hear our conversation she began talking in a voice just above a whisper.

"Well, my husband finally stopped drinking," she said.

"Great," I said. "I remember you said that was the one thing that was making you unhappy. Are you feeling pretty good about it?"

"Not really," she said.

"No?"

"Well, I don't really know how long this is going to keep up. I keep waiting for the other shoe to drop. I mean, I sleep less than I used to now because I'm so afraid this is temporary. And he goes to all those meetings. Who is he meeting there? This whole sobriety thing feels too good to be true. Someone is going to take this away from me. I'm up nights now like never before worrying about it."

You can see her problem—the other person has all the power.

When we have our happiness depend on what other people think and do, we have lost *our* chance for happiness in a relationship. Happiness will never come. Because happiness doesn't come from outside forces. It's a feeling we generate for ourselves inside. Relationships get great when we finally understand this.

Relationships get great when both people bring their own

good feelings to the relationship and share them. That's why people who focus on personal growth are not self-centered. People who buy self-help books and go to self-help seminars are not self-obsessed, as unhappy cynics like to say they are. Instead, they become the true difference-makers of this world. Because they are working on the only thing they can possibly change for the better—themselves. They know that the better they feel about themselves, the more they can give to other people.

There's a great old blues song that I used to love that sums up happiness in relationships. The name of the song is "Bring It With You When You Come."

55

Relax with money

Someday I want to be rich.
Some people get so rich they lose all respect for humanity.
That's how rich I want to be.

~ Rita Rudner

Paying attention is like buying stock in something. If I pay attention to my desires, I am buying stock in them. If I pay attention to my miseries, I am buying stock in *them.* I'm always investing in what I'm paying attention to. The dynamic of attention is really that simple—you pay it.

My own attention for most of my life, no, for almost *all* of my life, was a spoiled, underdeveloped, immature, stimulus-response thing. It went wherever the stimulus was. Like a puppy, responding to whatever stimulus is out there. My attention was uncontrolled.

After a while it became clear to me that I needed to choose a few priorities and focus on them. That was something I had never done before. So, I wondered, was I too old to change?

"We don't realize how short life really is," my friend and personal coach Steve Hardison said to me at that time. "If we knew how short it was, we would start choosing what's really important to us and then focus on that."

"But one of my problems," I said, "is that I'm not good with money. And that has led to other problems. I guess, because of my past history as a child, I don't think I deserve money, and that gets in the way of my behavior today."

"Not true," Steve said. "That's just something you have told yourself so often that it feels like a truth to you. But truth is a creation. You create the truth about yourself. So if you want to create a truth called *I deserve money, I love money, and I'm good with money* then that can be your truth the minute you say it. Just keep saying it, and never say the other thing again. In fact, you might want to put a tattoo on your arm that says *HFM$."*

"What would that mean?" I asked.

"That would mean *Having Fun Making Money.*"

It was then that I realized that age meant nothing compared to practice. Choosing what to practice, and then practicing that, meant everything.

But choosing where to pay your attention is sometimes tricky. Because many times what you want isn't really what you want— it's just what you imagine would *get you* what you want.

That's why a lot of people say "I want a million dollars," when it's not really what they want. The missing steps are the examination and validation of the intention. Is it really my deepest intention? If it's not, then it's not going to really drive me. Our deepest intentions drive us.

So it's important, if I tell myself that I want a million dollars, to ask myself this question: Why do I want it? Why do I want a million dollars?

56

Use your best weapon

I spent some time in the Army in psychological warfare. One of the first things you observe if you study psychological warfare is that fear is not the most powerful psychological weapon we know of.

Most people are unaware of this and operate as if it were. Most people think fear and intimidation are the weapons that will control other people, but this is simply not true. The most powerful psychological weapon known to man is love. This is why, when you are captured by the enemy, you don't give more than your name, rank, and serial number. The more they know about you, the more compassion they can show, and there is no defense against love and compassion.

Notice that when you've done something wrong in a relationship, the other person often won't want to talk to you. They won't give you much more than their name, rank, and serial number. That's how people protect themselves during vulnerable times. The more you know and understand about them, the more you can love them, and they have no defense against that.

Fear is something people can learn to dig in against, but there is no defense against love. No one can keep it out, no one can fight it off.

(Imagine our softball fans yelling at the umpires, "We love you! You're doing a great job! We appreciate the work you do.

You're wonderful!" Of course, it wouldn't feel like a real ball game. But the psychological effect on the umpire would be closer to what the fans really wanted because even crooked umpires have no defense against love.)

A recent devastating computer virus was transmitted by email. It had the words "I Love You" as the message line, because the criminal hackers knew that of all the messages in the world, this would be the one that would be most likely to be opened, and opened first, before the person could get to any other messages warning them of the virus. "I Love You" was something they knew would be opened immediately by everyone—even the darkest pessimists and most self-pitying depressives would go right to that message. Nothing they could have written would have attracted people faster.

When the American psychological warfare units went to Haiti a few years ago, they dropped leaflets on the island to prepare for the landing of the regular troops. Did the leaflets try to intimidate the Haitians? Did they try to use fear? Did they say, "You better cooperate with the American troops or you'll be wasted"? No. They used the opposite approach. They spoke of compassion and understanding for what the people of the island had been through. They told the people that the Americans cared for them and were coming to help restore peace and order and civilization to the island. The Haitian people responded, and there was virtually no violence at all when the soldiers arrived. Love changes people's minds.

When we fear other people in relationships, we'll do all kinds of subtle things to try to control them. The relationships get progressively worse. When we deliberately bring love in, especially to those who don't seem to deserve it, the relationships always gets better. You can't show you love someone and be afraid of them at the same time.

~ 50 Ways to Create Relationships

57

Be a servant

When you cease to make a contribution you begin to die.

~ Eleanor Roosevelt

When the serving of others is done in a happy spirit, relationships blossom immediately.

However, when service is performed in the mood of self-sacrifice, the service is wasted. Anything we do out of a sense of obligation is not a gift at all. We're better off not even doing it.

Obligation does not build relationships, it wears them out.

How do *you* like it when you realize that someone who has done something for you only did it out of a sense of obligation?

If I've enjoyed a wonderful romantic evening with my wife and tell her so the next morning, how would I feel if she turned to me and said, "Oh, I did it because I felt obligated. It was my duty."

I would not feel so great. It was not the kind of remark I had hoped for.

Obligation does not create great relationships. Voluntary and creative service does.

Serve someone else's purpose. Find out what another person needs and provide it. Just for the fun of it.

Steve Hardison figures out ways to serve people everywhere he goes. Sometimes he'll see a little family struggling with their groceries in the supermarket and he will step up and pay for them. He'll stop his car and talk to a postal delivery person in a small neighborhood and ask which family is hurting right now ("People who deliver the mail always know," he laughs), and the next day he'll bring that family an envelope with some cash in it from an "anonymous" donor.

One day he decided to "adopt" a person at a nursing home. He realized that he and his children had no grandmother figure in their lives living nearby so he went to a local nursing home and found himself one. The old woman, who had no one in her life, was thrilled. Steve brought his family by and they simply adopted her. He was so happy to have added her to his life that he begged me to come by the nursing home one day to celebrate it.

"Bring your guitar," he said. "We're going to sing to all of them."

"I didn't think you sang," I protested.

"I don't, but I'll be there to support you while you sing. They'll love it and so will you. And I'll dance. I may not sing, but I'm a great dancer. No one dances like I do."

"Steve," I said. "They're in wheelchairs."

"Doesn't matter!" he said.

So one evening the two of us went to the nursing home and I went to the front of the room and sang and sang and sang while Steve danced with the old ladies in their wheelchairs. I'll never forget the sight of him hopping around and dancing and spinning their chairs around while I was singing. He had an insanely blissful look on his face and the people at the nursing home were obviously enjoying themselves completely. Up until then they may have thought they had seen it all.

That's what Steve is like. A giver. Whenever he has a spare moment, he gives. I've seen him leave anonymous envelopes of money in people's mail folders at the office. I've heard of him sitting with a depressed person for 24 straight hours just to listen and talk to them. It was sometimes a person he didn't even know before that.

But here's the clincher, for me. One time, years ago, I was telling Steve about my many car problems and he was listening, as usual, with great compassion. It was in the winter getting near holiday season and I didn't think anything else about it. Until one day one of my children called me at work and said, "Dad! When are you coming home?"

"Why?"

"Just . . . when . . . when?"

"In about an hour."

"Can't you come home now?"

"Why?"

"We're not supposed to tell you."

So I went home from work and as I drove up I saw in front of my house a bright new car with a huge red ribbon around it. I knew right away where it came from. Although Steve Hardison made a ridiculous effort to keep the gift anonymous, I knew where it came from.

Feel the power and the grace

Service of others has gotten a weird reputation these days. We seem to have lost the fun and spontaneity that can be associated with it. Somehow we now associate it with dreary servitude and shuffling around—a kind of subtle inferiority.

In truth, when service is provided with the right spirit, it's a pure joy. The endless energy and spirit that my friend Steve shows is proof enough to me. I never see him happier than when he's helping someone out.

President George Washington was known for signing all his letters, "Your most humble and obedient servant."

No one questioned his power. What they didn't know is where he got it: in his commitment to serve. He knew the power and the grace he could get from service.

Service is the opposite of inferiority to another person because in service, the other person can't touch you. You are so high above your emotional center, you can't be intimidated. When your focus is on service, you are in the most spirited part of your being and it gives you the feeling of having wings.

People used to ask Mother Teresa how she found the inner strength to live such a life of self-sacrifice. All of her selfless service to the poor seemed so unimaginable to the journalists who interviewed her. However, as she often said in her interviews, "If people knew how much joy I was experiencing, they wouldn't consider this to be a sacrifice."

People who serve are way beyond the opinions of others. They are not worried about what other people think of them. They are too busy serving. And, as my mother used to annoy me by saying, "Busy hands are happy hands."

Studies at Harvard University show that helping others has a measurable impact on the immune system of the body. Even *thinking* about reaching out to serve others has a dramatic effect. Harvard researchers had 132 students watch a film of Mother Teresa helping the sick and dying in Calcutta. After the viewing they tested the saliva of the students for the level of immunoglobulin A, a vital defense against the cold virus. They found that students who watched the film, no matter whether they admired the work of Mother Teresa or not, experienced dramatic increases in immunity. Then the students were asked to watch a film about Nazi Germany and Hitler, and the same test was made afterward. The immune systems were depressed after the Nazi movie. This experiment has been called "The Mother Teresa

Effect" ever since, because it has helped scientists explain why people who are serving others live so much longer.

Dr. Allen Luks created a breakthrough study of what he called "helper's high"—the rush of endorphins into the brain that people get when they help other people. He compared it favorably to runner's high, and demonstrated that people who are in the act of helping others receive profound physiological and psychological benefits.

Meditation expert Dr. Herbert Benson also concluded that helping others gave the same kind of relief from stress that meditation gave, if not more.

Once when meeting with the Dalai Lama, Benson asked the famous holy man what one could do to maintain inner peace and joy once the meditating was over and it was time to go out into the chaotic world. The Dalai Lama replied simply, "Look at what's in front of you."

In the years that followed that conversation, Benson pondered that answer.

"For a while I wasn't sure what he meant," said Benson. "Then I realized that by looking at what's in front of you, you attach your thoughts to other persons. That breaks the message of stress. And now I see that a way to make that really happen for a lengthy period is through helping."

Serving others breaks the message of stress because stress comes from focusing on personal worries. The more I worry about myself, the more worried I become and soon I am even worried that I might be worrying too much.

But the moment I shift that focus to what's in front of me, I see someone who could use some help. And the more I help, the higher I get. That's the huge personal benefit to making a difference in another person's life.

~ 50 Ways to Create Relationships

58

Be your commitment

Do you know the difference between involvement and commitment?
Think of eggs and ham. The chicken is involved.
The pig is committed.

~ Martina Navratilova

I think the most often overlooked principle in relationship-building is the principle of daily renewal.

My commitments to other people will all grow weak if I never recommit to them. If I don't renew my commitment to you, the commitment must grow weaker. Whenever I have great relationships, it's because I am aware that commitment is a creation. The commitments I have to other people are created by me. If I'm clear on that, I can then move on to renewing all the commitments I want to renew each day.

Sometimes this takes only a few seconds, but it is very valuable time spent. It's a simple matter of reminding myself of my priorities and what I'm up to in life.

People who struggle with relationships don't understand the power behind renewed commitments. They think commitments are somehow external to the mind. They exist in the gut, or somewhere else. In fact, when I consult with people who are having trouble, whether they are CEOs having trouble with partners or managers or customers, or people having trouble at home with family members, the problems almost always begin with the same misunderstanding: the feeling that commitments exist independent of the person creating the commitment.

You can hear the misunderstanding in their language. They talk about commitment as if it began as something in the air, like a virus. "I'm not feeling as much commitment to my wife as I used to," they will say. I expect them to hold their stomachs, probing for the pocket of pain that went away. "I'm not feeling the same commitment to this job and this company I used to feel," some people say. To them, commitment is just a feeling.

But commitment is not a feeling. It's a decision. We can decide to make *whatever* commitment we want, to *whomever* we want, *whenever* we want. The world is divided between those who know that and those who don't know that.

Once we have made a commitment to love or serve someone it is a good idea not to put the expression of that commitment off. It's a good idea to act on that gentle commitment every day. Especially because it's so easy to do. A newspaper column by my friend Dale Dauten brought that sense of urgency home to me in a dramatic way not long ago.

Dauten recounted a meeting he had with his brilliantly eccentric friend Roger Axford (the man Dale based his main character Max on in his two wonderful books, *Experiments Never Fail* and *The Gifted Boss*). In that meeting, Dale had asked Axford a variation on the question of what life is all about. Axford told him to go to a hospital, any hospital, go into the chapel, and find the book where people write their thoughts about their loved ones. "There you'll find your answer," said Axford.

One day Dale took his advice and went into a hospital where he found the guest book in the chapel. He read many passages that people had written there, many prayers for loved ones in surgery, many touching thoughts written by people in states of shock and grief and hope. Among the messages written he found this one:

"Dear Lord: It's day 22. I am grateful that my son is breathing on his own. I hope you can let us have another little miracle and let him open his eyes or squeeze our hands."

Dale said that in seeing the people's passages, he found that the secret to life is that there is no secret. "It's all there," he realized, "we only need to experience it. Nine-tenths of wisdom is appreciation. Go find somebody's hand and squeeze it, while there's time."

59

Become a problem

The intellectual function of trouble is to lead people to think.

~ John Dewey

If you have a relationship problem right now, the fastest way to solve it is to *become* the problem.

To actually say to yourself, "I am the problem," because, as was revealed in the great study of American business, *Flight of the Buffalo*, it's only when you're willing to see yourself as the problem that you can become the solution.

If you're the problem, you're the solution. The willingness to say, "I am the problem," will take you up your ladder into pure creativity. Although most people think the opposite would happen—that you would go down your ladder into guilt, but that's not so.

Let me give you an example to show you the power—absolute power—of learning to say, "I am the problem."

Let's say I am the football coach and the players keep showing up late for team meetings. If I'm like most people, I'll waste all my energy and emotions blaming the players who show up late and trying to change them. (Here's that pathetic fallacy in relationship building again—the thought that we can change other people. If you believe you can change other people, you'll be uncomfortable in relationships for the rest of your life.)

If my players are showing up late, the only chance I have to solve this problem is to get alone with myself and say, "I am the problem." If my players are coming in late, I am the problem, and if I am the problem, I am the solution.

So now I want to go to work figuring out what it is that I am doing that permits this problem to go on. How am I allowing it to happen? All of a sudden, I see that my rules are not strong enough and my consequences aren't creative enough. I might decide to increase the creativity of my behavior. I might make some new rules: "Meetings start at 8 in the morning. There will be no one late for the meetings, there will be no such thing as late. At 8 o'clock I'll lock the door to the meeting room. Anyone not inside has *missed* the meeting." The players know that the penalty for missing a team meeting is significant, so all of a sudden I find that the players are arriving *early* for team meetings.

Problem solved.

Notice what happened to this problem. I never said that the players weren't responsible for showing up late. Of course they were responsible. Of course they were "to blame" in a certain sense. But the more time I spent blaming them, the more time I would have wasted.

When I said, "I am the problem," I wasn't seeking to blame myself or feel guilty, I was seeking a solution. It was for intellectual leverage only. It gave me a fresh new advantage over the situation to say that I was the problem.

60

Build the love in

A man without a smile should not open a shop.

~ Chinese Proverb

Love operates in the universe in a very mathematical way. Whatever gets put in to one side of the equation shows up on the other. Maybe not right away and maybe not in the same place you put it, but the love always comes back. People who have great relationships in life have a relationship to the idea of love that's very active. They experience love as something they can create. Something that they can build into their lives to whatever degree they wish.

People who struggle in relationships have the opposite concept of love. They see love as being "out there somewhere." They always talk about love as coming *into* their lives. They wait for love and they hope they'll get lucky.

Some even believe in a mythological cupid—a flying chubby baby armed with a bow and arrow who may or may not choose to shoot them full of love.

I know a woman who's jealous of her sister because her sister seems to be "lucky in love." This woman wishes that *she* were so lucky and believes life has been unfair to her so far. "My sister is very, very lucky," she says. "She had someone special come into her life at just the right time. I wish someone like that could come into my life. I have so much to give to someone if they would come into my life."

Love doesn't simply come into one's life. It must first go out. It must go out bravely and without guarantee. It then circles around awhile so that you'll see no connection. Finally it comes back in. That's the only way it travels and materializes. By going out into the world, connecting with someone else, and, later, coming right back to you, multiplied.

61

Try to understand

Living is easy with eyes closed, misunderstanding all you see.

~ John Lennon

We only fear what we don't understand. And the more we learn about what we don't understand, the more we realize that knowledge is power. Not power over the other person, but power over our consciousness. Power to relate to someone in a confident and comfortable way.

Many times, our habit is to worry about other people. A habit, by the way, that takes us right out of the possibility of creative thinking.

The people who create the best relationships are the people who think the most creatively about other people. The people who have the worst relationships are the people who worry the most about other people. Horace Walpole once made an observation about this side of human nature: "The world is a comedy for those who think and a tragedy for those who feel."

It's easier not to understand someone else. To just go with our gut feelings about them, our gut suspicions. Living is easy with eyes closed.

But great friendships and great professional connections are always made through understanding the other person. Taking an interest. Becoming a thinker and an expert on that person. Eyes wide open. That's what works. We only fear what we don't understand.

62

Celebrate your independence

*Hating someone is like burning your
house down to get rid of a rat.*

~ Harry Emerson Fosdick

People used to believe that their emotions were all caused by outside events and other people. People also used to believe that the world was flat.

People who still believe in what psychologist Dr. William Glasser calls the "stimulus/response view of the world" are making a mistake that is even greater than believing that the world is flat. By believing that you have no choice but to just *respond* to whatever stimulus is out there, you've surrendered all the power within you to create a life.

People do not have the absolute power to scare us. People do not have the capacity to make us mad. People don't intimidate us, and people don't frustrate or irritate us. It just *seems* like they do—in the same hallucinatory false way that the world *seems* like it's flat. Fortunately we know better about the world, but most of us don't know better about other people. By hallucinating that other people are the problem, we extend the hallucination into a futility by then trying to change other people. The way we know this is dysfunctional thinking based on mistaken beliefs is that it never works.   *~ 50 Ways to Create Relationships*

63

Make a difference

*Your life's meaning is the difference that it makes. If it doesn't
make a difference, it has no meaning.*

~ Lyndon Duke

At one time in my life my professional relationships weren't
what I wanted them to be, so I enlisted the help of consultant
Lyndon Duke.

Although Lyndon's lifelong research was on the linguistics of
suicide, he discovered during his studies that if you can
understand suicide, you can understand all human unhappiness.
It's just a matter of degree.

Soon he became a consultant to a wide spectrum of
professional people who wanted to learn his ideas. If those ideas
could stop a suicide, they could also stop all the unpleasant states
that fall short of that act. His focus was on showing people how
to have a life that meant something.

Meaning is nothing more than the difference it makes [he told
me]. If it doesn't make a difference, it has no meaning. When
you are on your death bed, what you will be asking yourself
is, What's different? What is different on this planet because I
was here? If nothing is different, then you didn't make a
difference. If you didn't make a difference, your life had no
meaning. That's all meaning is—the difference it makes. What
doesn't make a difference has no meaning."

I visited Lyndon where he lives in Oregon to learn his ideas. He told me his life story, and it was very similar to my own, with one difference: He began his adult life as an exceptionally successful man. He was a scholar and a respected professor. But he experienced a very serious bottoming-out after a while and remembered lying face down on his carpet in total despair. He didn't know how to go on. Then, as he was lying there, he heard a sound. It was his next door neighbor mowing the lawn. And above the sound of the mower he heard singing. His neighbor was singing while he was mowing his lawn, and it hit Lyndon like a light—that's what I want! More than anything! To have a life that simple and happy that I can mow the lawn and feel like singing at the same time.

He wanted that. That was his new desire: to be an average person enjoying life in a simple way.

Lyndon explained that he realized that one's lifelong desire doesn't have to be for anything exceptional. It can be for a very simple form of comfort and joy. It can be for the pleasure of singing while performing a chore.

Lyndon was an extraordinary intellect who wanted to make that fact irrelevant to his happiness. He knew he had a lot of work to do to get to the simple pleasure of being an "average person," but he was excited by the idea of trying.

As he sat telling me about his journey to happiness, he was speaking with a very excited voice. It was clear that he was now a very happy man who wanted to make a difference by sharing how he got that way.

"Happiness and a meaningful life come from making differences. But this is the most important rule to follow: Always make the differences you *can* make," he said, "not the differences you would prefer to make but can't. As you keep making differences, your skill will automatically and effortlessly increase. Anything human beings repeat they get more skillful at. Including misery!"

When he said, "Including misery!" he let go with a huge long laugh. That was his fun—exposing human folly and showing the way to avoid it.

Society pushes exceptionality

After my weekend with Lyndon, I flew back home to Arizona with my head full of wonderful ideas. Already I had begun to apply them. Rather than always trying to be exceptional at everything, I discovered I could be happy with simply being an average person doing what I could do to make a difference. This took so much pressure off. Because trying to be exceptional was wearing me out and I was never satisfied. I was never exceptional enough, to begin with. And sometimes being exceptional took so much energy that I had to take time off to just crash and be depressed for a while until I couldn't stand myself any longer and it was time to go out and try to be exceptional again.

The other problem with holding myself to the standard of being exceptional was that I often couldn't do it at all, and I got so discouraged, I would do nothing. And doing nothing is less than what an average person does.

The final downside to trying to be exceptional was how it distanced me from other people. Average people are not comfortable being around self-described exceptional people. Exceptional people, by definition, are isolated from others. They don't relate well. They are the exceptions.

Lyndon taught me to keep repeating my average day, and things would get better on their own. Anything repeated gets better. By small comfortable increments. None of the white-knuckled striving and jamming and forcing my way to the top of the heap. Just a happy average person having a happy average day. I was so pleased with how well this low-pressure approach was working for me, I even began mystifying my friends by signing my messages, "Have an average day."

I had realized that always telling myself to have a "great" day was putting a lot of pressure on. Telling myself that either I had to be exceptional or I wasn't worth anything was disconnecting me from the human family. Lyndon Duke had discovered how this kind of pressure led to suicide. The pressure to be exceptional. He had also discovered that when potential suicides learned to allow themselves to be average, the pressure was released and people could live again and experience the happiness of daily small improvements.

"All of society pushes exceptionality on us," Lyndon said. "Parents, especially, think it is their duty to urge their children to be exceptional. They don't know the harm it does."

I couldn't wait for my next meeting with Lyndon, which was to be the following weekend. I flew up from Arizona to Oregon and he met me at the airport to take me to my hotel. Our studies would begin again bright and early the next morning.

As I ate breakfast in the hotel dining room that next morning, a very strange thing happened. A rumpled, ruddy little man in an undersized hotel uniform burst into the restaurant calling out my name. I looked up and identified myself and he said, with fear on his face, "You have an emergency phone call at the front desk!"

My heart pounded as I left with him, wondering if my children were okay. When I got to the phone it was a nurse on the line who said she was from a hospital in Eugene. She was talking about Lyndon.

"He's had a heart attack. We think he has a hole in his aorta. He had severe heart pains early this morning and we rushed him here. He has to have an emergency operation, and he's in very critical condition."

I was stunned. Lyndon had been so buoyant and full of life the evening before at the airport. I remembered how happy he was to hear about how average my previous week had been.

"How critical is critical?" I asked. "How serious is this? Can I see him?"

"No you can't see him now. And this is very critical; there are no guarantees here. But I did want to call you because he insisted. It was one of the most unusual things I've ever seen. He not only insisted that I call you, but he also begged me to let him give his lessons to you. He wanted us to let him teach you while we were prepping him for this operation. I told him it was out of the question, but he kept insisting! I finally had to tell him once again that he'd had a potentially fatal heart attack and we were trying to save his life! First things first!"

"That's just like him," I said.

"What?"

"He lives for the differences he can make. He's been making a big difference in my life. He wanted to continue. That's all. Please save him."

"Please what?" she said as static came on the line.

"Please save his life," I said more clearly, pushing the words past the lump in my throat.

"Yes," she said. "We're going to do what we can."

I walked back to the restaurant in a sad state of shock. I gathered my books and notebook and walked slowly back to my room.

Although his recovery was complicated by a stroke suffered during surgery, Lyndon surprised everyone by fighting back and working to get his life of difference-making back. Soon he was out of the hospital and living with his daughter to continue his rehabilitation. The doctors were amazed that he had suffered so much and still made it through.

I was not amazed.

On the street where you live

There is a little old man in my neighborhood that I see out walking every morning. He walks slowly, with a slight limp (almost as if he's had a knee or hip replacement) and he's always cheerful when he sees people.

But if you watch him on his walk, as I do almost every morning as I get into my car, you notice something. Every time he finds a morning newspaper on the sidewalk, in the street, in a driveway or on a lawn he always picks it up and walks it up to the front porch of the home that it belongs to. He does this all morning, all along the street, with every house he passes. He picks up people's papers and puts them on the front porch for them.

I used to watch him before I met Lyndon, wondering why he did that. But after Lyndon's teaching, I understood. This was difference-making on display for me. It was difference-making at its most basic. Something is always different because of this man. With every house he passes, something is different than it was before.

Before he arrives, there is a paper out there someplace, in the street, on the lawn, wherever. A hassle. And after he passes, it is now conveniently located on the front porch. That's a difference.

This man is a true difference-maker. This might not be the difference he would *prefer* to make. If he were an exceptionality freak, he'd probably be drunk and depressed because he had not been able to make a bigger difference in people's lives. But this was the difference he was easily *able* to make. Lyndon's words come back to me every time I see this little morning man: "Focus on the differences you *can* make, not the differences you would prefer to but can't."

~ *50 Ways to Create Relationships*

64

Becoming the wounded one

I have a friend named Darby who was wondering how to respond to his young son one day when the boy came home from school after being terrorized by bullies on the playground. Darby decided to tell his son a story of how he himself had been frightened and humiliated by bullies when he was little. One of them actually held Darby down and forced clumps of dirt and grass into Darby's mouth. Today, Darby is a tall and imposing confident motivational speaker. To picture him as a terrified little boy with dirt being forced into his mouth must have been very dramatic for his son.

"I wanted him to know that he wasn't alone," Darby said. "I wanted him to realize that there was nothing wrong with him, and that he wasn't a coward."

After establishing that deeply compassionate connection, Darby and his son could talk about the action they were going to take to see that the bullying didn't happen again.

What Darby did to create closeness with his son was to reveal his own weakness and his own humanity. Contrast that to what many other people would do in a similar situation.

"You shouldn't feel afraid!" they would yell. "You should report those boys! You should stand up to them! You don't have anything to be afraid about. Why are you so afraid?"

When people are uncomfortable with another person's feelings, the first impulse is to make those feelings wrong. To tell them that they shouldn't be feeling that way. But that kind of communication only causes distance. Whenever we make someone wrong for how they're feeling, we put distance between us.

It is helpful to have the awareness that no feeling is wrong. All feelings are right. All feelings are exactly correct, because they are exactly what that person is feeling. There is no right or wrong involved. The feeling is a sensation being felt, just like a fever.

We would never say, "You shouldn't have a fever! It's wrong for you to have a fever! You have nothing to base that fever on!"

Feelings are the same thing as a fever. They are experienced in the body the same way. But we're always trying to make other peoples' feelings wrong, and, when we do, it *always* creates distance between us.

Closeness comes from revealing ourselves. It comes from dramatizing what we have in common.

~ 50 Ways to Create Relationships

65

Take your time

There is no such thing as constructive criticism.

~ Dale Carnegie

When a monthly women's magazine recently called to talk to me for an article they were writing on "How To Give Criticism Without Feeling Guilty," my impulse was to simply say, "You can't."

My first temptation was to say to them that you always feel guilty after criticizing somebody, and well you *should*.

In fact, there's a good reason for feeling guilty after giving criticism. Criticizing is a very unkind thing to do to someone. If your body and emotions are causing guilt to occur that's because they are only trying to protect you from eventually losing *all* your friends. The body sends that guilt signal because the body knows you need friends to survive.

But then after talking to the nice lady from the magazine for a while I finally agreed with her point that there were *some* circumstances that would come up in a person's life when criticism was appropriate (although, it sounded like her article was going to suggest that we have to give criticism all day, every day), and if it's appropriate then why should we have to feel guilty? The answer is, we don't.

So my ultimate answer was, if you have to deliver criticism, make sure you take your time.

The most important thing about criticism is not how it is said but how it is heard. How people are hearing you is more important than what you are saying.

Take your time to talk about what your fundamental commitment is to that person. If he is your employee, and you must correct some behavior, tell him first what your primary commitment is. You are committed to his success. You are committed to his career progress. You are committed to his happiness and fulfillment on the job. You acknowledge all the good he has done and what his potential is.

Then you relate your own past to his behavior. You let him know that you consider yourself to be human like he is. You've made bigger, more embarrassing mistakes in your life than he ever will. He is no worse than you once were.

Then you point out the behavior that is working against your helping him reach his goals. You highlight the behavior that goes against the fundamental agreement you have with each other, whatever that agreement is.

Finally, you make a request. You don't criticize, or judge him, or make him wrong; you make a request. A simple request. If he agrees to fulfill your request, you have a new agreement. Agreements are mutual, they are not one person lording it over another.

Turning criticism into agreement

Many years ago, I ran a small company. We had weekly employee meetings and a woman I will call Cleo was always showing up late to our team meetings. She would come rushing in, arms full of clutter, about ten minutes after the meeting started, with hushed apologies all around. When it came time for her to say something in the meeting, she always first mentioned her tardiness. She apologized to everyone for being late.

It was always something. Her daughter's teacher called. A client had kept her on the phone. She had to rush over to put out some business fire somewhere. There were always "good" reasons.

Finally I asked Cleo if she would meet with me. I applied my "take your time" formula. I started the conversation by telling her how much I valued her work, and how committed I was to making sure her career was succeeding. I mentioned some great things she had done, and I mentioned a few things she and I had done that had advanced her career. Then I said I was going to talk about being late to meetings, because I knew it was a source of discomfort and embarrassment to her to have it happen so often. I talked about my earlier life, when I was always late. I had cultivated a kind of legend around being energetic, creative, and completely disorganized. The disorganized part was affecting my professional relationships, but somehow I couldn't figure out how to time my life so that nothing would come up to keep me from being on time.

"I finally realized that it was immaturity," I told Cleo. "I don't know if this fits for you, but being late everywhere was my final stand against growing up. I would show the world who was in control. Not the boring grown-up world that wants me to be places on time. No! I myself was in charge of my life! I would suffer any embarrassment I could to keep that illusion of control."

"But I actually do want to be on time," said Cleo.

"I don't believe that's really true," I said. "Because if you really wanted to, you would."

"No, it's just circumstances," she said. "They keep coming up at the wrong time. There's nothing I can do."

"Let's see if that's really true," I said, smiling, and she could tell that I had one of my famous brain puzzles ready to present to her.

"Here's a question for you," I said. "Do you miss any airplanes? What I mean by that is, do you schedule flights and then not make the flight? Does that happen quite often?"

"No."

"Well, I wonder why not. I mean, all these circumstances that are preventing you from coming to our team meetings on time, they are still in operation when you have to catch a plane, right? Outside circumstances don't lose their power or stop occurring just because you've bought a plane ticket, right?"

"I guess not."

"Then why don't you miss those flights?"

"Well, I guess because flights cost a lot of money."

"Yes," I said. "That's part of it. And because they cost a lot of money, you have made them more of a priority. You've made them important to yourself and to others. In fact, I'd be willing to bet that you speak differently about them than you do about your other time commitments."

"No," she said. "Not that I'm aware of."

"I bet you do," I smiled, trying to encourage her to see the humor in this conversation. "When you've booked a flight to Chicago for next week, I bet you speak of it with the language of absolute commitment. I bet you say things like, 'I'll be in Chicago next week.' Or, 'I can't do that, I'm going to be in Chicago.' Or someone might ask you what you're doing next Wednesday at noon and you might say, "At noon Wednesday? I'll be on a plane to Chicago.' You are speaking the language of absolute certainty."

"Okay," she said, "I guess I do talk that way about planes and flights and things like that."

"And that's because you have made them important enough in your mind to speak about them differently, and think about them differently. Because you take on the language and thoughts of absolute certainty, you never miss any flights. If a circumstance comes up, you handle it, or get someone else to."

"And you think I could do that with meetings, too?" she said.

"If you gave your word that you would, I'd bet my house that you would."

"What about traffic? What if I'm slowed up by a traffic jam?" she said.

"The best way to make certain you're not late for a meeting is not to just barely be on time, but to be early. People who are early are never late. Don't you always get to the airport a little early?"

"Yes, I do."

"So I have a request," I said. "I am requesting that you treat our team meetings with as much importance as you treat your travel plans. I am requesting that you arrive early at every team meeting for the next six weeks, and just to show me that you're keeping the agreement, I would like you to come see me at least fifteen minutes before each team meeting. We can have a good talk, so your time won't be wasted. After the six weeks, I trust you completely to make it to every team meeting on time and set the standard for other people. You will do it because it represents your word, and your word is everything to you. Are you willing to do that? Don't just say yes; tell me if you are willing to make it a formal agreement."

"Okay," she said, smiling and reaching her hand out to shake mine, "I agree."

She left looking cheerful, and we never had another problem

with her again showing up late to team meetings. Often I would acknowledge her to the rest of the team for being someone who kept her agreements and someone I could count on.

So, if I *must* criticize someone, it helps to take my time. Take the time to set things up. This is the process that always seems to work:

1. State my commitments to the person.

2. Relate personally to the problem by revealing my own weaknesses.

3. Make a request.

4. Seek an agreement.

Agreements are mutual, and criticism is one-sided. Criticism creates distance between us. Agreements bring us closer.

66

Live your life forward

*Why don't we have a psychology that asks,
How do you change your marriage from okay back to great?
Or that advises you when your job doesn't give you joy?*

~ Martin Seligman

Some of us go back over the past too much. We never got all our resentment out about tiny past hurts and problems, so we carry them around. We work them into the next encounter with the next person we see.

But we contaminate our relationships this way.

The great philosopher Soren Kierkegaard once said,

Philosophy is perfectly right in saying that life must be understood backward. But then one forgets the other clause— that it must be lived forward.

The same is true of relationships. They are best understood backward. They're best understood looking back throughout the history of the relationship. All those conversations we had are there to learn from. In them, people tell us, if we pay attention, we learn how they want to be treated.

But to really grow a relationship into something fun and wonderful, whether in business or in life, the trick is to live it forward. The trick is to always picture what you want and live into that picture with every conversation, every small gift, every acknowledgment, and every act of service.

The experience is one of living forward into an intention.

When we get dragged by our emotions into the past, the trick is to gently return to what it is you *want*, the way a transcendental meditator quietly brings his attention back to a mantra. Make a mantra (a repeated thought) of your intention. Bring your attention back to it. Don't let your attention become a rolling stone. Or a wandering star. Or a spoiled child running wild in the grocery store.

Often what people want is simpler and easier to get than they realize. The things they desire are often hidden right behind the next door. Once, a company in Phoenix, Ariz., showed me internal surveys that revealed that some of their employees thought the company "lacked the courage and the will" to properly measure and manage each other's performance. I suggested that they did not lack the courage and the will (because no human really lacks these things). I asked them to consider the possibility that all they lacked was a routine.

Sometimes when I think I lack willpower all I really lack is a routine. If I want to lose weight, the easy thing to tell myself is that I lack the will to exercise. But that's not really the truth. All I lack is a routine.

Figure out what you want and begin a simple routine that makes certain you do something about it every day. Pay attention to your intention and it will become reality.

If I want a friendship with my daughter, my choices are to live backward into what I regret or live forward into what I want. If I think we have a problem communicating, I can dwell on that. But if I want a future in which she and I are friends, all I have to do is whisper softly to myself the word *friends* when I see her and my behavior is entirely different. Soon I am kidding around and having fun with her. Soon I am listening to her, as friends often do.

~ 50 Ways to Create Relationships

67

Learn to say no

Self-respect is the fruit of discipline; the sense of dignity grows with the ability to say no to oneself.

~ Abraham Heschel

Many people get sidetracked into designing and drawing up all kinds of wish lists in their lives without stopping to say *no* to what they really don't want.

In relationships, it's important to say no. "No! I will not accept that. I will not be with someone who cheats on me, who disrespects me, who abuses me in any way." That kind of "no" is a more powerful stand than all the wishes in the world.

Often when I am working with people trying to construct goals and missions we go way off track when we attempt to imagine what it is we want. However, when we start at what it is we *don't* want (in this company, in this relationship, in this home) then we get clear and decisive. Then what we do want emerges of its own logic and beauty.

"No" is the strongest of all words. Because by saying no, you are taking a stand. You are staking all your life's energy on stopping something. You are drawing a line in the sand. It's the strongest language we have to use, because it's the most powerfully decisive thought a human can think.

I have watched and lived and worked with people who wasted

their lives on a seemingly hopeless and incurable addiction to alcohol. Then they wake up one day after hitting a low enough bottom and simply say no. That one word becomes the strongest word they ever said because it changes their lives completely.

Later, the people would invent complicated sentiments about saying yes to a higher power or to sobriety or to freedom and love and peace and kindness, but all of that is just invented frosting when compared to the raw irrevocable power of the time they said no. No to this. No more. Not one more drink.

Often when people are having difficulty negotiating something it is helpful to return them to the core strength of no. What is it that you absolutely do not want? What won't you tolerate? Once the no's are all on the table, the yes's often emerge and become obvious. But when we hide the no's they fester inside us as primordial urges and fears. Soon the secret knowledge of them undermines a long negotiation full of wishes and hopes and empty dreams.

In all relationship-building, it's most effective to first take a stand against what you don't want and will not accept. For example, if I would love to have a romantic relationship in my life, the best thing I can do is first take a stand against its opposite.

Because if I spend all my time wishing and hoping and dreaming of what I would like to have, I'll probably carry those wishes into the nursing home with me.

If, however, I wake up one day and realize that I am lonely and not making a difference anywhere and not enjoying any part of this solitary life in which all I do creatively is try to figure out how to entertain or pamper myself today then I might have worked up enough inner strength to say the strongest word there is in this situation, "No!" No to this life. No to this isolation. No to this loneliness. I'm ending it. It's over. I won't permit it in my life for another minute.

And then, emboldened by my stand, I will head out the door to meet people and help people and connect with people everywhere I can.

68

Get engaged

It is better to be happy for the moment and be burned up with beauty than to live a long time and be bored all the while.

~ Logan Pearsall Smith

When people are young and immature, their minds are always going on "out of body" excursions. It's hard for them to stay focused on any given conversation. You often see kids' eyes glaze over when you talk to them for more than a few seconds.

But as young people mature, it is possible for them to gain more and more control over their roving minds. Soon they can reel themselves in and settle down to really listen to someone else. Soon their minds are experiencing the poet Rilke's "stillness like the heart of a rose." That's when relationships get better and better.

The best ways to create relationships are also the best ways to listen to people. That's because listening creates such an immediate bond.

The kind of listening it's most fun to keep practicing is *engaged* listening. In that format, when I'm listening, I'm totally engaged—like gears in a machine are engaged—totally locked into what you are saying.

A few years ago in one of our seminars, a guy at the back of the room raised his hand and said, "Hey, Steve. I think I know what you mean by engaged listening. When I was engaged to my wife, I listened to her a lot differently than I do now."

That was his idea of engaged listening. He wasn't far off, because humor rarely is. If you really think about it, he was probably more correct than I realized as I laughed at him and mocked his observation.

When we are in the process of falling in love, we're using the full scope of our imaginations to listen with. Somehow, during courtship, we drop the habitual worry and fire up the imagination again and use it like we did when we were children—to create with, and be clever, and be thoughtful and imaginative. So we listen differently, too. What would be a boring night of talk to other people, in courtship becomes some enchanted evening. We listen with all we've got. We listen in a way that honors and adores the other person. In more ways than one, we tend to become engaged.

I can only get better and better at engaged listening through repetition. When I find my mind has left the room, I simply bring it back. I repeat this process every time it happens. Pretty soon bringing it back gets easier and easier, like reeling in a fish. After practice, I can even catch the fish on its way out of the room. Soon I can even catch it right at the point of impulse, as it's *considering* leaving the room.

It's harder to think about practice than it is to actually practice. That's because we think of practice as boring and dread sets in. Practice is the last thing we want recommended to us. But practice, in itself, really isn't boring. What's truly boring is *thinking about practicing* ahead of time.

Once I'm actually practicing something, I know I am getting better at it. I can sense it and feel it. Repetition increases skill. And anything I'm getting better at becomes more and more fun to do. This is especially true of engaged listening.

~ 50 Ways to Create Relationships

69

Jump into action

Regret for the things we did can be tempered by time. It is regret for the things we did not do that is inconsolable.

~ Sydney J. Harris

Colin Wilson once pointed out that one sure way to cure people of feeling depressed would be to throw them down a flight of stairs.

Their feelings would change immediately.

In this age of compassion, sensitivity, and reverence for depression, that would probably not be a popular sentiment. But inside the idea is something worth considering.

One day Steve Hardison invited me over to his home for lunch and conversation and he spent some of our time together explaining his system of personal coaching. Given his huge influence on my life, it was fun to listen to him talk about his personal coaching theory.

"It's all about action," he said. "People's relationship problems can all be traced to a lack of willingness to take action. If I can get someone into action, I know my coaching will be successful."

"What if it's not the right action?" I asked.

"It's not a matter of right and wrong so much as it is a matter of being in action and not being in action," he said. "Let's say you come to me with a problem. If I can get you into action, *any kind of action,* the magnitude of the problem will start to diminish right away."

We were at his kitchen table enjoying sandwiches when he gestured toward his backyard, which we could see through the picture window.

"Let's say you come to me with a problem in your life and we go out back here to talk about it. And as you're describing your problem to me I have a little ball I am throwing across the lawn and asking you to go get for me. As you talk, I keep tossing the ball out there, and you're telling me this huge problem in your life as you go get the ball and bring it back to me each time. And as you go out and return each time, your problem is getting smaller and smaller in your mind. If I had asked you to rate your happiness in this matter on a scale of one to 10 before we started discussing it, you might have said it was a two or a three. I guarantee you that after retrieving the ball for me over and over you would rate your feelings about this problem much higher."

"Like getting a dog to fetch?" I said.

"Yes," he laughed.

"Well, what would that action have to do with this particular problem?"

"That's my point!" he said. "You asked if action would be valuable if it wasn't the right action, and I am saying action is what is missing, not doing the right thing. So, obviously, fetching a ball wouldn't relate to much, but your problem would diminish in your mind. It would become more manageable to you."

Think of someone right now. Have it be a person that you have a difficult relationship with in business or in personal life. Now, immediately, take some kind of action. Get on the phone with them to acknowledge something, send them an email of gratitude for something, make an appointment to see them, anything. Any action will do. And then sit back and evaluate. How did you feel about this relationship when you first thought of the person? How do you feel about it now?

Mind

70

Who died?

My niece once wore a tee shirt that said, "Who died and made you Elvis?"

Elvis! After my father, Elvis was my first true hero. Elvis Presley! King of rock and roll. He must have dreamed big, don't you think? Given his achievements in the world of entertainment, and his legendary status. I was sure he dreamed big all the way.

Look at what he achieved! The title of his second album of gold records was *50,000,000 Elvis Fans Can't Be Wrong.*

Feeding my assumption that he dreamed big was his movie called *Follow That Dream,* in which he sang, "You've gotta follow that dream wherever that dream may lead."

I assumed he meant follow that *big* dream.

But when I study the Presley biographies and interviews I find out that there was never a big dream. Never. In fact, it seemed like Elvis only dreamed small. (He wanted to be a truck driver.)

And what was his musical dream? To make a recording for his mother. That was it. Not to sing for millions of fans, but just for his mother.

This dream would cost him four dollars. That's how small it was. He paid his four dollars and went into a recording booth in Memphis and sang one song to give to his mother. After they recorded him they made him an acetate that he could put on his mother's turntable and play for her. A dream come true. (As small dreams always seem to do.)

But there was something about that recording that had the recording studio owner listen again and again. Something about that voice. Such an unusual combination of vulnerability and strength. There was innocence in it, but underneath there was swagger too. The owner would play it for people and say, "Believe it or not, this guy's white."

Months went by and Elvis was invited back into the studio to see what else he could do. He tried some more soft ballads with a couple of musicians, and it was okay but not amazing. Then during a break they started fooling around with an up-tempo rhythm and Elvis sang a wild and rocking version of "That's All Right Mama," and the studio owner came out of his chair.

The rest is history. And yet . . . no big dream was ever involved. Just a willingness to sing from the heart. And though his initial dream was small, his fame became huge.

And his story is just one of many that show us that even though big dreams are great and exciting, they're not necessary. You can go the other way too. You can *shift your mind* down to the smallest imaginable intention.

And the reason this is worth realizing is that so many people I have met become confused and feel inadequate when they can't come up with some kind of big dream to commit to and follow.

Wouldn't it be good for them to know that it's not always necessary?

~ Shift Your Mind, Shift the World

71

Opportunity is already here

I used to wait around and hope somebody would give me a *big* opportunity. I used to think that was what I needed . . . a fresh start . . . so that I could show what I could do!

When you are like I was, chronically dissatisfied with life and unhappy with yourself, you often think something BIG has to happen OUT THERE IN THE WORLD to turn an inner feeling around.

I know I did.

So I tried hard to dream big. I didn't know this was an inner game, and that the perceived world wasn't going to "shift" without my awareness shifting first. I didn't know that.

I also didn't know that I could be happy with what I had. That happiness didn't have anything to do with exceptional achievement. Instead, I thought I probably had to be some form of a rock star like Elvis for this inner unhappiness to change.

And here's the irony: not even Elvis needed that. A major part of Elvis' appeal to the world was the joyful energy he was *already demonstrating* when he sang, even at the very start. People felt that.

The joy came first, not later after some kind of achievement or recognition.

Recently I found an old quote by Elvis in *Esquire* magazine in which he said, "All my life, I've always had a nice time. We never had any money or nothin', but we never were hungry, you know. That's something to be thankful for."

All his life he always had a nice time? Not just after he got rich and famous?

For most of my life my thoughts and beliefs kept me from having that kind of nice time. Those were not good days for me. Those were the days before the mind shifts started . . . those were the days when I thought thoughts like these:

"If only someone believed in me."

"When someone gives me the right opportunity, then I'll be on my way to being happy!"

"When I luck into the proper career that's my true calling, then I'll be able to display my true talent—the real me."

Then one day it shifted to this: *You can come from happiness right now.* You can have it be in every encounter. You can light up even the smallest task with enthusiastic creativity if you want to. That's the whole meaning of shifting in the mind. It happens in a heartbeat.

Just like shifting gears in a sports car. The shift doesn't take time. It's a roll of the wrist.

~ Shift Your Mind, Shift the World

72

Stories can put you in a prison

Some people *think* they don't get out on the road because they're lazy. They think they don't write, paint, make music, build bird houses, design homes, etc., etc., because they are lazy.

But laziness is just a story. We like to make stories up like this . . . stories about what we are like.

But soon they become chains. All of them.

Because the real fun is in the *action*—not the story. The real fun happens once you are up and riding. Therefore the story is, in fact, the very thing that keeps you off the bike.

But anyone can rise above a story. Or below it. Or beyond it. It's a mind shift. Anyone can leave any personal quality like "laziness" in the dust. Laziness will eat your dust. Shift the mind and the world shifts, too. Always both. Always simultaneous.

Q: What makes us spin all these stories?

A: We get fascinated with ourselves.

We become intoxicated just thinking about ourselves. Then we share with others what we think we are like. All the qualities we think we have, negative or positive, it soon doesn't matter. Lots of people even *brag* about being lazy.

"I was just too lazy to do that! I'm soooo lazy, ha ha ha ha ha. I *was* going to do that, but I was too lazy. I'm also too lazy to work out. I'm too lazy to learn a foreign language, so I'm going to take an interpreter with me when I go to that country. I know, I've been appointed ambassador, and it probably would be more professional of me if I learned the language of the country I was going to be in, but I'll have interpreters all around me, so let's just do it that way. I'm lazy. But you knew that. You knew that, didn't you? Have I told you about myself? Pull up a chair."

It's amazing how many American ambassadors refuse to learn the language of the country they are in. They say things like, "I'm not good with languages," but to themselves or to their family they'll say, "I'm just too lazy to learn it. I admit it! I've always been lazy. Goes way back. All the way back. As a fetus I was lazy. Ha ha ha ha ha ha ha."

All these "lazy" personality traits we adopt are merely facets of fear. Because when we are in joyful and pure action, or joyful and pure relaxation, there is no fixed personality anymore. Certainly no laziness.

Buckminster Fuller used to say, "I seem to be a verb."

Maybe you were *not* too lazy to do that one thing in your life you always wanted to do. Maybe you were *afraid of something*.

But once you can see that, your mind is open. And the mind that is open will always shift.

~ *Shift Your Mind, Shift the World*

73

How do I set myself free?

Truth is beauty, and beauty sets you free.

Beautiful movement, like that of a dancer or an athlete, can be where your awareness of freedom comes from. It can also come from venturing forth. Going places I didn't know I could go.

Happiness is not some kind of pleasure I get eating chocolate bunnies or binge-watching vampire shows. That is really not happiness. That may feel like short-term pleasure. But it is often used to get myself out of my personal thinking and story-telling. Temporarily.

Spinning and then believing a story of laziness is a way of lying low instead of rising up. So when I'm "too lazy" to make my calls, I'm lying low instead of rising up. I am hanging back, instead of venturing forth. That's what my laziness story really is. It's a pause button. It's a retreat into passivity. It's a retreat into the seeming illusion, the false illusion (illusions are false by definition, aren't they?) that hanging back or lying low is SAFER for me than venturing forth.

So you see a person on the couch, and rather than being out this Saturday, going to his son's game, helping his neighbors, cleaning the yard, painting the bird house, taking a long walk— doing wonderful things, active things, the person is instead on the couch vegging out; and we say he's lazy, but really, deep down, he wants to hang back rather than venture forth. For safety's sake.

On the other hand the great dance teacher Martha Graham said, "I am a dancer. I believe that we learn by practice. Whether it means to learn to dance by practicing dancing or to learn to live by practicing living, the principles are the same."

Most people would never practice living. Ever. They are too busy trying to please others to enact and practice a vision of their own . . . not realizing that the very thing they might practice, like a Martha Graham ballet, or a Steph Curry jump shot, becomes the most pleasing thing in the world for others to behold.

~ Shift Your Mind, Shift the World

74

What have we done to money?

Around the pure loving energy that money is, we have wrapped beliefs such as shortage, obligation, hard work, loss, manipulation, security and survival. We have then wrapped layers of emotional consequences such as fear, frustration, anger and shame.

~ Arnold M. Patent

This is an "insecure"-looking universe! How beautiful that it all changes daily. It ebbs and flows and comes and goes. The tide comes in and the tide goes out.

And such good tidings come to all who can see that clearly.

Because then it's possible to welcome the "hard times," because they allow us to rise up and play well. They allow us to renew our comprehension of money as pure, loving energy that flows to those who best serve others.

The award-winning novelist Walker Percy had some very interesting questions about this paradox. He asked:

"Why do people often feel so bad in good environments that they prefer bad environments?"

"Why is a man apt to feel bad in a good environment, say Short Hills, New Jersey, on an ordinary Wednesday afternoon? Why is the same man apt to feel good in a very bad environment, say an old hotel on Key Largo in a hurricane?"

I think we know the answer to these questions.

Challenges and problems can give us a new feeling of life.

Standing beside you, with my arm around you, in that old hotel in Key Largo, with the hurricane winds and rain whipping at the windows, we had adventure. That sense of wild challenge, dancing with the elements; we really felt *alive* again. Our minds were shifting all by themselves.

I can allow that same context of adventure to flow in to my "problems with money." The same way I felt when I was a small child entering a new field of play.

75

Just allow your games to begin

People can improve their careers faster if they relate their careers to a game. Or a playful contest . . . or a Bruce Lee martial arts tournament.

They need to take it out of the category of "grim reality" and put it into the game mentality, so it can free them up to find their best thinking.

So today I'm going to see if I can picture a possible game. Instead of picturing what's wrong with life. That's the whole formula right there.

When I'm depressed, I meditate on one non-transformational mantra: Me. Me. Me. Me. Me. So today I will try a change of course. Rather than obsessing about my unique personality and ego, I will pick a game to play. Once I decide what that is, then I'll just be whoever I want to be to get that game going.

When I hit a speed bump, I might simply step back a little, in prayer or meditation or on a good long walk, and observe the patterns of thought that clouded up my brain and see how all those patterns obscured my spirit. I let them fall away. I love the dissolution. It's beautiful, like fireworks in the sky as they fall and fade.

I want to remind myself that the body takes each thought and translates it into a feeling, which is a wonderful system if I understand it. If I know how it works, how it always goes thought-to-feeling, then I can allow that awareness to effect a mind shift.

Falling out of self-centered, self-conscious seriousness, I fall in love with the game.

76

You know how to do commitment

I love people who say "Done" when you request something.
Look at how time disappears when that happens! When the person is committed, the task is not "*going to* be done" in the future; it's done. Already. Done even before it's done!

The task is no longer in the past or in the future, because with commitment, there is no more time. That's why tenses are meaningless in the face of a commitment.

"Can you coach me by phone Friday at 3:00 p.m.?" someone asks, and I say, "No. I will have just gotten off my plane to New York."

Look at that weird tense. Will have just gotten. It's striving to express something definite and guaranteed! What you're seeing is my commitment to be in New York. It makes mincemeat of time. And tense.

People say, "I'm in New York that week." That's present tense! Why use present tense when it's the future? Because commitment is there. Commitment makes it *already done* right now even though it is technically going to happen in the future.

I know I am going to be on that plane. I've made that commitment. Therefore, in my mind, I'm already there! My mind can shift time. And time is the stuff life is made of.

That's the beauty of a created commitment. Certainty arrives!

And certainty is so different than belief. The etymological root of belief is to "fervently hope" something is true. To try to believe in yourself is to fervently hope you can do what you say you can do.

But a commitment is different. It's the internal voice that says, "I am *certain* I am doing this."

No matter what. No matter how hard.

This is already done.

~ Shift Your Mind, Shift the World

77

My terror was you'd set me free

There is a radical, controversial, powerful poet named Frederick Seidel. At the beginning of a recent book I wrote I used his lines:

> Don't cure me. Sickness is my me.
> My terror was you'd set me free.

I think those lines express so beautifully what happens when we go to a coach or a therapist or a mentor. We don't really want to be cured of our sick beliefs because we think that's who we are! We get confused and think our sickness is our identity. If I lose that, maybe I'll be nothing. Don't cure me. Sickness *is* my me.

The second line by the poet says, "My terror was you'd set me free."

I know that terror! I felt it before going to Byron Katie's nine-day school. Many people assume Katie is some kind of diaphanous being, a new age priestess with feel-good, pseudo-spiritual rituals for the gullible. Well, not really!

Her work asks that the worker of the work bring great courage to the party. She calls it "the great undoing." One woman stood up halfway through the school and said, "I feel like I'm going to die" and Katie said, "Let's hope you do."

How cruel a thing to say! Or so it would seem. But Katie

merely wanted that woman's false identity to die so that her true, healthy, infinite being would be set free to just LOVE EVERYTHING. Terrifying. Sickness was my me. My terror was she'd set me free.

I like these words from John Lennon, from a desolate song he wrote called "Isolation":

> People say we got it made.
> Don't they know we're so afraid?

People thought John and Yoko had it made. They had fame and fortune. They could do anything they wanted. While you and I? Who screams for *us*? And we do things because we HAVE TO! The Beatles had it made.

So why, then, were they so afraid? Why? Can we even imagine the painful isolation that comes with fame? People loving you for all the wrong reasons? People loving you, not because of their true experience of the real you, but because of the fame you have. The mere name and face recognition. Hey, look! Isn't that one of the Beatles? Or is it one of the Beastie Boys? What does it matter? I've just seen a *face*! Can I have your autograph? I want to be able to show it to people back home. I want them to see that I saw someone whose face is famous. What? You're having dinner with your wife? What are you, some kind of snob, better than someone like me?

No wonder it feels like isolation. No wonder he sang, "Don't they know we're so afraid."

But the antidote to all of this isolation and fear is sweet, and fun to watch being put into play. The fearless life is no more than this fearless moment . . . the one your mind will always shift to when you finally know about it. Soon you'll become inseparable from the gentle awareness that shifts your mind to joy.

You won't be upset even when your brain is grinding out in the gear of personal thought and worry. You'll see it and smile. It's just a train of thought; it's not who you are. And if you can see the train, you're not the train.

Just as in real life, if you're watching a train pull out of the station, you are not on that train.

It's no longer a mystery to understand that a train of thought is only that. Not who I am. But when I believe my thoughts they become like the *Mystery Train* in the song written by Junior Parker and recorded by Elvis, The Band and the Doors:

> Train, train rolling down the line
> Well it took my baby
> And left poor me behind

78

Why do children teach us so much?

And you, of tender years,
Can't know the fears that your elders grew by,
And so please help them with your youth,
They seek the truth before they can die.

~ Crosby, Stills, Nash & Young

It's fun to watch children. To talk to them and really see how they love to learn and grow. We can observe so much.

Children spend most of their time in the alpha brainwave state. That's why children learn so effortlessly. Notice how they easily learn a second language. As Peter Ragnar says, "All an infant needs to do is listen and imitate. But adults, with an assortment of concerns and mental stresses, struggle with it as if it were a great task. An infant raised in a relaxed, carefree, mentally enriching environment absorbs like a sponge."

Accessing this alpha state is a true mind shift. It happens when we dream. It happens in meditation. It happens during hypnosis. And it happens during any kind of deep relaxation and falling out of personal thinking.

The anxious, left-brained beta state is another story. It's a version of the worried mind most people bring to their day's work. But sometimes just closing your eyes and taking a deep breath and picturing the ocean within can allow the shift that gives you the peaceful idea you've been waiting for.

79

Optimism is a user-friendly program

Once while I was in the airport waiting to fly away, I noticed people running around, frantically opening laptops and chattering into cell phones and dashing from gate to gate. I began to wonder, what are they chasing?

It had to be stories, right? Chasing the stories about the things they think they need. Chasing relationships, money, new cars, granite countertops and validation of their excellent parenting.

I do this, too? Oh yes. Looking for life in all the wrong places. Not understanding the word "within." Not stopping to allow everyday good fortune to inspire me. Drawing my sword and seeking better kingdoms in distant lands.

And why do I forget that the kingdom is already here? It's the kingdom that has been described for thousands of years as "within."

I'm here in Atlanta working with my clients at a large company to show them that the technology of the mind (that knows how to shift) can match their peerless technology on the factory floor. Or at least that's the language I use to avoid sounding like a practitioner of new-age, "soft" training.

I'm showing them on a slide that the brain can use the "technology of optimism" as a proven biocomputer program to open up creativity and solution-thinking.

And without such a shift? They will buy into the common (erroneous) wisdom that says optimism is a personality trait you're either born with or not. Like a hardwired sunny disposition. And the "optimist" in the common, everyday perception is a happy, glad-handing idiotic, beaming, smiling, false front of upbeat mannerisms.

Actually, optimism is tougher than all that. Optimism, when it's real, is a powerful, precise, teachable tool for unlocking the right side of the brain—and all its practical functions.

Dr. Martin Seligman conducted studies of over half a million people for twenty years. He scientifically validated two important findings in those studies: 1) Optimism is more effective than pessimism, and 2) Optimism can be learned.

Shocking. It can be learned! Aren't we stuck with our personalities? If a person is moody, is she not permanently moody? As permanent as her blue eyes?

Goodness, no. When you read *Learned Optimism* you learn that you can dispute—DISPUTE!—any pessimistic thought that appears. It's nothing permanent. It can disappear like a rain cloud across the sky of your mind.

Dispute it. Challenge it. Question it. Make the case for a greater possibility than a thought can hold. Make the case for more options open to you than gloom.

It's as if you had a higher self that you don't call on much. Except in a huge crisis. But if you called on it more and more, it would become more present. It would reveal itself to be . . . the real you.

Because that pessimistic voice in you is a very small blip on the radar screen of who you really are. Why let it rule? Just allow the shift in your mind up to optimism.

~ Shift Your Mind, Shift the World

80

Looking for love in all the wrong places

It's just like the time I was getting ready to go to a football game and looking all over—and I do mean ALL OVER—the house for my binoculars while they were, all the while, around my neck.

We search far and wide for the friends and lovers who will reassure us that we are worth something. Instead of finding the love inside we have to give. Always already there.

But then we make up a story that we need to find it in other people!

But the wonderful psychologist George Pransky teaches about how the mind can shift on this subject of love. And when it shifts, it has a calming effect.

Pransky says, "When anyone has even the slightest inkling of an understanding of the role of thought in creating perception, it has a calming effect. One avoids becoming consumed in a spiraling intensity of their own perceptions. One doesn't get carried away and upset. One goes the other direction, tending to calm down, to get a little humble about it, thinking: Maybe I need to take a fresh look at this, let my intelligence behind my thought evolve my perception, see it in a more understanding, functional light. That is the nature of life: to create more options, more possibilities."

~ Shift Your Mind, Shift the World

81

If you're not enough please stand up

W hen you take the merely linear road, nothing will ever be enough. When you strive and struggle to live out a story's narrow path from birth to death, nothing you do will ever feel like it's enough.

"I love the way you've fixed up your house! It's so charming!"

But you say, "We're not done yet. We've just got started. There's so much to do. It's really a mess."

"Oh." And here I thought it looked great.

It's a story that some people can't shake loose no matter what. It's the story of not enough.

If I tell you, "You've done well at your job," you don't agree. You say, "I really want a Division Manager position. I should have had it a year ago."

Okay. You look good, though. You've lost weight. I tell you, "You look like you've lost a lot of weight."

You say, "Not enough. Not nearly enough!"

I remark later how well your son is doing in school. I heard he almost made the honor roll.

"Well . . . yes. But he's having some problems in math that we can't seem to solve."

So he's not enough. Even your beautiful son is not enough.

Sometimes just standing up will take you out of your

horizontal "not enough" story and into the real vertical universe of *always enough for now*. It's a true mind shift. The mere act of standing on your feet forces oxygen into your lungs that wasn't there before.

Elizabeth Barrett Browning said, "He who breathes more air lives more life."

Ask your class to stand and take a breath. Look how the stagnant story they were stuck in disappears and they look so fresh and relieved. Relieved! Relieved of bored thought. Relieved of a mind mired in the tales from the crypt of not enough.

82

Let this ladder shift your mind

When two people get together in a coaching session, you now have the brain power, the mind power, the soul power, the life power of *two* human beings working together. It's not so much one plus one as it is two squared.

You may say, "Why would one need a coach for that? Why doesn't that synergistic power just happen every time *any* two people talk together or get together?"

Because they're not consciously there to produce change.

In fact, quite often they're there to belabor a conflict! That's why so many relationships slowly go south. They lapse into conflict. One person wants and expects so much from the other person that disappointment becomes the theme.

But in coaching, mind shifting occurs upward. Because the minds are after the same thing.

Some people also have a shift occur in a musical setting when they are in tune with the vibrations of the song. Other people when they exercise. Toby Estler wrote a book on the spiritual power of getting out there and running. When the body is open, the spirit enters.

Sometimes I draw a ladder to illustrate this phenomenon. People who see the ladder suddenly have a visual picture of what's happening inside their mind. Previously they wondered

"Why am I stuck?" Or: "Why is life not seeming to work for me?"

Now they can see that the answer is pretty simple and open. They are low on their ladder!

But this ladder—a ladder of human consciousness—can be ascended, with a series of shifts in the mind.

This is hard to see when you are stuck in your own story and stuck in your own belief system.

So I draw the ladder, either on a piece of paper or on the whiteboard, and at the very bottom of the ladder I put the word "death." (I want people to be mildly shocked into a realization that that would be their lowest level of consciousness. I then say after writing the word DEATH at the bottom of the ladder, "If you are trying to persuade someone at *this* level of consciousness to purchase something from you, you've got to be surreally good.")

The next step up is fear. Fear is the next step up from death. It's almost the lowest possible level of living human consciousness. It is really where everything stops. If we could see that and understand it, we would understand people so much better!

We'd understand ourselves so much better, too. We'd shift. Because once that first shift happens, up from fear, all the other shifts are now possible. Courage returns. (We were born with it.) And courage is the virtue that makes all the other virtues possible.

~ Shift Your Mind, Shift the World

83

All my anger comes from fear

Anger is a mask for fear. It's a way people transmute fear. So whenever you're angry, know that it's based on a fear. It was caused by a fear. There's no way that you could be angry without feeling threatened. The two can't exist apart from each other.

Anger feels more powerful than fear. That's why people execute the mind shift. It's a way that the ego strengthens itself so that it feels like it finally has a little power around this fear.

Because I feel helpless when I just feel the fear. Helpless is not a great feeling. It doesn't hold a candle to being royally ticked off.

So now I am angry and I can push my focus outside of me to an object. I can now identify who or what I want to blame. There's got to be somebody causing this fear in me! It's *you*, or it's the corporation, or it's the government, or it's the market, or it's some other person.

Now go up the ladder a step higher and you'll find resentment. A less dangerous form of anger. It's milder but more ongoing. It can permeate the day. If I resent this person, it can pull me down, creatively and energetically, every time I think of him. It disconnects me from any possibility of enthusiasm.

Enthusiasm? It's the place where all great things in life are created. Emerson saw this. "Nothing great," he said, "was ever created without enthusiasm."

When you jump to the highest part of the ladder, way, way up there, way above worry, resentment, anger, fear and death, there is spirit. There is absolute enthusiasm, there is humor, creativity, joy, and infinite energy, and that's where we want to keep allowing the shifting to take us, because when we can access that (the ultimate mind shift) problems look hilarious. Problems really look like the funniest things we could think of. They're not "real" problems anymore. They're just an adventure.

And that comes from the ultimate mind shift to the very highest level.

This ladder is something I draw so people can actually get a picture of *where they are,* vertically, at any given moment. Where am I? Am I down low? Stuck in worry or fear? If so, I'm not accessing my creativity, or my greatest energy, or my imagination (those states of mind are high on top of the ladder).

Creativity doesn't live down on the lower rungs. Those are the rungs that keep me stuck. I only see yes and no, black and white, bad and good—a narrowly critical mindset trapped in a small part of the linear left side of the brain.

But if I can shift and go! Oh man! I'll be in spirit, I'll be in creativity, I'll be in joy. Now I'll keep shifting so my life opens up. So I can expand myself into that joy I felt when I was young, because that was the real me. I knew it at the time.

I don't actually have to shift before I take good action. I can take the good action in a low mood. I don't have to wait. And sometimes just getting into the game allows thought to drop away, and the rising up the ladder happens on its own.

~ Shift Your Mind, Shift the World

84

You can become a liberated circle

The great novelist Vladimir Nabokov was the first person I know of to point out that a spiral is a liberated circle.

A mind full of expectations is nothing but a vicious circle. Stories about how others don't appreciate me add weight to this vicious circle.

Soon this mind of mine is grinding like a sports car stuck in first gear, crying out to be shifted.

My own mind cries out to be shifted when I'm in some vicious circle story about how *you should be* acting. When SHIFT HAPPENS the circle is liberated. It is now a spiral . . . opening languorously upward in a heavenly swirl, and there is no upper limit.

In the courses I teach on mind shifting I use Nabokov's observation that a spiral is a liberated circle. I draw the vicious circle of an unshifted mind on the white board. Then I draw a spiral. Up from fear and anger and worry and resentment. Up toward creativity, compassion and spirit. There's a gold mine in that sky. And up there at the top, beyond the gold mine, there is even more . . . things too wonderful to even talk about in linear language, or sentences that have beginnings and endings.

What keeps us trapped so low and so far away from that level?

Thinking there are "other" people. Thinking negative thoughts about those people. Unwillingness to forgive other people for being human.

There is an old saying that pretty much says it all: "To forgive is to set a prisoner free and discover the prisoner was you."

~ Shift Your Mind, Shift the World

85

Stop trying to break habits

My client Mickey said, "I know I've got to try to break this habit."

He wanted to oppose his habit, and be angry at it, and take a stand against it, and then break it into pieces.

The problem with that, Mick, is that it will push back. It will persist *because* you are fighting it and trying to break it. It will grow even stronger in significance because you've created inner conflict with it. You're feeding it with your resistance.

Also, on some strange but true level your ego believes it *needs* that habit. A habit always has some subconscious "survival" value for you so it's going to try to maintain itself if you try to force it out of your life.

So don't fight it. Replace it. Replace it with an upgraded, healthier look-alike. Habits cannot be broken, but they *can* be replaced and that's really the approach that works for me and the people I work with.

Let's look back on my life as an example. I was stuck in the habit of addiction to alcohol use for years. It was a horrific habit. It was a terrible addiction, life-threatening, life-destroying—all the things you've read and heard about if you haven't been through it yourself.

So, I could try to fight it off and just use willpower and go on a dry drunk and white-knuckle it through the rest of my life, fighting off the temptation to drink every time I went out to a social occasion or suffered an emotional story. But that's been proven not to work so well.

What does work is to replace the habit—not break it. What works—better than medication, better than psychology—is a spiritual program of recovery. That has the best track record and there's a reason for that.

When a person works a spiritual program of recovery from an addiction, they're actually *replacing* false spirit with true spirit. They're not just eliminating alcohol and going back to zero. They are replacing the "freedom" that they thought alcohol gave them, or the "release" it gave them, with something similar but better.

It's interesting that in the Old West, alcohol was described as "spirits." It's also interesting that alcohol was referred to as "false courage."

In a good program of recovery, alcohol gets replaced with true spirit and the courage to change the things you can. You are blessed with the serenity to accept the things you cannot change. Spiritual progress is now happening in life as opposed to the false chemical spirit you were pouring into an anxious human body.

The problem with addictive drugs and alcohol is that they always eventually backfire. They turn against you. What they were intended to do turns back around and goes at you. Stephen King couldn't have invented a greater horror. (But maybe *The Shining* was his attempt. For "Johnny" had a bit of a drinking problem, didn't he?)

My good friend Lindsay Brady is a hypnotherapist with a great track record for helping people quit smoking. He gets great results in just one visit.

He replaces a person's self-concept on the matter of smoking.

They go into his office perceiving themselves to be a smoker and after the session, they walk out with a new self-concept, a new self-perception that says, "I am a non-smoker." And as a non-smoker they naturally build healthy lungs with deep breathing; their health becomes vibrant, it increases, and they get better feelings about life because of the way they can breathe now as a non-smoker.

Non-smokers don't smoke.

So it's not just "quitting smoking" that's going on—smoking is being perceptually replaced by something that's even better, and that's really the way to get rid of a habit.

If I have a habit, for example, of having a messy workspace I might decide that I don't want that—I want more organization. Then what I can do is *replace* the messy workspace with something that I like better and that functions better. I don't just want to get rid of the mess. I don't want to just break the habit of being disorganized, I want to create a new system that I actually like better. Otherwise there's no replacement. It won't hold. Ever.

So always look for something you can replace your habit with that's better. Because subconsciously your habit is there as a survival mechanism. At some level you think that this habit is something you need. So in order for that subconscious clinging to the habit to be let go, you want to show your subconscious mind that the new system you've introduced into your life is even better! Then it can let go.

That's the law of creation. Create a replacement for the habit you don't like. Do not react to the habit by fighting it off. The law of creation is a law that can kick in at any stage when you're ready to allow a mind shift.

~ Shift Your Mind, Shift the World

86

How most people get it wrong

When people believe that they have a particular fixed personality it can become a prison for them. What was once formed to give them, perhaps, a hoped-for sense of safety, identity and individuality, now can put them in total lockdown.

When I work with people who want to excel but aren't excelling, one of the first things I see getting in the way is what they believe their fixed personality is. What they believe they are like, and therefore must always be like.

Now it's true that people have various belief systems inside themselves that have been created from childhood by repeated thoughts. These systems become what everyone else calls "personality," but it's anything but fixed.

There's nothing permanent in them, or anything else out in the physical world under the sun.

Yet people's imaginary permanent characteristics can become like a religion to them. Something to believe in! They might have been indoctrinated into the dogma early: they were told they were lazy, or disorganized, or cowardly, or that they weren't thoughtful about other people. Soon these various personality characteristics became their beliefs.

Who among us can really see that they are only fleeting *thoughts?* Very few do, but everyone can!

Let's use the example of a house burning down across the street. I run out of my house and I hear a small child crying inside the flames and I run in, I grab the child and I bring her out. All of this was done in a heightened state of *action beyond and without personal thought*. I was swept up in and then carried by what I felt simply needed to be done. It almost felt automatic. No time to think! Just did it! So it certainly wasn't the result of any particular personality showing its stuff.

We read accounts of a grandmother lifting the back of a car to free a trapped child or animal. Incredible feats of courage and improbable strength.

But we can't see that it comes from dropping the illusion of a permanent personality and allowing the fertile void to replace it with immediate action. A noun drops away to get replaced by a verb.

Your restrictive, permanent personality was never anything but repeated thoughts. They were repeated enough times to make a made-up illusion of "you," just the way a sparkler at night waved in a circle looks like a glowing whole circle. It's not a thing! It's a rotation of disappearing light. That's who the personal "you" are.

In the moment of *now* you can drop all of that rotating thought you call you. You can be whoever you choose to be given the higher purpose calling to you. You can have your actions called *forth by* the game you are playing, instead of trying to *come out of* your personality. Such good news for those (including the old me) hung up inside pathological limitation.

87

Shifting out of the unreal

One of the most important ways to shift the mind on our way to success is to shift from what's unreal to what's real. When you are working with what's really *real* you can get to success so much faster.

Imagine you are walking down the narrow road toward home, and there's a boulder in the road and you see it and say "I've got to take a side road now—I've got to do something different—I've got to go through the woods to get to my home, because there's a boulder in the road."

Now you're in the woods plowing through the thicket, trying to find an opening to get back home—to success, to wherever you want to go in life.

But what if that boulder in the road were not real? What if the boulder was just an illusion—something you thought was real— it looked real—everyone said it was real—and because you *believed* it was real, you are in the woods, pushing through the poison ivy, the poison oak, trying to get back home?

Absurd example? Well it happens every day. We are sidetracked by imaginary fears every day. That's why reality is so important to work with.

Because the real road to success is often so clear we can't see it.

So we stop and take side roads, and soon that's called "being busy" or "fighting fires" or handling big problems. Most people do this. They are overwhelmed by their distractions. They become too busy to succeed.

What if, instead of busy, I were "focused" in a relaxed, but paradoxically, energetic way. Focused, locked in, excited, enthusiastic, one-pointed.

I got a call the other day from a person who was apologizing to me for missing a phone appointment he had with me.

He said, "I'm sure you understand that a person like me, running businesses that I run, is very busy all the time and I'm so sorry. This time of year it's very busy and I'm sorry I missed the call. You probably run into that a lot, and you're probably even more busy than I am."

I said to him, "No, I am not busy."

And he was stunned, and he waited a minute and said, "What do you mean by that?"

I said, "Busyness for me used to be my story. But it was a surrender to all the things that seemed to call to me throughout the day. It was a cowardly white flag of surrender. I was throwing down my weapons and saying 'OK, take me! Take me in, put me behind bars, torture me!' I was allowing every single thing that called to me to take me away from what it is I really wanted to do. And yet I called it being busy."

I explained how one hour of uninterrupted time is worth any two other hours during my day. I shifted in my mind with this realization: When I'm *selecting* the things I'm going to focus on today, deliberately, based on the road I want to be on, then I can say *no* a lot more easily. I'm more relaxed saying no. Because I have already chosen something else.

When I say yes to what it is I have chosen to do, *no* comes easily. When something comes up or puts its head in the door and says "Got a minute?" I can easily say "No, I don't now," instead of what I used to say. What did I used to say when interruption poked in?

"Okay! Yeah, yeah, sure, sure come on in. Have a seat. What is it? What's going on?"

"Well, I'm kind of upset with Sally. She said she would do this report . . . but it's like before, she has no respect for my department . . ." and pretty soon my whole life was pulled into the gratuitous drama of other people's victim stories . . . boulders on the road, all false.

The road was actually clear. There was a clear, reality-based path to success all along.

~ Shift Your Mind, Shift the World

88

Helpless is the face of opportunity?

Tracy Goss in her book *The Last Word on Power* wrote:

Death is not the most profound loss or tragedy in life. That which dies inside of us as we live is a far greater loss. The loss of possibility. A loss that comes from running our personal rackets, has ravaged the lives of too many individuals who could have otherwise transformed the world.

So these rackets that we run are really belief systems built on a house of cards (of lies we tell ourselves). These are lies about how weak we really are and how helpless we are in the face of life's opportunities.

Ponder that irony! People become helpless in the face of opportunity!

Opportunity threatens them!

Because rather than grabbing the opportunity and creating something wonderful, they react negatively. They react with caution. They try to be safe. They fear making a mistake. They become paralyzed "trying to decide" what to do with the opportunity.

At any given moment, with any given opportunity, I am either creating or I am reacting.

If I'm creating, I'm coming from my highest self. I'm coming from the infinite creativity of the universe that is my very essence.

Our common mythology teaches us that *it's just so rare* that we really create. It's some kind of "epiphany!" when it happens. Like writers who believe they have to wait for inspiration to write. And they haven't been inspired for years. Some writers go into depression and get what they believe is "writer's block." Writer's block is just a concept, but they can't see it. They think it's a real block.

A creative life is simpler than that.

Begin by thinking in terms of creating rather than reacting. See the choice that's always present. If you catch yourself reacting, all that means is that you are low on your ladder. You're stuck in your left brain. You're trapped in there and you're condemning things. Condemning and judging is how you know you're there!

Notice how opportunity arrives and rather than welcome it, you start to judge it! You might spend your whole day looking that gift horse in the mouth.

Let the shift happen. Right then and there. See whatever is in front of you as an opportunity, and then use it to begin creating what you want.

89

A soothing rainbow of relaxation

Language is the house of Being. In its home we dwell.
Those who think and those who create with words
are the guardians of this home.

~ Martin Heidegger

L anguage is the house of being! And this house of being is
built with words. So it should not be so surprising to see the
lasting effect that these "mere" words have.

You can test this effect any way you like. But do test it. Test
it with yourself. Start with three words that are positive for you.
Let's say, "soothing," "rainbow," "relaxation." Those are three
words that are usually positive for people.

So now say to yourself, "soothing, rainbow, relaxation" and
notice the feeling in your body when you say it. Say it again out
loud. And again. Notice how you feel as you ponder these three
words. Notice that there's really a change in how you feel. You
start to breathe a little more easily and deeply, you're a little more
relaxed, and all of a sudden life looks a little more attractive to you.

And it was all from pondering the words soothing, rainbow, and
relaxation. Those three words (as you reflect on them) will alter the
chemistry in your body, will completely change the biomarkers, as
they can be measured, and will shift your brain waves.

Now think of the words, "fatal," "pornographic,"

"life-threatening." Those three words usually put people on edge. If you were to keep saying them to yourself you would become edgy. Soon you'd be deeply upset.

Just words, though, right?

You can also test this by sending an email to someone. Send somebody you know an email that says "soothing, rainbow, relaxation" and then sign your name, and see what kind of reactions you get. Send it to twenty people and then send the email that says, "fatal, pornographic, life-threatening" and sign your name and see what kind of reactions you get to that! These are just words. But look at the emotions they trigger in people!

Always, all day, night and day—even when you are asleep— certain words and phrases pass through the mind. When you are in the dream level of consciousness (at the Alpha brainwave state) words are still seeding their impact. Certain words and phrases that went into your mind during the day can manifest at night in a really bad dream. Because the brain at night tries to resolve the unfinished business of the day, and it will try to complete those word pictures for you. Really bad dreams and nightmares occur because certain thoughts keep coming in that you haven't seen for what they are. At night the dream tries to complete the unfinished thoughts of the day. It can be frightening.

But they're words—that's all they are.

Let's just pick one word for now and see its impact. The word will be "problem."

Most of us have a very negative emotional history with the word problem. If someone calls you and says, "We've got a problem," notice how you feel. It's not good. If you grab it and cling to it, it can take you down the ladder.

The very use of the word "problem" diminishes your problem-solving ability. What a double-bind that is. By identifying and naming a "problem" I've lowered my ability to solve it. No wonder I have so many problems piling up!

The very use of the *word* shrinks the resources I once had to solve things. That was the last thing I wanted when I brought this problem up. I thought I had courageously spoken about this problem in order to see it and solve it. Yet now I've created my own weakness. Because the mere mention of the word has lowered my mood, and therefore lowered my consciousness and creativity, the very things I need to solve things with.

What a load of quicksand that is. The mind has undercut itself with language! When it does this, language is truly the house of being.

So it's time to allow an immediate mind shift. Because if I open my mind, it will shift my perception of the world around me and its "problems." So now I'll try describing this situation (the one I was tempted to call a problem) as "a real adventure." I might now identify it as a real *opportunity*. And the more I use this new language, the faster my mind opens and rises.

Try sending ten people an email with just the word "problem" in it, then sign your name. See what they come back with. Watch all the nervous responses! "Hey, what's going on? Call me! What problem? What do you mean? What are you referring to? Do you mean that voice mail I left? I'm sorry, I might have been too harsh!"

It will trigger all kinds of negative response. But it's just a word. Now, find ten different people and send them a one-word email that says "opportunity." And sign your name. Watch what happens to *that* email. "Hey, great to hear from you! Wow, I want to talk about that opportunity whatever it is. Opportunity for me and you? Call me!"

You have a completely different response. Because you shifted the language.

~ Shift Your Mind, Shift the World

90

You either own it or you don't

I'm often asked to give a public speech or a workshop on my book *Reinventing Yourself*, which contains the owner/victim distinction.

My workshops are always about contrasting distinctions. The workshops are never just downloads of information. People already have too much information.

Clients who are considering whether to hire me have asked, "What's the information in your speech?"

"There isn't much."

"Are you joking?"

"No. There's just a distinction."

"You'll have to explain that."

A distinction is different than information. If I went in front of a group of people for an hour and gave them a ton of new information, they'd simply have more information. Now they'd have to try to remember it all! They might have taken notes, but a month later they would have forgotten most of the information. Sounds like a waste of time. No wonder most leaders tell me, "Training comes and goes and nothing's ever different."

I agree with that. How could anything be different when you're just filling people with information?

These days we already receive more information than ever

before in the history of humankind. We are overwhelmed with information. We get so much. The minute we wake up, the television might be on, or the radio, or we flip the computer on to get our early morning information, or receive a series of texts, and soon the information just overwhelms us. It's like a rush of polluted water . . . a tsunami of information.

And then throughout the day we are given more and more information.

So if you go into a seminar and I give you even more information, then it's a disservice!

A single contrasting distinction is different than information. Because a distinction is simply a vision of separation. Over here is this, over there is that. The intention is to inspire an insight. And when you get a new insight, it never leaves you with anything you have to "try to remember."

Like the distinction between perceiving the world like an owner and perceiving it like a victim. A clear distinction. An unforgettable contrast. When you see it and when you "get" the contrast—it is yours forever.

You own your insight. You're like the young King Arthur of legend pulling the sword Excalibur from the stone. (Now the sword was his, and he would be the once and future king.)

When you clearly *get* how distinct two things are you'll never lose that distinction.

For example, life and death. It's a contrasting distinction! I believe you've already gotten that one. Because when you were a young child there was a point at which you learned about death, and how it was different and distinct from life.

I remember when I was three years old and there was a dead bird on the road. My father was pushing me in a stroller and I pointed at the bird and he explained to me that that bird was dead.

And for the first time, I got the distinction. Something could be living or something could be dead.

Once you get a distinction, you've got it. You don't have to revisit it and continuously remind yourself of it.

I have had people contact me who were in an owner/victim distinction seminar over ten years ago and tell me that the main distinction has stayed with them throughout all these years.

When the sun goes down, it is night time. We know that because we learned the distinction between night and day. We only had to get it once. We never had to put a sticker up on our refrigerator saying, "Remember: dark equals night time and light equals day time." We never have to *remind ourselves* of a distinction. We've already got it.

Distinctions are like good jokes. You get it! When you get it, you own it. It's yours. You are now moving through the world interacting with others *with a distinction in you* that you have and can use. Distinctions help you simplify life. You have new mental leverage that wasn't there before. Shifting becomes easier.

91

Victim thinking drags me down

A victim is someone who wakes up in the morning and interprets natural, normal events as threats and injustices. He then talks all day in victimized language, which deepens the problem. Language is the house of being for a victim, and it is a bleak house.

It's a self-fulfilling prophecy to think I'm a victim. Because when I speak victim language it carries me down to the lowest levels of productivity and creativity. And at those low levels I am less capable of solving problems or creating wealth or even creating relationships. All the things I wish I could do!

So now I become even *more* of a victim. My victim self-concept creates more victim language! Soon other victims gather around me to reinforce me. They tell me they are victims, too, and that it's real. They say it has nothing to do with the mind. It's just out there.

Meanwhile victim language causes low energy. So the problems are now piling up. Who has the energy to solve them? Who has the willpower? Who has the heart anymore?

Predators and manipulators see my vulnerable and weak state. Now I'm taken advantage of! And it's real stuff and true! Not in the mind at all! Now other people use me for things, and I never really get respect.

A victim talks about people who made her feel inferior. Later in the day she singles out people who made her feel stressed. That's the victim's life. Her emotions are all caused by other people. Or so it seems.

No wonder she's now mildly afraid of other people. Can you blame her? Look how everyone makes her feel.

If I say to her, "Have a really great day," she might say to me, "Well I sure *hope* so, but how would I know if I was going to have a great day? How in the world would I know ahead of time whether today is going to be great?"

Whereas owners can actually say, "I will appreciate this day as a great day," and that's a primary difference between the two people. (Sometimes known as a distinction.)

When I'm a victim, I'll start my day by reviewing what I dread. I have dread for breakfast! What do I hope doesn't happen to me? What should I watch out for today?

"Oh, no, I have this darn meeting."

"Oh, my goodness, there's so much more to do today than I have time to do, what will I do?"

I'm already stressed just thinking about my day. And this thought-produced, stressed-out state makes me less effective. So I make mistakes. I forget to call someone back. I lock my keys in the car! My judgment is bad. I waste time needlessly. I avoid what's important.

Ownership is the opposite of that downward spiral. Its starting point is gratitude and awareness of my essential creativity. So rather than a desired state to *get to*, creativity is the beginning place—a place to come from.

A lot of times when people attend the owner/victim seminar, they'll come up to me later and say, "Now I've really got to be more of an owner. I heard what you said. I can see where that would really help my life and I know it's going to take a lot of work for me to do it. But I just know I'm going to be able to get there. Someday. If I read your book again and really practice?"

My answer is it's not a place to get to.

It's a place to come from. In fact, it's very natural. You're already there. Only thought can change that. Circumstances can't.

In the seminar I like keeping it as simple and distinct as possible. I have two flipcharts. That's it. No PowerPoint or multi-media overheads. I don't come into the course descending from the ceiling like David Bowie in *Ziggy Stardust and the Spiders from Mars*. The loud speakers aren't singing "Ground Control to Major Tom" when I walk in.

Some "motivators" like those approaches, but I'm not there to motivate anyone.

I'm there to uncover a gentle distinction.

One of the flipcharts I label "owner," the other I label "victim." I begin to put words on each flipchart. I write simple phrases. People sit and watch and look at the two different flipcharts as I walk back and forth between them. They can see victim thoughts. They let them sink in. They sit back and look at them in a very objective way. And then they can look at ownership thoughts (the language of owners of the human spirit, people who don't offer their spirit to others to be broken during the day).

I might quote Eleanor Roosevelt to further the distinction of owner. She said "No one can make me feel inferior without my permission."

I can see people reflecting on that remark. I actually see some of them realizing that no one can make them feel inferior without their permission.

The mind shifts.

~ Shift Your Mind, Shift the World

92

Take care of yourself first

I was coaching someone today—call her Simone—and she had lost a lot of the luster and enthusiasm she'd had in a previous session. She finally admitted that she was fatigued and sleep-deprived . . . up with her child until four in the morning, nursing coughs.

I asked her to take care of herself, to get plenty of rest.

I told her that sleep heals. I was drawing on painful personal experience. And success, when it's enduring, is always mind-body-spirit, never just one of those three, but always all three. You'll only fly high when all three are tuned. I told Simone, "Take care of yourself first."

But for a lot of people this is not easy.

They love serving people but they can't see that they themselves are also part of the "people" category. Part of the team. A vital part of the ecosystem. And always the best place to start when living a life of creative service.

Like the announcement in the plane that tells you to secure your own oxygen mask first, before your children's. If you try to do your children's first, everyone's in trouble. Because you yourself could pass out before they get their masks on. So serving yourself first is not selfish. It actually leaves you in better shape for helping others.

I know what it's like to care for children. My children's mother was taken away from them when they were very young. She was hospitalized and was never able to fully return to the family setting. So there I was with full custody of four little ones! What an adventure.

But I learned quickly that to take care of them, I'd have to take care of me. Later it really hit home for me. The greatest gift I can give my child is the example of my own life working.

When a child sees a life that's working, it's a gift to that child.

So many parents think they need to be noble martyrs sacrificing their health and well-being for their children. But the children never wanted that. They would rather you be happy as a person. Do they really want a bitter, depressed, self-sacrificing parent who is giving all their time to *them*?

Delmore Schwartz wrote a short story called "In Dreams Begin Responsibilities." I choose to see those responsibilities as opportunities to *respond* compassionately to the people I love. To life. To opportunity disguised as trouble. And the more I rest and dream, the more enjoyable those responsibilities become. Rather than burdens, they are now gifts.

~ Shift Your Mind, Shift the World

93

No more newspapers to read?

Newspapers everywhere are going out of business, and many people are alarmed and worried. Some are even saddened.

But I always remember what Maria said in *The Sound of Music*—"When the good Lord closes a door, he always opens a window." It's reckless and foolhardy to ignore the wisdom of Maria Von Trapp, wouldn't you agree?

That same wisdom was the whole point of Emerson's profound essay, "Compensation." Everything is always compensated for. You can't lose something without gaining something else.

And, as Byron Katie says, "Loss is a concept." It's always and only just a concept.

So here I am loving and enjoying cable TV's many choices, all the great things on Netflix, and my favorite websites and blogs and news sources on the internet—far, far better than any newspaper is today, and yet I can still remain unaware of the divine law of compensation, always at work in the universe. I can still make myself sad. Over anything. With my thoughts. (If I don't focus on and cling to those thoughts of sadness in there, the sadness simply can't happen.)

The media feeds this sense of sadness. Today a TV show like *Meet the Press* should really be called something else . . . it should be called WHY YOU SHOULD BE DEPRESSED.

Some people view all change with deep alarm. Oh, no! Just when they thought they had it all figured out, major changes sweep through the world. And, oh no! (I used to watch my favorite duo Bud & Travis perform, and in between songs while they were tuning their guitars Bud said, "When I get this guitar tuned I'm going to weld it.")

The sun comes up. The paper is inside now. I look through it. It only takes me seven minutes to read everything of interest. Most of what's in the paper I knew about yesterday or the day before—because of the internet.

So I set it aside and open the book I'm reading (for the third time) by Brenda Ueland called *If You Want to Write*. In it she says (and I see I have highlighted it in yellow) William Blake has inspired her on this subject of being creative. Blake said, "Imagination is the Divine Body in every person."

Brenda Ueland then says, "Blake thought that this creative power should be kept alive in all people for all of their lives. And so do I. Why? Because it is life itself. It is the spirit. In fact it is the only important thing about us. The rest of us is legs and stomach, materialistic cravings and fears."

She was a brilliant woman. Her book was written in 1938! Yet when I read it she is sitting right here in my kitchen with me. I can listen and really hear what she says—life is for creation—or I can turn on the news and be a *reactor* in life. That's the choice I always have.

When we're at our yellow-highlighting best we are creating the future together. The paradox of creating a great future is that it always takes place in the present moment: this little communication right here in front of me will have more to do with my future than any series of worries I may string together.

That next task you do, whatever it is, will have more to do with creating your future than any fearful, worried brainstorm of projection ever will.   ~ *Shift Your Mind, Shift the World*

94

Eventually you must serve someone

People today spend hours doing their social networking, getting connected and linked. I had a friend I'll call Charlotte who spent a full year linking people to her network, up to twelve hours a day at her computer weaving her virtual web, and at the end had to declare bankruptcy and move out of her foreclosed-upon home.

She never figured out why such successful computerized hooking-up never made her successful.

"Who is being served?" I would ask her about her "business."

"Tell me what you mean by that," Charlotte said.

"How are the people whose names you are now linked to being served?"

Silence.

Laurence Platt is a contemporary philosopher whose fascinating website is full of essays:

http://www.laurenceplatt.com/wernererhard/

Platt recently wrote this: "There are occasions of absolute greatness which come on the world from time to time, carefully orchestrated events which seem so simple, so effortless in their execution, so *natural* that they appear to be deceptively *easy*. Almost always predicating such events is herculean preparation, heroic, inspired *bringing forth*, driven setups, corrections, testing, then more corrections, still *more* testing and still more corrections before the final product is ready for the world."

This process that Platt is describing is so much more powerful and committed than hooking up and giving shout-outs. I am stunned by how beautifully he finishes his observation:

"When the finished product finally appears, it's hailed as masterful, as *genius*, as a *champion of the genre*. We know something happened prior to this to get it into the shape it's in. But we almost aren't ever privy to exactly what it takes. *We weren't there* to see what it takes to bring it forth in the state of mastery."

To shift in the mind from mere social networking to really and truly working on something great that *profoundly serves people* is to shift from living on the shallow surface of life to diving toward the treasures of the deep.

~ Shift Your Mind, Shift the World

95

To make more money, go non-linear

What is it that when I am doing it, time really is not an issue? In other words, when I am doing that thing, I can look at the clock and say "Oh, my goodness, where did that hour go? I can't believe it's six o'clock!"

When I can't believe time has passed so quickly it's because I have left behind the linear world of measured time. You know that linear world. It goes tick-tock, tick-tock. That's its soundtrack. Time just creeping by to the beat of a boring drum.

I remember jobs, and classes I had to sit through, where I kept looking at the clock . . . and that clock looked like it was the slowest thing in the world. I couldn't wait for that time to be over.

I remember working in some factories where that clock would just go by so slowly. We would watch the clock, then we would try not to watch the clock. That was a good sign that we were not engaged in our best work. Nor did we have the shifting capacity to have that not matter. (Because with the right number of mind shifts, everything I do becomes my true calling.)

If you want to start something exciting on your own, you don't have to quit your job to do it. You can do a little bit of it here and there and let it grow nicely on the side. Once you get the signs that it's up and running and that it can support you, boom . . . you're gone and that's what you do.

Other friends of mine have left the company they are with, and then sold themselves back to that company as a consultant, so now they only go in one or two days a week, do their very best thing, get a nice fee for that, and use the other four days for things they love to do even more.

So in today's global market, with all the leverage that the internet gives you to reach out to the world instantly, it's much easier to find what you love to do and tap into it.

We have the ability to link love, service and wealth together! In the past those three things were rarely linked. That was not the key to making money. Today it is. If we're enlightened enough to see it, the global internet marketplace is fertile enough to receive it. It's a mind shift: Love, service, wealth. Love, service, wealth. If I can get that pattern going—get that rhythm—get that chanted mantra in my mind, I can succeed. What do I love to do for people? How can I serve more people with it? Wealth will come as a result of that.

In the past, it was different. In the very near past it was loyalty to an organization, duty, and obligation. You had to figure out a way to earn a living, then win a position, somewhere. It was all a STRUGGLE in which bootlicking and apple-polishing were indispensable tools for advancing. It was often about manipulating, office politics and winning people over. Playing the game of sucking up! All the old style, hierarchal structures of companies and governmental organizations are based on the old monarchical systems of the past. People mastering the licking of boots. People becoming more and more skillful at polishing apples for the teacher.

Those systems emphasized that there were superior humans and subservient humans. But that whole paradigm is being dissolved by powerful individuals who do what they love, then sell it, and make a lot of money, and keep the world turning. It's a positive mind shift that has shifted the world.

~ *Shift Your Mind, Shift the World*

96

You can focus or you can spray

Living from my anxieties is a completely different way of life. Unlike living from purpose, there is very little energy available.

And most of my anxieties come from trying to protect my personality, my ego, and my smallest sense of being a separate self. And because this separation is false, it is fraught with problems.

My egoic personality can be constantly wounded and disrespected. It's whole purpose is an everlasting fight for respect. A battle I can never win.

But living from purpose has other people's opinions of me not feel so important.

When I am up to something, energy flows *into* me. But when I am focused on the isolated and separate self that I think I am (my personality), energy flows *away* from me.

Personality fixation leaves me weakened because everyone and everything else looks so threatening and powerful. Other people look like they have all the money and all the power my personality needs. Institutions look overwhelmingly intimidating. Health problems, no matter how small, now look like they could take me down. Everything looks frightening when I'm living from my personality.

We read a lot of amazing stories about people who become more and more successful with age. People like Clint Eastwood, or Frank Lloyd Wright or Helen Mirren, or Judi Dench or P.D. James, who really start to blossom in their 70's and 80's because they've stayed on their curve of artistic purpose . . . a curve that keeps eliminating what's not important.

I've always loved this quote by the great ballet director, George Balanchine. He says, "I've got more energy now than when I was younger because I know exactly what I want to do."

He has *more* energy now than when he was younger. And it's because he knows exactly what he wants to do.

When Balanchine was younger (like so many of us) he had so many things he was trying to do at once. Energy is robbed by this kind of indecision. Not choosing freely what to do next. Trying so hard to decide which course to take. It wears you out.

That's why I love the old saying, "Winners focus, losers spray." It's really true.

When my sense of purpose floods me with energy—single-minded energy—it's really a beautiful thing.

There's a story I love to tell about Harry Bernstein. People misinterpret the story sometimes to be about doing great things in your old age. It's not about that. It's about mind shifting from personality to purpose. Shift the mind, shift the world.

Harry was ninety-three years old. His wife had just died of leukemia and he was sad and he didn't know how to go on because his purpose prior to then was taking care of her, and being with her and making sure she was happy. So all of a sudden—at ninety-three years old—this man's purpose drops out from under him and he wakes up—and there's no more energy for living.

That's depression. He was depressed—what's the use—why bother—why go on—that's the whole concept of depression—

I'm up to nothing. There's nothing I'm enthused about or excited about. So now the focus is back on lonely personality . . . me . . . my feelings . . . how I'm feeling about this and what I think about that and my sadness. My sadness, my remorse and my regret—a totally self-centered focus.

But Harry Bernstein didn't stay in that world for long. His body shifted from depression the moment his mind shifted from personality to purpose.

He did something unusual and we don't know quite what inspired him. When the mind shifts, spirit has a way in. Like Leonard Cohen sings, there is a crack in everything, that's how the light gets in. Harry Bernstein decided to do something illogical.

He sat down and decided he would write about his life. So many things had occurred in his life, so many fascinating things. He would no longer just react to the death of his wife and take it personally.

Instead, he would create.

He would create a book that other people could read that would be all about the excitement, the sadness, all the amazing things that can happen to a human being who is ninety-three years old and has lived such a full, interesting life. He decided to create his life one more time, and this time he was going to create it as a book that would give other people great pleasure.

He was ninety-three! He wasn't twenty-five years old and learning to be an author and making connections with posh people in the publishing world and getting on a social network and finding out who the good agents were, planting seeds for the future. How much of a future is there when you are ninety-three? Anybody?

Most people waste 90 percent of their days on the future. And maybe I'm just guessing at that. I can say however, that I used to waste 90 percent of my own days thinking about my thoughts about the future. I was always trying to find other people to connect to who would make me successful someday. It's just a sad scattering of intellectual power and imagination with the false idea that I have got to know someone else who is powerful who will pull me up into the lofty and exclusive ranks of power.

But what Harry Bernstein did is what anyone can do—what all of us can do—even if we're eighteen years old. We don't have to wait until we're ninety-three. We can create a purpose. We don't have to focus all day on the feelings we are feeling produced by thoughts about our personality—we can have a purpose, and the purpose will then drive us.

Harry spent a year working around the clock on that book and then Harry found a publisher (after all the New York publishers rejected his work) at the London office of Random House. (This was back when you had to have a publisher for your book to get it out to the world.) His manuscript sat there for over a year and then it came across the desk of an editor by the name of Kate Elton, who read his book and said it was "unputdownable" (that was her word). Unputdownable!

That's what happens when you are working from a central purpose. He woke up with his purpose and he lived with his purpose, just like the guys breaking out of prison, just like me fighting to reach the surface of the lake in the water—there was nothing but that purpose.

Some people worry that if they shift their mind from their worries to a purpose it would be dangerous. It might make them fanatical. It might rule out other people. It might bring on disappointment.

Not so. Purpose can be more gentle than that. It can rest easy on the soul. It can be a very sweet presence that you wake up with in the morning. You can bring it with you. It's a friend to you. It never has to leave you. It's not something that you *try to remember* what it is, or *try to find out* what it is—it's there with you now. Just let it guide you. Get your thoughts out of its way. Allow your thoughts to be irrelevant to what you are creating.

97

How to use whatever reality gives

When I live life based on my personality anxieties, my whole world can be about hurt feelings. I've been there.

My daughter hurt my feelings when she didn't call me on my birthday. You hurt my feelings when you didn't answer my email. I swing like a monkey from hurt to hurt because it's all about my fragile personality that I'm trying to hold together. This *thing* I think is "me" that can be hurt and can be bothered and disrespected—unappreciated.

When people live from this personality anxiety and not from their purpose, life is not creative and life is no longer fun.

When people live from a created purpose, everything simplifies. Soon they can be like Fats Domino singing that he's simply "walking to New Orleans." (I remember when I was a teenager listening to him rocking and rolling and singing "I'm walkin' to New Orleans" and I just thought about how *simple* his life had become! That's all he was doing—he was walking to New Orleans. That was it. That was how joy worked.)

The other side of that (the dark side, the flip side) is my complex personality. The thoughts and beliefs about little old "me" that drive me crazy. Soon my mission on this flip side is to change other people so they won't hurt my "me" so much.

But if I pay attention I can allow experience to show me that wanting other people to change how they relate to me is a

non-starter. It's dead in the water.

Wanting *myself* to change is where the juice is. Learning my spiritual nature is how it happens.

Because maybe I'm up to something and maybe the way I'm behaving or the way I'm spending my precious imagination and mental energy is not taking me there. So what can I change in me? I'll sit down with myself. Or maybe I'll even sit down with a mentor, or my coach, and I'll say, "Here's what I'm up to, and here's where I'm stuck."

He says, "Are you willing to change and see something that you're not used to seeing?"

"Yes."

"See it until realizing it becomes second nature to you?"

"Yeah, sure, because I'm up to something big."

"OK, let's work on that."

So now I'll be open to seeing something.

Recently I saw on the sidelines of a pro football game one of the players screaming at his coach. He was just losing it. Yelling at his coach and the coach was telling him to "knock it off," and yelling back at him. Pure public tantrum.

"You hurt my *feelings* when you don't put me in! I'm being disrespected! How do I look on national television when I sit out two plays that are important to the team? How am I coming across allowing myself to be disrespected like that?"

There was another player on the same team who for almost the whole season wasn't put in the game at all. He *used* that situation for his higher purpose. He took what reality gave him and said to himself, "I will rest. I will save my strength. I will learn. I will train. I will work out. I will be so fresh and ready when they *do* put me in that my purpose will be fulfilled."

And so it was. In the playoffs, that player was stronger than ever.   *~ Shift Your Mind, Shift the World*

98

How did he learn to be happy?

I have no money, no resources, no hopes.
I am the happiest man alive.

~ Henry Miller

Why would you be the happiest man alive, Henry? How could that be?

You have no money. No resources. Don't you know that people strive to amass resources so they can finally be happy? And yet you are happy without them?

You have no hopes! You are just the creative, compulsive, rapid-writing, productive and prolific Henry Miller. Clue! There's a clue in there. There's a blaze of light in every word you write.

You can tell from reading his quote above and other ebullient writings from the ecstatic Henry Miller that he had experienced some glorious mind shifting early in his life. You could tell it shifted his world. And because of that, ordinary circumstances held no negative power over him. He wrote about them and made them poetic.

Most people aren't there yet.

But any mind can shift like his.

I once thought that mind shifting would be the ultimate

success course. Once I taught my attendees the things I've put in these books, they would be breaking free! But the very phrase "success course" implies lots of learning and lots of information.

I finally saw that mind shifting is not like that. It's a different kind of course. Rather than a course of study, it's more like the way a river "courses." That's the kind of course it really is. A river courses through the woodlands into the valley. The clear water courses through the land, and runs to the sea, building momentum all the way. All by itself. Without my controlling it, or trying to grasp it.

I can just step back and celebrate it.

~ Shift Your Mind, Shift the World

Choices

99

A lonely cell, my only hell

Part of my own path was to look back and see that everything I used to complain about in my past was actually there for my benefit. That rather than thinking I had a hard victim's life, I now realized that I had a fulfilling, encouraging adventure full of challenges—right out of the adventure comics and books I used to escape into so I wouldn't have to face life. I thought I was a victim of real life, so I escaped into fantasy life, reading about Superman and Robin Hood. If I had been one of those comic book characters they would have called me Victim Hood.

Most people, including those I coach, have painted a similar hard-knock life inside their own minds.

The song "It's the Hard-Knock Life" from the musical *Annie* refers to the tough situations and circumstances that the little orphans were up against. Later Jay-Z rapped out a hip-hop version of the same song in a more adult context. Featuring what *he* thought he was up against. ("Fleein' the murder scene, you know me well, from nightmares of a lonely cell, my only hell.")

Seeing life as full of hard knocks is the most common and widespread perception of life. I referred to it as "victim thinking" in an earlier book, and that whole book circled around just how automatic victim thinking had become for most people on this planet. (People believing they were lost and afraid in a world they never made.)

But because it's so conditioned, so pounded in, so deeply ingrained, it's hard to call it a conscious choice to think that way. It's more like a family tradition. A tradition of the human family. It's more like a hypnotized, knee-jerk response to everything. A *default setting* in the mind.

We are blind to it most of our lives, and then something beautiful happens and we can see. And once we see, we can't un-see. Which is cool, to put it mildly.

What do we see? What do we wake up to?

We wake up to the choices.

It's in these choices that we regain our power.

I may be stuck in victim thinking, temporarily, but if I step back and breathe I can see that I don't have to be. I don't have to believe the victim thoughts. I don't have to see my life through hard-knock glasses.

I can choose freedom, and if I choose freedom enough times, my life becomes better than good. It flies out there *beyond* good, into the realm of *crazy* good.

~ Crazy Good

100

Dying from alcohol and morphine

I sent Amanda a link to the Hank Williams, Jr. song, "Family Tradition." I invite you now to set this book down and go to YouTube and play that song and float around inside its message.

In Hank's song he asks himself why he is ruining his own life. He sings, "Hank, why do you drink? Why do you roll smoke?" and then he asks us to put ourselves in his "unique position. If I get stoned and sing all night, it's a family tradition."

Of course he's referring to his famous father, country legend Hank Williams, who died quite young of an overdose of alcohol and morphine. He was famous for "Your Cheating Heart," and his last single was prophetically called, "I'll Never Get Out of this World Alive."

Amanda said, "I don't see what this has to do with how I've been living. I'm not like a drunken fake cowboy who sings."

She was right about that. But addiction was addiction and Amanda was addicted to her victim stories and the morphine-like downer she experienced when she thought about her past life. However none of her thoughts and beliefs about money or men or life were original. She picked up most of the beliefs growing up in her family. None of her beliefs really had anything to do with the truth about life, and they were all dragging her down.

"I guess I need to replace my negative beliefs with more

positive thoughts," she said. "Maybe we should start with money. I picked up a lot of frightening beliefs about money growing up in my family. In my house, whenever money was mentioned, fear filled the air. People would yell and scream. And *that* was a family tradition for sure."

I had asked Amanda in an earlier conversation who she thought had a crazy-good life in this world. She named a few people, and they all had big money in common. So I knew money meant a lot to her in both negative and positive ways.

But I had a question for her. Why did she want to create positive beliefs about money? What if she simply had no beliefs at all about money? What if she, unburdened by belief, could just let money flow in and out? Wouldn't that be pure freedom? Nothing to maintain. Nothing to feed and care for.

"Why is neutral better than positive?" she said.

"Because *your* positive has to be forced. And neutral can just be."

I asked if she was open to seeing money the same way she saw paint. It's just something that's often useful. But nothing you have to maintain a belief in one way or another. When you decide to paint the walls in your bedroom, you figure out how much paint you need and you go to the store and get the paint. Do you need positive beliefs about the paint? No, because paint is just paint. It's all right the way it is. It's perfect because it's neutral. It doesn't have to be given some hyped-up affirmative shock charge in your mind.

It would not be useful to try to force a positive belief in paint. To say an affirmation like, "Oh, paint! Divine paint. Paint is the liquid manifestation of my expressive soul."

What if you got yourself to believe that, and then you spilled a bucket of paint? Instead of just getting a new bucket of paint, you'd have to deal with watching the liquid manifestation of your expressive soul running all over the floor! That would take a long time to process. You would definitely have feelings around that.

So, therefore, just realize that money is only money. It can be useful to you without all the moaning, noise, tears and dreams about it.

"But . . ." said Amanda. "It wouldn't do any harm to have a positive affirmation I say about money every day in order to create a new belief."

What Amanda wasn't seeing is that loading the mind up with beliefs, positive and negative alike, burden it and make life unnecessarily heavy and hard to walk through (much less dance with). It is the *clear* mind that enjoys a life that's out beyond good.

Amanda found, over time, that there were choices available to her that could free her from her serious life, full of heavy beliefs. Through these choices, she would become more light-hearted when she thought of things like money and men. And from that light-hearted state of mind, she would be able to enjoy life however it showed up.

Now we will look at the rest of the choices that Amanda (and I, and so many others) can discover and re-discover—and use.

~ Crazy Good

101

How you can lose your marbles

I can spend forever trying to decide something.

The variables worth considering are infinite. I will never run out of variables to study. And so valuable time is lost. Not only that, but my mood declines the whole time I am trying to decide.

That's me in the corner. I sit on the floor, like a child with his spilled marbles, lost among the variables. Losing my spirit as the world passes me by. I would have been better off just *choosing something right off*, one of the options that felt right at the time, and going with it, to hell with the consequences.

Trying to figure out whether something is a "good decision" ahead of time can become an endless thought-maze to wander into. Besides, whether the decision is a "good one" is something I have a lot to say about *after* making the choice. If I choose to take a certain job, it's my work at that job that can turn it into a good decision. I can *make it into* a good decision by what I do and create after the choice.

Trying to have it all figured out *before* I choose keeps me dancing with fear. Like those quarterbacks who never know who to throw to, so their feet are dancing in place, faster and faster, until they are leveled by a 340-pound professional opponent. On the sidelines, lying on a stretcher, they tell the team neurologist that they were having a difficult time deciding who to throw to or whether to just throw it away.

"Trying to decide" is a popular way of losing the moment. A way that leads to always thinking about life instead of living life. For a life to become crazy good, it has to be *lived.*

On the other hand, there is an option. It's called choosing! Choosing has a great thrill in it. That's why your body tells you it's the better way to go.

Your life can be thrilling, or it can be endlessly debated in your mind.

And it's so fun when you find out that you can choose.

Recently I went to a very enjoyable concert in which I heard the rocking jazz band of Hugh Laurie, the star of the TV series *House.* Hugh Laurie is actually a British actor who plays blues piano and sings and chooses whatever career excites him at the moment. He just jumps right in, ready or not.

In an interview he said, "It's a terrible thing in life to wait until you're ready. I have this feeling now that actually no one is ever ready to do anything. There is almost no such thing as ready. There is only now."

~ Crazy Good

102

You must think you're something

So what are you choosing to *be* in life?

Are you being a verb or are you a noun?

Now if you don't remember your grammar (many of us don't want to remember our grammar) let me remind you that a noun is a person, a place, or a thing. It is something. It is an entity. It is a solid object that you can describe. Is that you?

Most people want to be that noun! They try to sell you on that concept, that they are a separate thing, apart from everything else. Flying solo. (Actually, sitting solo. Living solo.) But it's only a concept. It's only a belief. What's the reality?

Well, a more accurate understanding (a stronger choice) than the concept that you are a noun (or a thing) is that you are a verb! You are energy, action and movement. Verbs move. They dance, they sing, they embrace other people. They smile, they laugh, and they communicate. That's what verbs do.

Nouns are just there. Until you somehow motivate them, they just sit there.

Nouns have enablers that keep them in the noun state. They are called adjectives—descriptors.

This is starting to sound a little like English class, but please stay with me, because many people, including myself, have had an AHA! in understanding the possibilities of a crazy-good life based on realizing that *in truth I am a verb*.   ~ *Crazy Good*

103

Am I that kind of person?

I received an e-mail from Amanda that asked me whether I
thought she was generous.

She was worried. Maybe she wasn't generous enough as a
person to really utilize a service-based system I had taught her for
acquiring clients.

"I just don't know that I'm a very generous person," she said,
reflecting on the noun she thought she was. Was that noun
generous?

I had been working with her for quite some time and that's
why she felt I could pass judgment on this. Notice that she was
testing an adjective (generous) to describe her noun (herself).

I was not willing to further the myth that she was a noun. I
was not going to reinforce her perception of herself as being an
entity, an identity, or a thing. I was going to help her get into
action, if that was what she wanted to do. I was going to help her
move from noun to verb because that's where all the fun is.

So my answer to her question was simply, "What act of
generosity would you like to perform?"

"Oh," she said. And then she told me the action she was
resisting taking. We saw a way to take it.

Why would I want to participate with her in labeling her and
limiting her with the labels—you're generous, you're not

generous, you're kind, you're not kind, you're courageous, you're cowardly, you're organized, you're disorganized. None of these things help anybody. None of them are even accurate for more than one or two seconds before everything changes. Life itself is nothing but changes. Change is another word for life.

Why not celebrate the great dance of interconnectivity?

Our breathing takes in oxygen from the plants. And that dance of breath makes us inseparable from the plants and the earth and all other things we are moving and dancing with whether we see it or not! Why do we try to freeze ourselves into feeling like static, disconnected objects?

What Amanda really is is a verb, and that's good. That's crazy good. That is Amanda at her best. And so by asking what act of generosity she would like to perform she could move out of her static, stuck position. No longer was she trying to figure out how to describe herself, trying to decide what she was really like.

Now anything was possible.

You will want to find the verb in you if you are going to live a wonderful life. Because the verb in you is who you really are. All the cells flowing and dancing through your system, all the atoms dancing inside of every molecule, all the molecules dancing in the cell—even *you* dancing as a great song comes to your ears and you feel you *just have to* get up and move—that's the real you.

~ Crazy Good

104

Coloring the world with my mood

M oods are like blobs of paint on a palette. Once I react to something, I drop down into a bad mood. Then I try to describe what's going on. But the only paints I have to paint the picture with are the gloomy paints of a low mood. So innocent situations look like unbelievable challenges when I put them up there on the canvas. Ordinary, everyday events get painted as catastrophes. In that low mood "life sucks," as our celebrities and children say.

But what if I stop reacting and start creating? What if I just start noticing when I am reacting? What if I then back away and breathe? "Given this situation, what can I create?" What if I just start doing that as a practice? Almost like a hobby that I get more and more into?

Would there be any problems left?

~ Crazy Good

105

How could a problem be good?

Peter Diamandis says, "I think of problems as gold mines."
He is the successful founder of more than fifteen high-tech companies.

Just that thought gets my own creativity going. How could this problem be a gold mine?

My coach Steve Hardison trained me in this always-available choice between creating and reacting. He is like Diamandis! I realize now that Steve, too, sees problems as gold mines.

I sit down with him for a coaching session and tell him my latest problem. He listens carefully and compassionately and I see his eyes start to sparkle. I can start to feel his impatience with me as I keep trying to finish my story about my problem. He is about to come out of his chair and embrace me with creative joy. I see once again that problems excite him.

After I finish talking he asks me a simple question, "Given what is happening, what would you like to create?"

But when I'm in a low mood, I don't always immediately warm up to that line of questioning. What is this, art class? Am I back in kindergarten with finger-paints? Should we get out the Legos?

Yes, Yes and Yes.

~ Crazy Good

106

I needed to make a big, magical leap

I used to think I had to do that magical leap myself.

If I was cowardly, I had to change completely into super courageous. If I was weak, I had to become amazingly strong. If I was overweight I had to become rail thin.

It never worked because it was a dysfunctional approach. It was a dream that divorced me from reality. I had no idea back then that reality was kind, and that reality was on my side, ready to work with me, ready to support me in everything.

Before Dr. Branden, I had always been stuck inside the innocent malfunction of using self-criticism as a motivator. But the problem with that is that after you condemn yourself as being wrong or bad you immediately disconnect yourself from reality.

Self-criticism is like pulling a lamp's plug out of the wall because it isn't giving the room enough light. But now the room goes completely dark.

Oops.

~ Crazy Good

107

Just whose side are you on?

To produce something you have to start with something.
You have to see the good in who you already are.

You have to acknowledge that you've done the best you could so far, given what you've been believing and how you have seen your life.

You have to take that walk over to *your* side of the courtroom. So that you are no longer the prosecutor in your life. Now you're on *your* side. You are your own attorney. *You represent yourself from now on.*

~ Crazy Good

108

The deathbed question

I like people to imagine their upcoming deathbed experience. What will happen when you are on your deathbed looking back on your life? Will you ask yourself, "How many people have I pleased? Did I really please people? Did I win enough of them over?"

Probably not. Those won't be the questions you'll ask yourself on that deathbed. Really what is asked on the deathbed is this: "Who have I served? What difference have I made? What difference has my life made? Is life different because I was here on earth?"

That's what people truly wonder. They don't wonder how many people they pleased. How many people they maneuvered into liking them. What they think of is this: Whom did I serve? Did I spend my days serving? Yes or No.

And if the answer's yes, what a beautiful feeling.

~ Crazy Good

109

Motivation will no longer be necessary

We can actually become addicted after a while to things that are fun. If you have young people in your life you know how hard it is to pull them away from the games they are playing—the video games, the computer games, the games on their smart phone, the games in the driveway . . . because those games are fun.

Games do that for people. Notice that a lethargic group of people sitting around in the living room thinking they are too tired to do anything but watch the Kardashians and eat doughnuts can come to life immediately when someone proposes that "we all play a game." It isn't long before everyone is laughing and shouting and having fun because they are now *playing*. This is the game element! If we really understand it and appreciate it, it will change our lives.

Once a game is joined, there's no need for me to also try to motivate myself. I am already tapped into that playful game energy.

Contrast that to my saying to myself at the end of the day that *I should have exercised more. I should have taken a walk or two.* Or at the beginning of the day saying, *I should go to the gym today. I should get on the treadmill so I can trudge and trudge . . . I should do that.*

"Should" deflates and contracts.

Games inflate and expand.

They get me out of the stands and onto the field of play.

~ Crazy Good

110

It's time to move your mouse

Our shaming thoughts are not original. We don't "create" them from some dark internal place as so many people like to believe.

We've picked these thoughts up from other people. They soon become the dialogue we can't get out of our heads, but they're borrowed. Many of us have grown up and hung out with other shame-based individuals, and so that's the language we learn.

This borrowing factor is good news when we can see it. We don't have to identify with these thoughts any more. We don't have to take them seriously. The jump (the shift, the choice) from a shame-based approach to a game-based approach then becomes as easy as shifting gears in a car, or moving your mouse to a better place to click.

~ Crazy Good

111

Shouldn't I take this more seriously?

"**I** really have to do this," said Amanda in a low, sad voice. We were talking about her new work project that was not getting off the ground. She was sad and scared.

"I'm so afraid of failure," she told me. "And I have a pattern of procrastinating and eventually giving up."

"What do you think the solution is?" I said (which is what a coach says when he himself doesn't have the solution).

"I need to be more committed," said Amanda. "I need to grow up. I need to take responsibility for my failure thus far and get more serious about the business."

"Sounds like fun," I said. And she could hear in my voice that I was only kidding.

"What do you mean by that?" she said.

"I mean it *doesn't* sound like fun."

"Well," she said, "it's not *supposed* to be fun, is it? It's work. That's why they call it work."

Amanda was trying to find a vein of shame to tap into. She thought she had let herself down, and if she became ashamed of herself—*really* ashamed of herself—she might force herself to succeed.

"There's no lightness in this," I said. "There's no way you're going to enjoy this."

"So you think positive psychology can paper over something real and serious?"

"No, I think you are at your best when you are having fun. And the only problem your business has had is your own lack of time and attention."

"I don't see the connection. I believe if I took it more *seriously*, I'd give it more time and attention."

"Well, no. I've never experienced that. Seriousness is stressful. By definition. Seriousness is not fun and addictive. Seriousness does not bring out the best in us. Games are addictive. They get our attention."

"Games!" she said. "This is not a game to me. I have bills to pay. I have a child to raise. This is no game."

"Precisely the problem," I said.

~ Crazy Good

112

You don't know how to do it?

When Sam Beckford and I wrote a book about small business owners and the lies they tell themselves, Lie #1 was about people saying they really just need to know *how* to succeed at their business.

They were fooling themselves.

And it's not just the business owners. We all seem to do this all the time.

We think we just need to know *how to* get clients, or we need to know *how to* increase cash flow or *how to* hire good people, or *how to* be happy, or *how to* communicate with our children, or *how to* lose weight. We think we don't know *how!* It is a self-deception that spills way across business boundaries and runs into personal life as well. It's a floodwater of self-deception.

Let me give you an example of this: If my teenage son is not cleaning his room it will never occur to me to go to him with a manual or a little e-book that teaches How to Clean Your Room. I know what's missing is not the how-to. What's missing is the want-to.

The want-to is almost always what's missing *whenever* something's not happening. It's not that we don't know how to do things. With the right level of desire, we can find that out very quickly.

~ Crazy Good

113

This can be a work of art

Agreements are creative by nature.
It's two people designing a work of art together. Therefore agreements are a lot more fun than expectations. Expectations are stressful. They lead to anxiety. I'll even say they are cowardly. Because my expectations allow me to put the blame for everything that goes wrong on other people. It's not me. It wasn't me. He didn't do what I expected! Really, I expected better from him.

But here's the good news: Expectations are not necessary. Oh, yes, they are rampant. Everybody seems to have them. But they are not necessary. In fact, it's actually possible to have no expectations of anyone, and to only have agreements when you need them.

~ Crazy Good

114

A house built on shouting

I know a family who argued all the time. Their house was filled with shouting and name-calling. Sometimes "Screw you!!" was all you'd hear on an otherwise sunny Saturday morning. One daughter kept quoting Amy Winehouse by yelling, "What is this fuckery?"

So I met with the father, Stewart, to see if we could sort this out.

"Maybe you could create an agreement," I said. "All of you, together, when the mood is relaxed and happy, maybe sitting around a friendly table together."

Stewart was skeptical. He said this shouting thing ran deep in his family history. His parents used to throw plates and stuff.

"It runs deep," he said.

"We respond to fleeting, ethereal, negative thoughts," I said, trying to sound like I was from India. "Nothing runs 'deep.' That's a myth. That's a geological metaphor that doesn't apply. You're not a planet. You won't understand your mind or your family by thinking that way."

Stewart was listening. But he was not understanding. Do you blame him?

So I decided to take a different tack. I decided to shift from India to Little Italy in New York. I asked him if his family ever ordered pizza.

"Yes."

"When the pizza delivery boy or man comes to the door, how do you treat him?"

Stewart said he wasn't sure if he understood my question. He said, "We're nice to him."

I asked if they were *extremely* nice to him, if they smiled at him, joked with him about the weather, and called out a cheerful, "Thank you!" and "Take care!" and "Have a great evening!" and Stewart said yes, all of those things.

I said, "Do you always do this, no matter who the delivery person is?"

"Yes, I guess so."

"And when you have your box of pizza in your hand, do you then return to your bickering, hostile family and start the arguments back up?"

"A lot of the time, yes."

"So you're all treating some unknown person far better than you are treating yourselves, your family—the people you love the most."

Stewart nodded his head. I asked him if he were willing to lead a family meeting in which they all agreed to communicate with each other with a baseline of kindness and courtesy—the same level of kindness they find *so easy* to give the delivery boy.

"We could try that," he said, "but it will be hard. At least at the beginning."

"You'd be going against family tradition," I said.

"Right!"

I asked him if it would ever occur to him to open the door when the pizza delivery boy arrived and yell at him, "Damn you! You *never* listen to me. You'll never change, you selfish a**hole!

Screw you!!!!"

Stewart stared at me without any expression. We both knew I was being a little strange, but I wanted to do that to make this insight work for him.

"I have another idea," I said, "in case the family meeting doesn't produce an agreement."

"What is that?"

"You could go to Domino's and buy one of their uniforms and hats, and the next time some family member starts arguing with you, you can go into your room and put the uniform on and re-emerge. I think when they saw you in that pizza uniform they would treat you really differently. Maybe your whole family could get fitted for them."

~ Crazy Good

115

What have we fallen into?

One young woman told me she yelled at her husband and called him all kinds of humiliating names because that's what her mother did to her father. She thought it might even be "healthy" to vent that way and then try to have "make-up sex" and make it an even better relationship in the long run.

"And," I said, "does it work?"

She said she was surprised that it was *not* working out.

"How did it work for your mom and dad?"

"They got divorced."

"What am I missing? I can be slow at times."

As we talked on she became hopeful and excited when she learned there was a choice available to her between expectations and agreements. And that agreements could be what she and her husband could use to feel better about each other. And that they might work even better than "healthy, vulnerable, transparent venting."

~ Crazy Good

116

Expectations weigh a lot

Amanda wondered whether she was willing to look at how many expectations she had of other people (with an eye to dropping them).

"How do I find out what my expectations are?" she said.

I asked her to make a list of her disappointments. That would do it. Who was she disappointed with? What are some of the behaviors of other people recently that left her feeling let down or upset? She had a good, long list after thinking about it.

Because expectations lead to disappointment, you can trace it backwards from disappointment to expectation. Any disappointment she had in life would not have been there if she had no expectation.

"I'm disappointed when my husband doesn't volunteer to clean the dishes after I have made a dinner for us," she said. "It's like he doesn't get the work I've done. Or else he thinks I should be doing all this dinner stuff and be cleaning up afterward as well."

I said, "Is there a gentle request that you could make?"

Amanda thought for a while and then said, "Maybe."

"What might you say to him? Something that could encourage a new agreement."

Amanda said, "I could say, 'Hey, Jason, would it kill you to participate a little bit in our evening here?' "

"Okay. Maybe something even warmer than that."

"'Jason, dude, could you stand to step outside of a world that's all about you, all Jason, all the time, and show a brief gesture of partnership? Might you just do the mother-loving dishes? You can return to your inner world right after. I'll go downstairs to call my girlfriend. I won't bother your introspection any further after that. I'll even sleep in a different room if that will help you hold your focus on yourself.' "

I nodded my head. "Okay, that's a beginning."

Amanda looked pleased with herself and a little more relaxed. Then she said, "You know, I think he's actually just innocent in this."

I waited for her to continue. She was seeing something important. Then she said, "He's just a little clueless, you know? I guess I could say, 'Could we have an agreement? I have an idea for one, but only if you agree.' And then I could ask if he'd participate. The more I think about it, the more I think he'd gladly do it if I put it that way."

~ Crazy Good

117

But what if we are not saints?

A lot of people think, "If I have negative feelings, if I'm judging someone critically, if I'm upset with someone, it's *healthy* to say it. It's *healthy* to attack, it's *healthy* to hurt someone else, because that takes the hurt out of *me*."

Now how sensible is that, really?

I had a client who said he had a fight with his wife and I asked him, "How was it?" and he said, "Well, you know what that's like. You've had those."

And I said, "No, I really haven't."

And he said, "Oh, come on."

I said, "I really haven't. Kathy and I have been together for over twenty-five years, and we've never had a real fight."

He said, "Well . . . I . . . Oh, yeah, okay . . . I forgot that you're a saint, right? But I'm not. I'm a regular person."

I said, "No, no, it's not that, I'm not a saint at all. In fact if you look at my biography, I probably shouldn't be allowed to walk the earth a free man. So I'm not a saint, but I'll tell you that I don't fight with her, and it's for the same reason that I don't punch the mailman when he's late, or I don't strangle that cat in my backyard and kill it. Same reason exactly—I just don't want to. I've decided it's not the kind of behavior I want to indulge in. I won't do it. I just won't do it. It's not useful."

You hear so many people say, "Oh, fights are great, aren't they? They clear the air, they purge things, they're so wonderful."

The only people I've ever heard say that are now divorced people. Because, no, they are not wonderful. They're hurtful. They're unforgettably hurtful, and they're mean and they're demeaning and every fight is just bitterly selfish. It's like two children scratching each other's eyes out. When little children do that you separate them immediately. You put them in different rooms and explain that we humans don't do that to each other.

But when grown-ups do it? Oh, how therapeutic! How wonderful! How authentic we are! How transparent and vulnerable!

Expectations are what lead to fights, arguments and negative judgments of another human being. If we have no expectations, only agreements, fights don't have to occur.

~ Crazy Good

118

Did you think walking would work?

When you were a little baby, you didn't have to *trust* that walking would work. You didn't have to believe in yourself or have specific faith that you would learn to walk like grown-ups walk.

And so you stumbled around, and you fell, and you giggled, and you fell, and you cried. But then you got back up and you stumbled a while more and finally, days later, you were walking.

There wasn't really a trust in there that you had to master first. There was only your innate willingness to *test*. The human gift for adventure. (That we eventually talk ourselves out of.)

Now as you got a little older you saw that your friends in the neighborhood were riding bikes. And your brother and sister had a bike and they rode theirs. And it seemed like everybody had a bike. But the more you looked at a bicycle the more you saw that it didn't really seem to make sense that these two wheels would hold you up. It sure looked like you would just tip over if you got on the bike. And so you got up on the bike and it tipped over and you fell.

But somehow you knew that you didn't have to trust that the bicycle would hold you up in order to learn to ride it. All you had to do was be willing to keep testing it.

I know when I learned how to ride a bike I didn't trust it at all.

So my mind's internal mantra was, "This will never work. This will never work!! I don't see how this could work. Oh, it might work for others—but I don't think it will work for me."

But then, after I fell, I got back up on the bike. I kept doing that. Soon I was riding the bike.

But I was young. I was not a grown-up yet. A grown-up in a similar situation, with a similar thing they are trying to learn how to do, gets on the bike, falls off the bike, and then sues the bike company.

Then they join a support group with other people who have fallen off *their* bikes. And they meet in the old church basement every Wednesday night and share their stories about what victims they are and how horrible it was to get their hopes up about riding a bike, and all they did was fall off when they tried it.

That's what grown-ups do. Living in a world that is so hard to trust.

Failure is embarrassing and something you should never put yourself in a position to experience, right? Not if you're a grown-up. You shouldn't expose yourself to public failure for any reason ever—so, therefore, be careful, don't even *try* to ride a bike until you can believe that it will work.

Meanwhile the child (their mind clear of sentiment and fear) is yelling, "Look, Ma, no hands!" Because this first time around the block on a bike?

Well . . . it's just crazy good.

~ Crazy Good

119

Life as a series of experiments

Testing means experimenting, and as the brilliant business author Dale Dauten says, "Experiments never fail."

Experiments never fail because when you are experimenting you are just as eager to find out what *doesn't* work as what does. Whatever you find out helps you grow. There is no failure in that.

Experiments give you a way to play with the universe. They allow you to interact with the real world and get some interesting answers. What works? What doesn't? Let me try again. This is starting to energize me.

~ Crazy Good

120

All we are is dust in the wind

I was not a purpose-driven person growing up. (For me, growing up took about fifty-five years. That's normal, right?)

I walked around with this idea that I was programmed and coded by this thing called my personality to be a certain way. A way that left purpose out of the equation. (And how convenient it was to be run by a robotic program instead of making choices. Robotically living the almost-good-enough life and not even seeing that I could have a crazy-good life if I'd known about the choices.)

Permanent personality, for me, was such a no-brainer. Doesn't it seem obvious? And simple! I believe I have a permanent personality and then *allow it to run me!* Sure I was suffering, but who wasn't? (Nathaniel Branden once said to me, "Suffering is the easiest way to live.")

The underlying, hidden problem with my approach to life was that the central premise of my life was not true. It was an illusion. This thing called personality is *not* permanent. It's an illusion that it's permanent. It's an illusion that it even exists. It's just a collection of opinions, memories, fears and judgments. Swirling in and swirling out. Like dust in the wind. And until we know that we can choose our purpose, this dust called personality is *all we are.*

~ Crazy Good

121

Today I question every thought

Today I question every thought that arises about my so-called personality.

And the most fun part of doing that is that I get to invent all day. Like I knew to do when I was three years old. Before I got talked out of it! (By myself and others.)

When Ralph Waldo Emerson saw that we were being talked out of our natural playful selves he said, "Society everywhere is a conspiracy against the manhood of every one of its members."

(Today he would have said ". . . a conspiracy against the personhood of each of its members," but you get his point.)

Most people in adulthood have dropped invention out of their activity. They don't invent. But if they could set aside the illusions that they have bought into about their "personality," then all of a sudden what would be left?

Pure creativity.

~ Crazy Good

122

It's clouds' illusions I recall

When we are young we are given a name. That name is usually fairly arbitrary and always just dreamed up by our parents. But soon we cover our name with stories about who we really are. We believe we are becoming significant.

If somebody says to me when I am young, "You're never on time. You're always running late. You never plan ahead!" I just believe that automatically. Why wouldn't they know the truth? OK. That's me. That's significant. That's part of who I am! Instead of realizing *I made a choice that had me show up late.* I don't see that. I immediately see a pattern emerging from my identity.

It's obvious, looking back, that personality traits are just randomly thrown at us. Like paints thrown on a canvas at random. We could have all been named Jackson Pollock. The paint spots and splatter could be from the words of a father, or a sibling who says one thing, my best friend or a teacher who shouts something at me when I am young (about *me*), and all of a sudden I am gazing at a multi-colored canvas called my permanent-personality-art-museum self.

No wonder we go out into the world unaware of our choices!

No wonder we're always scared of who we are, and worried about whether we have the capability to do the things we think other people are doing so easily because of who *they* are.

The truth is better than all that.

The truth is we can be whoever we choose to be in any given moment. That's all we do anyway, we just don't see it. We don't have to be who we think we already permanently are. Look at all the nervous energy it takes to hold that illusory, multiple mosaic of a person together all day!

A second-century Indian scholar named Aryadeva, writing 1,900 years ago, said, "Could it be that this highly-knit sense of self is not what it seems? Do we really need to hold everything together, and *can we*? Is there life beyond self-importance?"

~ Crazy Good

123

My life was stuck in the mud

What happens if I have a choice but I don't know it? What if I don't see it?

Now that's the most interesting part (I believe) about these choices and about the very real possibility of living a crazy-good life.

In my life (looking back over the years) I was really *stuck*. I didn't know I had a choice to become unstuck. Like a car is stuck in the mud, I was stuck in so many categories, and for more years than most of you have been alive.

Now that's a pretty sad thing, because I didn't *need* to be stuck. I just didn't see the choices.

Sometimes it starts with knowing the difference between information and transformation.

Let me give you an example of this choice. With this example, I'm going to sound like I'm mean and uncaring and stereotyping. But I'll do it anyway, even exaggerate it a little bit, to make a point.

When I give seminars these days I notice some people when they first come into the room. They sit down and they are looking up to the front of the room, and I can almost see it in their eyes— they are here for information only.

They have that edgy look in their eyes. Impatient. Wondering if they should really be somewhere else. One last double-thumbing of the smart phone. Now they look pensive. Did they leave the oven on at home? Will they return to a whirlwind of smoke and ashes? Is this seminar a waste of time? Don't I already know this stuff?

These are the information people. It's in their eyes. They walk the earth like info-zombies. Life to them is only about knowing stuff.

But let's look and see: who else is in the room?

Oh, yes, there they are: the transformation people!

The transformation people look different. Their eyes are sparkling with a look of quiet excitement. They laugh with the person sitting next to them. They have one of my books under their chair and I notice it has a multitude of little colored stickers coming out of the pages, some pale blue, some pale yellow and some pink. Oh my. They are already *using* this stuff!

These are the people who are the most fun to teach.

~ Crazy Good

124

This can make your life a joke

Now you're in my course on learning to make money. I am teaching you that learning to make money is just like playing the piano.

It's the same process.

If you want to make more money, you will step into transformation and test the outer edges of whatever you do to make money now.

If I want to learn to play the piano, I won't just read books *about* the piano. I won't just watch videos of people showing me how to play the piano. Because I could do that for years, and people might challenge me to actually *play*!

"All this information you have, show us. Show us what you can do with it."

And I would sit at the piano and, of course, there wouldn't be anything I could do with it—nothing at all. The audience would grow restless. I'd try to make a joke. Turn the theme of the evening from music to comedy.

That's information for you. It can make your life a joke.

So why do I pursue it?

I keep thinking it will show me *how to* do things.

But that's the problem with information. It pushes you into a how-to world. It's a lost world. You're starring in *Lost*. Its inhabitants are all the people who don't know *how* to do what they *want* to do. Or so they think.

You can read a lot of books on piano playing. Or on *how to* ride a bicycle. You can go to a seminar on bicycle riding, and you can get all the information in the world. You can even read Lance Armstrong on how to ride a bicycle (with or without supplements). But if you are not out there experimenting with riding the bicycle, you won't be able to ride a bicycle.

~ Crazy Good

125

Fifteen minutes and then you can bail

Sometimes my clients who are writing books tell me, "I'm stuck! I'm stuck and I just bought three books on How to Write Your Book! I've been reading these books, so why haven't I made any progress on my own book? I've got to finish reading these books because they're giving me wonderful information about how to write a book."

But no book. No real writing. Just wonderful information!

Nassim Taleb says, "To bankrupt a fool, give him information." To bankrupt an author, same thing. Tell her she doesn't have enough know-how yet.

When I'm coaching authors I might ask them to accept my challenge: fifteen minutes a day on your book. You don't have to write anything great, just darken the page. That's all you have to do. Start with the blank pages, and darken them. Just do it. Fifteen minutes and then bail on yourself. You can go longer if you're loving it, but never shorter.

And again it sounds kind of silly, but so many people that I work with don't know they have a choice to transform. What they tell me is that they are dumbfounded and disheartened by all the information they have taken in on the subject and by their total lack of progress in the real world.

They're pretty downhearted, but what are they now looking

for? Are they now looking for what's wrong with their premise? Where their system is broken? No. They're looking for *more information*—better information.

And they call me and say, "Hey, I just found out about a new guy who teaches how to do this in a radical new way—I think I'm signing up for his course!"

That's just more information.

If you write fifteen minutes a day, radical changes occur in the world. Creation happens. Whether you want it to or not. Once you open yourself to that channel, productivity happens, and there's nothing you can do to prevent it.

~ Crazy Good

126

What do I fear might happen?

I can start my day with this question: "What would I love to do?" And then make my list of things.

Or I can start my day (as I did for years . . . no, decades) with, "What do I fear might happen today? What should I try to avoid?"

All these choices are versions of love versus fear. For example, when I choose transformation over information I am choosing a love of adventure and growth—versus fear of not knowing enough.

When I choose to live as a verb instead of a noun I am choosing an innate love of movement. A love of dancing with the universe. A joy I can take in motion and self-expression, versus the fear that pushes me into the corner where I learn to be a wallflower. I can bury my personality in a scrapbook and yield to the flood of life's beauty.

My friend, the author Lori Richards, likes to ask the question, "What would love do?" whenever she is unsure of her next action or communication. It's such a useful question! When choosing how to respond to that nasty email, or how to communicate with *anyone*, it's the perfect question. It leads me away from merely reacting. It leads me into the wonderful world of creating.

What would love do?

~ Crazy Good

127

A podcast host was interviewing me

A podcast host was interviewing me about some book I had written.

He wanted to know how I wanted to be remembered.

I asked him, "Why would I want to be remembered?"

Is there no end to our desire to impress other people? Does it get so obsessive that I even want to keep doing it after death?

He said, "What legacy do you want to leave?"

I said, "Open minds. Clear minds. No trace of me."

~ Crazy Good

128

I saw the news today, oh boy

In the house across the street, someone is helping her friend recover from alcoholism. That will not make the news today.

They are sitting on a couch and talking gently about the steps of recovery and what it means to live one day at a time. The wild, affirming rain hits their window.

A life is being changed for the better. Gentle hope is replacing depression.

Now I turn my head a little, away from the picture window, and I stare at the TV screen next to the window and someone is beheading someone who doesn't agree with their religion. I am stunned. What am I to learn? What are the depths of human cowardice? Oh well. News, sports and weather are just trying to make a buck. It's been proven, it's been measured: ratings go up whenever the viewers feel threatened. Demetri Martin says all TV news shows should be called *What's Wrong.* Good evening! And welcome to the six o'clock edition of *What's Wrong!*

But if I shift my eyes back away from the screen a bit I can see the house across the street again. I enjoy realizing that something very beautiful is happening in that house and no one knows it because it is not on television. Across the street I see the choice that has to come before all the other choices. The choice for living.

It's later that night. Now the sun has gone down. And I hear the sirens as I lie in bed. The sounds of the city. Before crazy good, the sirens bothered me. I would always think they meant trouble. Someone is hurt. Some crash has happened. Someone is being rushed to the hospital. The sirens were sad to hear.

But now the sirens are comforting . . . relaxing. They reassure me. They are the sound of someone helping someone else.

~ Crazy Good

Presence

129

Labels that stick me to the past

I was sitting with clients around a table when one young woman told us about her personal life and how she balanced it with work.

During the course of her conversation she talked about nutrition and food and then said softly, "I'm a cake person." She was confessing to a weakness for cake.

But her words hit me like a ton of bricks. What she said. I'd never heard it described that way . . . *I'm a cake person!*

Up until that very moment I didn't know I could *be* a cake person. I thought it was always about the eating of the cake. I assumed I had to discipline myself to eat less cake. I thought it was all about bad choices in the moment. Choices that lead to my plump stomach.

But what if? What if I'm a cake person?

Then when someone points out that I'm violating my paleo diet commitment by eating cake, I can simply let them know that the choice is not mine. Why? I'm a cake person.

I mean, hello! If you're a cake person you eat cake. It's no longer rocket science.

And inside this enlightenment experience I saw exactly what it is that gets in the way of our unlimited freedom and creativity . . . what produces our inability to thrive inside the present moment.

We can't thrive right now because we are covered with labels. We have labeled and classified ourselves. And the labels have seemed to increase our significance.

But what are they doing really? They've only strengthened our separation from the universe.

We slap labels of permanence and frozen characteristics onto what was formerly unlimited joyful energy. (Watch the family video of yourself running around and laughing at age three.)

We pin ourselves down this way. We chain ourselves up. We end up like those people who enjoy being chained to a big brass bed. We become twisted. We now struggle and strain against life . . . but we are really just struggling and straining against the way we have labeled ourselves.

We say things like, "I'm a cake person. And because of that, and only because of that, when I go to a birthday party or a funeral . . . I eat the cake."

It's a choiceless process. Seamless limitation! Organic captivity!

"I'm a progressive." "I'm a conservative." "I'm a Scorpio." "I'm an atheist." "I'm a foodie." "I'm an introvert." "I'm a 2 on the Enneagram!"

It goes on and on and with each label I get smaller and more paranoid. No wonder all I think about is how I can somehow get into a better future, a better now than this now.

But what's the answer? What's my solution?

Find someone who will steam these labels off my body. And take these chains, as Ray Charles sings, from my heart.

~ RIGHT NOW

130

Anyone can find someone

I know what you're thinking. You're thinking, What do you mean find someone to steam the labels off of me?

I mean find someone!

It might be someone in a book . . . or someone who does classes on the internet . . . or a spiritual mentor or teacher . . . or a colleague . . . or a grandparent . . . or a friend . . . or someone who has passed away but has left behind audio recordings that will inspire you to be free.

That's what I did. I went from mentor to mentor, hero to hero, inspiration to inspiration. I was finally ready to have them put on full steam. People who saw past the labels to the fearless heart inside of me (and also inside of you too).

And you can even become your own mentor, steaming off labels by entering the silence within. No distractions there. Allowing meditation to occur. Wisdom surfaces. It will be found inside once you get out of the past, get out of the future, and sink into the expanding and infinite present moment.

How present am I willing to be to what's going on? To the person I'm with? To the service I'm providing? To the skill I'm developing?

These labels drop off the minute I enter the beauty of the present moment. Because to "exist" they require a busy mind continuously spinning stories about the past and spinning worries about the future.   *~ RIGHT NOW*

131

Mastering the beauty
of the present moment

Today I'm learning to enjoy a satisfying, meditative mindset throughout the day by enjoying every little thing I do. The practice is to take anything that feels like a means to an end and slow down enough to make it an end in itself.

I am beginning to understand what the great songwriter Hoagy Carmichael meant when he said, "Slow motion gets you there faster."

Whether it's taking out the garbage or washing the dishes, I can slow down and have it be an end in itself. Not a means to an end.

If I'm talking to a potential client, I can do the same. If I'm not targeting them as a potential client—a target of opportunity!—(as if my life were a battlefield)—I can enjoy the human connection we have.

I can actually do this with everything. When I make washing the dishes something I need to grind through (a means to an end) I am no longer fully present to what I am doing and I don't allow happiness or satisfaction to be felt until the **end**, a clean sink, is achieved.

So happiness always gets pushed into the future. And the job I do isn't as thorough and complete as it could be. Because it isn't getting any love. It's a means to something else.

I used to live my whole waking life as a means to an end. Everything was something to get through. I raced through everything. If it hadn't been for the restful sleep I got at night I'd have gone insane this way.

Sleep was restorative because once I let go of my thoughts it became an end in itself, and therefore healthy. I didn't notice this at the time. In fact, I even wanted sleep to be a means to an end. I studied ways to hack my sleep so I could make it "powerful." I read up on "power naps." I looked for ways to learn lucid dreaming and impregnate my subconscious with wealth-producing affirmations while I slept! I wanted to work while I was sleeping! But fortunately I was usually too tired to do any of that so I just drifted off at night, allowing my sleep to be just sleep.

I eventually saw how my frenzied, sped-up days were reducing the quality of my life. Everything I was doing all day was a frantic, reckless means to an end. I was doing that because I thought it would mean something good would happen in the future.

This slowing down to appreciate life isn't a new idea. All the great spiritual teachers recommended loving every moment of God's creation. But I always worried about the downside of becoming "spiritual." I had friends who had become spiritual, and yes they seemed happier and more relaxed, but I feared that if I allowed myself to be happy and satisfied with the ordinary day's work, then I'd lose my drive. I didn't want to become a lazy idiot pleased with anything you handed me. I was convinced that my goals would not be reached unless I held my personal happiness hostage to their achievement.

But in doing that I missed something important. I missed the fact that happiness can lead to creativity. Even more so than relentless drive. Happiness is lighthearted and inventive. Happiness invites brilliant, unexpected solutions to pop into my mind. When I'm happy, problems no longer look frightening.

I was wrong to think that happiness would lead to passivity. I didn't understand that it could also invite in a pure and graceful kind of energy.

And I finally caved. I started reawakening a forgotten spiritual path I was on years ago. It was back when I was recovering from addiction and attending 12-step meetings and seeking conscious contact with a higher power. I wanted those days back again, so I sat with meditation teachers. I read spiritual books. I went to seminars and retreats that my coach recommended.

Soon I started seeing the wisdom in having everything I do be an end in itself. And the more I did that, the more my life got better. Even my profession got better. My prosperity grew. My life changed. All by itself.

~ RIGHT NOW

132

Let's give everyone a fresh chance

Sometimes I like to assign movies for my clients to watch. One of them is *Finding Dory*. The little fish character voiced by Ellen DeGeneres has short-term memory loss in that movie, and much of the humor comes from her forgetting who the other characters are.

She might have a long scene with a character and see the same character two minutes later and have no idea who she's talking to. Then cheerfully she says, "Oh hello! My name is Dory!" How exciting to find a new relationship! And for Dory, they're all showing up as new.

What if I can try being Dory? When I arrive at a gathering and I see someone there who I have had judgmental memories of, this time I approach them as Dory. I am happy and cheerful. I am open and empty and so glad to run into them. There is no story about them that I have to filter their words through.

When I show up empty, I am right here right now in the present moment. Like falling out of thought and like falling in love.

I have to be present to fall in love. Only in the here and now can I fall in love, because falling in love is an experience of pleasant surprise, or, as G.K. Chesterton said about his spiritual awakening, it's like receiving "absurd good news."

And I can fall in love with anything. I recently learned to fall in love with taking the garbage out. I noticed that I dreaded it every week, and when it came time to do it I slogged through it as a means to an end. It never occurred to me that I could make it an end in itself.

So I slowed it down and treated it like a sacred Zen practice. It wasn't long before I couldn't wait until garbage day. I'd even say to Kathy in a voice that sounded like elation, "Tomorrow's a big day."

"Oh really? Why?"

"Tomorrow is garbage day!"

She began to worry about me. She started looking online for what she could find about the first stages of dementia.

It is only stories (elaborate webs of thought) that make it hard for me to give something (like taking the garbage out) or someone (who once said something critical of me) a second chance. Someone criticizes me and I'm caught up into thinking they've done something deliberately hurtful. I try my best to forgive them, but built into my idea of forgiveness is the conviction that I am the person who was right and they are the person who was wrong. When I forgive them it feels like it's big of me to do that. I now sense that from now on I'll never be on the same moral level as they are. My forgiveness elevates my ego.

Isn't that right? Is it not from a superior level that I throw my pennies of forgiveness down to them? A magnificent being . . . that's who I am.

Dory would be kinder than that. Dory wouldn't even remember what that other person had done or said. And our love of her character comes not from thinking she's ignorant, but from feeling the kindness behind it all.

~ RIGHT NOW

133

You can do it right now

To me, it was a true revelation: There are things you can do right now.

I know that doesn't sound like big news. But I still like breaking it to people. Because it's not something they always notice.

Tamara said to me, "I want to have a better relationship with my mother. She lives back east. I don't talk to her very often."

"Why don't you call her?"

"I keep meaning to."

"How about right now?"

"Right now? I'm in a coaching session with *you* right now."

"Yes, but we are working on improving your relationship with your mother. So call her. I'll get off the line. We can pick up after your talk with her."

And so the new relationship between Tamara and her mother began. In that present moment. Not in our always well-meaning future. A much better use of time than me talking to her *about* calling her mother.

There are so many things in life like Tamara's relationship with her mother. Things we can do right now. Honoring the opportunity inside the present moment. Mastering its beauty.

For example, I love how Isaac Asimov wrote his books. He wrote over 500 books! Can you imagine? What about writer's block? Where did that thought go? Asimov wrote many

304 | *The Very Best of Steve Chandler*

bestsellers, like the *Foundation* series. I know that his output was absurd, and few writers really aspire to that level of productivity. But I love reading in his autobiographies (he actually wrote three of those) about his writing habits.

His favorite thing to do was to be writing *right now*.

It was his secret system of productivity.

If he was sitting in a doctor's waiting room and there were ten minutes more before his appointment, he delighted in that, and pulled out his notebook and wrote a short chapter for his current book. He wrote anywhere and everywhere throughout the day. He didn't have a sacred sanctuary of time set aside for his writing.

Or, actually he did, and it was called the present moment. That was his sacred space.

What is it *you* always wanted to create? What if you set this book down and started it right now? Would that upset your apple cart?

This opportunity can be applied to the relationships in your life, too. Who in your life have you neglected? If I asked you to name someone in your family, or an old friend who you have lost touch with—someone who, when you think of them, a tiny shiver of guilt passes through you—who would that be? It's not a good feeling, I know. What if you just contacted them? What if it was no longer a big deal that had to be thought about forever?

We often turn things into a big deal by blowing them up and floating them into the scary future. We fill these tasks with helium. Their importance and significance expands. Now they seem too big to hold on to any longer, so off they go into the distant future.

"This is too big. I can't do this right now."

There's a poster up in the gym I go to that shows a boxer strapping on a glove, and the poster says WHO'S STOPPING YOU? I love that poster. I love that question!

~ RIGHT NOW

134

Let me take you down and lift you up

Falling in love is the experience of returning to the eternal now.

When I'm in love, where else would I rather be but right here right now? It's a form of being "out of my mind." Falling out of my mind into a moment of truth I was not expecting.

Love, truth and beauty seem to be at the heart of all this. Because many other beautiful, amazing things inspire the same drop into the present moment. A sunset in Tucson. A street full of autumn leaves in Michigan. A certain painting, a sad and beautiful song. Holding my new grandson in my arms. They all take me down, or lift me up into the beauty of the present moment.

What if we could live there?

What if we already live there?

~ RIGHT NOW

135

I cannot create abundance

I cannot create abundance. It already exists everywhere.
The only thing I can create is scarcity.

~ John D. Vehr

The John Vehr in the quote above is a friend of mine and before I moved to Michigan he and I would have a monthly lunch together to talk about life, business, love, parenting, political outrage and whatever felt interesting.

Despite John's provocative views on a lot of popular issues his optimism is always shining through and his remarkable successes in the world of business tell you that he walks his talk and has skin in the game.

So what's the deal with that quote up above? What are we to make of that? Is it true? Does abundance exist everywhere? And when I experience scarcity, have I myself actually created it?

"Your thinking creates it," John says.

Let's set aside the issues of famine and poverty and social and political systems that have put people in situations where material and financial scarcity has become a physical reality. Some people have argued online with John's quote based on their looking at it through that lens of social justice.

I prefer to look at the quote from a personal lens. That way I can see how it applies to individual people like me. Let's take the quote personally. One example comes immediately to mind.

If I want to increase my income, there are people out there waiting to be helped and served right now. (Not at some future date when I get my act together, or when I become fortunate.)

Opportunities for serving people are out there in abundance.

When I couldn't see that reality I struggled financially because my thinking was always creating scarcity. It was making things look hard. It was making people look intimidating. It was pulling me down.

My thoughts of scarcity developed into a judgment cascade and then solidified into serious beliefs about personal limitations. I became a believer! I believed in my personal permanent characteristics, which unfortunately were weaknesses and shortcomings. Then those beliefs weighed me down further. I was drowning in debt. I started to think I was depressed. I was scaring myself.

All in my thinking.

Those images were blocking out reality. When I pulled a worried thought down and made it the truth it was exactly like pulling the shade down on my window and losing the light of the sun.

When I awoke to the possibility that lives inside John Vehr's reflection on abundance, everything changed. I saw that there were things I could do *right now* to connect my service to abundance. Once I saw that and took action on that insight I was able to help clients do the same.

~ RIGHT NOW

136

Waking people up to the abundance

There was a community college in a state out West that hired me to help them deal with what they saw as an external, real-world problem.

They thought that in their state there was only so much money to go around and the major university down the highway was getting it all. The donations to the little community college were scarce and the donations flowing in to the big university looked abundant.

"We have a hard time raising money here because of who we are," the Director of Development told me when I arrived to consult with them. "We are a small college without connections to the kinds of people who make large donations."

That's what she thought.

Fortunately I had learned by then how fleeting and insubstantial any thought was. She was believing an arbitrary thought. Maybe that seems obvious from the vantage point of where you and I are right now. But it was the very insight that allowed me to help turn things around at that school. One thing led to another and soon we had larger and larger donations coming in to help that little community college.

If I had taken her thought to be actual solid reality, I would have had to try to help them go to war with that reality and see what kind of changes we could make to the prevailing negative circumstance.

We didn't do that, because it wasn't reality. It was virtual reality.

What we did instead was set those thoughts of scarcity aside so our minds could settle and be clear. Like a glass of muddy water, we allowed the dirt to settle and things got clear. Inspiration and creativity showed up inside that relaxed clarity and we began to see how we could serve donors.

My own history with scarcity thinking helped me. I had been a poster boy for Dr. Martin Seligman's studies on "learned helplessness." I had become like the singer in "Old Man River" who sings, "I get weary, and sick of trying, I'm tired of living and scared of dying."

The fundraisers at the little college were also weary. They were sick of trying to create abundance. They were tired of asking for money and yet scared that their school and their department might soon be dying.

My job was to show up as Old Man River himself. Someone who could show them that they could just keep rolling along. Let's sit down around this table and get the flow going. Let's stop focusing on us and start looking at our donors. Let's be open to the abundance that is already there.

The system they learned, of serving their donors instead of serving their own goals and needs, is a system I learned from Michael Bassoff, my co-author of the book *Relationshift: Revolutionary Fundraising*. Donors want to make a difference in the world. That's why they donate. And if you show them the exact difference their donation is making, and if you build strong and lasting relationships with them based on that, they will become more and more inspired to help.

So the development team watched as their thinking changed. They began to see that they were actually serving the donors by giving them a way to make a difference in life. They got to know their donors better and appreciate them more. Their relationships began to be built on gratitude and close collaboration. No longer were the donors seen as impersonal targets. No longer were donors "set up" for the next uncomfortable "ask." They were now seen as real people you could communicate with heart-to-heart, instead of distant, clueless, stingy people you had to give a dog and pony presentation to, or people you had to beg your own board members to "hit up" for small, reluctant donations.

Scarcity, for this little school, had been a thought posing as reality. It was a thought everyone agreed to believe. It spread through the college like a religion. And then it was gone.

~ RIGHT NOW

137

The music in this very moment

Now I may not be an award-winning singer, but I can sing a song right now.

And just as William James said, "I don't sing because I'm happy; I'm happy because I sing."

And I may not be a talented dancer but I can get up and sway to the music this very moment.

And I may not be a great romancer but I can write someone a love letter and send them a flower the minute I finish this sentence.

But what if I have patterns of failed attempts at things? What if I have started previous projects and quit? What does that say about me?

If I am coaching you, it says nothing about you. So I will answer those questions with another question: What do you want to make of this moment together?

What if you saw that the past does not create the present? What if you could see that the present is what creates the past? It creates everything. It even creates the future.

Or, at least that is what seems to be my experience. And I want to base everything I say here on experience. I can trust that.

Which isn't the same thing as trusting myself. (My smaller personal self.)

People used to tell me, "Trust yourself!" And that was hard to do once I saw that I had made myself up. It was as if I had played the Phantom in a musical and out in real life, off-stage people kept saying to me, "Learn to trust the Phantom!" How could I if I knew I wasn't really the Phantom?

No, it's stronger to just trust my experience.

You ask about your past patterns and it's my experience that your patterns don't have to matter. You only make them matter when you believe that they are significant . . . when you believe that past patterns can cause behavior.

The patterns you perceive aren't the cause of behavior; they are the result of behavior.

So you can write them off as past history. Maybe interesting, maybe not. But merely history. And if you're willing to see them as past history, you and I can meet each other right here right now in the present moment. From here we can create a brand-new future.

~ RIGHT NOW

138

What's the name of that actor?

You're trying to think of his name. You know, that actor! He was in that movie with Jennifer Lawrence. He's in a TV series now. You try and try to think of his name but you just can't.

So you drop the whole thing, and you decide to carry some dishes to the sink in the kitchen. You start to scrape and rinse the dishes and then BOOM! The name appears!

What just happened?

You were trying to utilize highly-controlled personal thinking to access something that comes from somewhere else. This will happen any time you try desperately to figure something out. You keep feeding it into the cyclotron of your neocortex and it whirls faster and faster, colliding with other particles of thought. But the answer is never there.

The answer comes from somewhere else. It comes when the grip is relaxed.

Here's an even more important example.

You're writing something creative, say a book or a song or a blog, and you keep trying to figure out the next lyric or line. You think and you think and you pace and you fret. After you give up writing for the day you step into the shower and BOOM! the idea flies in.

The grip was released.

314 | *The Very Best of Steve Chandler*

And we start to understand that creativity and inspiration do not flow into a mind that grips and clenches.

I can release my death grip and drop out of my whirling thinking. Dropping out of my personal thinking is like telling my inner editor to take a hike. I will call on him later. If I'm letting him judge my writing as it is happening the flow stops.

The Dalai Lama keeps teaching that when there is no judgment we fall in love. Without that judgment, love is all there is. When I stopped judging the garbage as a dreary, boring chore, I fell in love with doing it. I had slowed it down to the speed of the present moment. I gave myself a chance to experience the *beauty* of the present moment.

It's the same thing as dropping into the now. I don't force my way into the now. I don't achieve the now. I don't "deserve" the now because of my efforts. I fall. Just as I don't deserve or achieve the love I feel when I fall in love. I just fall.

When I do that my creativity is unlimited. It is not governed by my personal history. It does not pay any attention to whether I think I am "a creative person" or not.

~ RIGHT NOW

139

What makes you feel this way?

D o you think like a victim? Do you take things personally? If so, join the club. I did for decades.

And it wasn't because of a character flaw or a pathological personality defect (as much as I thought it was). I was simply unaware that I didn't have to give credibility to my victim thoughts. I didn't have to follow them all the way down the rabbit hole, holding on for dear life all the way down.

In the past I always gave each successive negative thought a lot of depth and weight. I was letting each thought bring in clusters of related and equally discouraging thoughts.

But once the awareness checked in . . . the awareness that I could just let it go . . . it isn't true reality . . . it is just a thought! . . . my life changed for the better.

From that point on I defined ownership as taking whatever life gives you and welcoming it in. Owning it. I defined the victim thought cluster as one that sees circumstance as all powerful . . . and often those circumstances look negative and emotionally overwhelming.

I first got the idea for my victim thinking seminars from the many books I'd read by British philosopher Colin Wilson, whose philosophy was that humans have an endless innate capacity for optimism and creativity already built in. However, they bypass and ignore that resource in favor of the mistaken pessimistic viewpoint that life is difficult and oppressive. When we live long enough in

316 | *The Very Best of Steve Chandler*

that viewpoint we humans become weak and miserable.

Wilson said we could drop the pessimism in a heartbeat the moment we understood the depth of our untapped resources.

Wilson's optimistic philosophy struck a chord with me and the more I understood it, the more I experienced it to be true. When I believed my victim thoughts it felt like life was presenting me with a series of difficult situations I had to learn to "get through." But when I chose to believe my ownership thoughts (thereby acknowledging ownership of my built-in, powerful human spirit) I saw the same situations as opportunities for learning. I went from "get through" to "get from."

Organizations who took the training also woke up to their previously unrecognized power to create and innovate and bring good energy to everything they encountered. They started to ask what they could "get from" any situation that used to be automatically thought of as another problem to "get through."

One reason the training clicked and became useful was because it was allowing people to see the true origin of their victimized feelings. Those feelings were not caused by the situation itself, but rather by the way they were thinking about it.

So the real difference between the owner (of their inner unlimited human spirit) and the victim was that the owner realized that situations by themselves could not cause morale or energy to deflate. It was always just the thought. And you didn't have to go with your first thought about anything.

Colin Wilson put it best when he wrote, "When I open my eyes in the morning I am not confronted by a world, but by a million possible worlds."

It is not an easy thing for people to see what Wilson saw . . . that we live in a thought-projected world of infinite possibility. They just assume that we live in one real, external world, and that that world is a consistent challenge. They have been conditioned to believe that circumstances and other people are the cause of what they feel.

So they feel zapped by others, and zapped by fate, and zapped by this and zapped by that and no wonder life becomes hard to live. They are like flies flying into one of those electronic insect zappers. Who's not going to buckle under all that zapping? Who's going to wake up into that world singing, "Oh, what a beautiful morning!"?

We have been heavily conditioned by culture and society to interpret our feelings this way. We learn at an early age that they come from outside sources. People who loved us kept telling us they hoped something good would "happen" to us. The thought was that something would come from the outside world and envelop us with its inherent goodness!

People referred to those good things happening as "being blessed." If something came along, a new romantic mate, a job offer, a newborn child, a good day at the race track, they would say, "I've been blessed."

It didn't occur to them that the biggest blessing of all, dwarfing all those outside happenings, was consciousness itself. What they wake up into each day. The true miracle of present moment awareness. That inner, seemingly empty resource that is actually pregnant with optimism and creativity.

That's the ultimate blessing right there.

If I believe blessings must be bestowed in the form of good outside circumstances, then no wonder the outside world seems to contain all the power over my feelings. It feels like one day I could be blessed by life, and the next day cursed by life. Truly an anxiety-producing set up. Could that really be how life works?

Like Alan Watts used to say, if you were God would you create life so that it worked that way? Not if you were God. No way.

~ RIGHT NOW

140

Disconnecting from the source of happiness

My own disconnection happened because I was gathering discouraging beliefs as I got older. They were negative and pessimistic beliefs that soon became heavy in my heart, like stones.

They were heavy like the stones that Virginia Woolf filled her pockets with on the 28th of March in 1941 before she wandered into the water to drown herself. That kind of heavy.

The older I got the more I was walking the earth filled with many cold stones of belief.

It wasn't until my coach introduced me to the work of Byron Katie that I began to understand why he'd ask this powerful question: "What are you believing about yourself that would cause you to feel the way you do?"

That's where feelings come from? Our thoughts?

I was feeling discouraged, defeated and, as my mother used to put it, "down in the dumps." And I would point to situations and circumstances that I thought were causing those feelings. And then my coach would guide me back inside to look for the belief. And that always turned out to be the answer.

Or, as Byron Katie likes to ask, "What is the thought that kicks you out of heaven?"

Once I really heard that question, it became the most useful question in the world to me. I began to use that question with myself and my clients. I even do an exercise in my seminars where I put a volunteer up on a stool in front of the room and simply ask that question, "What is the thought that kicks you out of heaven?" and we take it from there.

After doing that enough times, more and more light comes in. It becomes a great unraveling. It is an effective way to deconstruct and disentangle a negative belief system. It's an opportunity to start fresh right then and there in the beauty of the present moment, seeing the role of thought.

Without thought and belief, there is nothing left but truth. And truth is beauty. As the poet John Keats wrote, "Beauty is truth, truth beauty, —that is all ye know on earth, and all ye need to know."

Beautiful moments occur up on that chair in front of the room. We originally called it "the hot seat" to acknowledge the courage of the people who volunteered to sit there and do the inquiry. Later it got the name "The Clarity Chair" because of the head-clearing truth that kept arising from the exercise.

~ RIGHT NOW

141

So sad it became funny

It would be puzzling if we actually disconnected from our inner fire *knowingly*. If we woke up and deliberately chose to spend the day toggling back and forth between a badly-remembered past and a completely fantasized future, all the while losing energy and hope.

But once I saw that I was doing that, I started asking myself some questions. Is my memory of my past accurate? Did my father really never believe in me? For years I crafted resentments from fleeting, faded memories. I had begun thinking I was never given enough encouragement to have good survival skills. I started picturing worst-case scenarios for the future. I saw myself as a homeless person.

I heard an interview with Larry David (the major writer for the *Seinfeld* TV series) once in which he said he had such vivid fears of ending up homeless that he'd actually picked out a spot on the street for himself.

He discovered humor to be his road to freedom from all this illusion.

Sometimes being funny can be a way to bring the truth in. To realize what the sages and mystics of old meant when they said that enlightenment was "the restoration of humor" to human life. (Notice how many times a day children laugh.)

My friend and colleague Jason Goldberg and I created a little internet show called *The Not-So-Serious Life* as a playful experiment that explored the potential of lightheartedness. We had viewers send us real-life questions about real-life problems, and although we didn't try to dismiss the pain that (thinking about) these problems had produced for our people, we had fun offering creative solutions and enjoying the challenge of the problems. We were playing with solutions instead of desperately seeking them. (You can see these episodes on YouTube and other places on the internet.) And although some critics said we were taking people's problems too lightly, I've never regretted exploring the function of fun as a problem-solving system.

Another example of seeing how humor can open up a mind closed down by beliefs is in a short video done by Fred Knipe, as his comedic character Dr. Ludiker gives us advice on the subject of credentials. You'll find that on YouTube too. I've used it to help professional coaches and consultants who are stressed out about whether their credentials are impressive enough. They laugh when they see it and their hearts are suddenly lighter.

I've often wondered what would happen if you gave people an honest, real-life choice between humor and self-improvement. Let's say you had three theaters on a theater row and the first one had a religious figure who could lift you up spiritually and maybe even save your soul, and in the next theater you had a motivational guru who could give you great ideas for self-improvement, and in the third theater the funniest stand-up comic in the country. Where would the lines be the longest? I think it would be with the comedian.

And it wouldn't be just because people would rather be entertained than improved or spiritually saved. I think it would be because something deeper calls them to the humor. We secretly know that there is something explosive and non-linear about humor that can open us up in a heartbeat. Instant freedom from our thinking. Whereas those other disciplines can take lifetimes of practice. (And there is still no guarantee of freedom.)

A laugh is a spontaneous opening. It instantly opens even the most tightly-closed mind. It's a burst of childhood happiness that blows the confetti of your serious thoughts back out into space. It's a bodily eruption of total surprise. An unexpected and irresistible surge of joy in the line, a power surge that can momentarily shut down your analytical biocomputer altogether!

Even on a biological level the flood of endorphins that comes from laughter is proven to be healing. A good joke stops you from taking your previous thinking seriously.

So the next time you have a serious problem that you are bringing to your coach to solve you might get your best result by saying, "Help me have some fun with this."

~ RIGHT NOW

142

He never finishes anything

L evon is the name I will give to a person who hired me to help him with a debilitating problem.

He admitted that he didn't know if I could help him solve this thing, given his long history with it, but he was willing to try anything. He called me at our appointed early morning coaching hour, and I asked him what the problem was.

"I never finish anything," he said.

I asked him to talk more about that and he told me it ran through his whole life and it caused him all sorts of problems with his wife and family and he was really discouraged and down on himself.

I decided to ask him some unusual questions. I thought I might find an opening in the way he saw the world.

I knew Levon was a dedicated outdoorsman so I asked him what kind of shoes he was wearing. Just as I'd hoped, he said he was wearing hiking boots.

I said, "Are they the kind you have to tie? Do they have laces?"

"Yes, of course. Are there hiking boots that don't?"

I had to admit that I wouldn't know that. But I continued by saying, "Are they tied right now, all the way up?"

"Yes."

324 | The Very Best of Steve Chandler

"And this morning when you put them on, were they tied? Were they tied before you put them on?"

Levon said, "No," and I could hear that he was getting impatient.

"Okay, good, so you put them on, and then you started to tie them and then you finished tying them. So that's something you started and finished."

"Well, yeah, but . . ."

I said, "Did you finish high school?"

There was a pause and then he said yes.

I said, "Oh good, so you started high school and you went all the way through high school and you finished high school."

"Right," he said.

I told him that was another thing right there that he started and finished and not to think it was a minor thing. I'd read an article that said over 45 percent of students in Los Angeles County don't finish high school. They start but they don't finish.

And there are a lot of people who sit around the house with their laces untied.

We inquired about three or four more things in his world, all of which he had finished. Soon he'd had enough.

"I don't see where you're going with all this," he said. "These things that I did finish are not that big a deal. Well, maybe high school, but . . ."

I said I understood that, but I wanted to make the point that if we inquired long enough we'd also find a lot of things that were very important to him that he did finish, and that my point was to show him that his belief—"I never finish anything"—was not true.

"You finish almost everything," I said.

He was silent but he didn't disagree.

So we talked about the consequences of living in a world of falsehood. A world of labels. What exactly happens to someone who finishes almost everything but then they see the world, and themselves, through the filter of "I never finish anything"?

Levon said he wasn't sure what happens to those people.

"They end up like you!" I said.

He tried to laugh.

I told him that when someone walks around believing something false and disrespectful about themselves they limit their capacity to love life and take action. Who would want that? They get bogged down in a false identity that they think *explains* their behavior. Even produces it! So just as Kevin Costner's character in the movie had the Indian name "Dances With Wolves," Levon now walked around his house with the identity, "Never Finishes Anything." Imagine that his family sees him come into the room and they cheerfully cry out, "Oh look, here comes Never Finishes Anything!" At least that's how it feels. And when you feel like that it gets harder and harder to finish things.

He was seeing it. It began to look funny to him. But I knew we hadn't addressed the problem behind the problem . . . the actual reason he was calling this a problem. So I asked him what was it, specifically, that he hadn't finished that was the focus of his downhearted thinking.

"The basement game room," he said. "I started painting it a year ago, but it was such a big project I had to postpone work on it and I've never gotten back to it and my wife keeps bringing it up."

I told Levon that one of my biggest epiphanies ever was realizing that there were always things I could do right now. Things that didn't have to wait. And if he was willing, I'd be an accountability partner for him in painting this basement right now. But it was up to him.

He said he would love that.

For the next two weeks Levon sent me phone pics of the painting progress in his basement and, as we'd agreed to, he was completely finished with it by our next phone call.

Levon saw himself in a different light. He understood that his thinking was the only thing that was getting in his way. He got the difference between "I never finish anything" and "There's a basement that hasn't been finished." The first thought pulled Levon into a feeling of being personally defective. It disempowered him every time he believed it. And it wasn't even true. The second thought was just a neutral observation about the basement and an opportunity for action.

Colin Wilson once observed that if people saw life for what it really was—pure and endless opportunity—pessimism would become "a laughable absurdity."

143

Does self-esteem have to be earned?

In the old psychological theories, self-esteem and self-confidence were something you either had built up or else you didn't have them. And if you didn't have them, you'd better learn to develop them!

They were identifiable outcomes. They were also sought-after labels. For example, "high self-esteem" was a label we would hope to stick on ourselves after steaming off the "low self-esteem" label.

But Dicken Bettinger has a more optimistic view of this subject. For me, he has been a master at interpreting the light.

In an interview with Sebastian Eck (available on YouTube) Dicken explains his viewpoint. It's based on decades of experience counseling young people and grown-ups (like me) on the true nature of psychological well-being.

As for self-esteem and self-confidence?

"We're born with them," he says.

They emerge, not from heroic practice and personal development, but whenever we drop out of our insecure thoughts, worries and judgments. There they are: self-confidence and self-esteem. They have been there all along.

When people feel anxious and uncertain for a period of time, that feeling gets labeled as low self-esteem. It becomes a condition you think you have. A condition that you might want to have fixed and corrected.

"We think that if somebody has a feeling of insecurity for a long time, that must be their true nature," Dicken says. "So we'll say, 'They don't have self-esteem.'"

But what's really occurring is that the person is feeling low as a result of their passing thoughts and the temporary feelings they create. Nothing worthy of a permanent label.

Dicken says that when those thoughts drop away, "that's what we would call *living in the now*. Anybody who is living in the now, free of worries and judgments, is going to have perfect self-esteem and self-confidence."

So it occurred to me that self-esteem actually looks a little like Kansas.

Dorothy asked Glinda the good witch how she could get back to Kansas and the good witch laughed because she knew Dorothy *was already there*. Oz was a dream. If she just clicked her heels she would wake up.

Dorothy had obviously been dreaming. But we are dreaming too when we see the world (and ourselves!) as projections of our insecure thoughts and beliefs.

~ RIGHT NOW

144

Like waking up from my longest dream

My longest dream was not a good dream. It truly was the dream of low self-esteem.

But my life didn't start that way.

Because I remember when I was three years old, running with absolute abandon across a yard of green grass and feeling like I owned the world . . . I *was* the world in that moment. No problem with low self-esteem because I was living in the moment and loving life.

In my adult years so many beliefs clouded my connection with life that the love that lived inside felt like it had to *break through* those beliefs to be fully felt and expressed.

That predicament comes from confusing a negative belief with the truth, and from confusing virtual reality (a thought) with true reality.

I tell myself, "My father doesn't trust me or believe in me," and now his facial expressions look like suspicion, when in fact they were neutral. His encouraging words, "You can do better," sound like hurtful criticism. Because they are being perceived through the lens of my beliefs. If I put on purple sunglasses everything looks purple, even the rain. If I put on beliefs of any color, the world and my father look like they *are* that color.

One day Dicken Bettinger told me he had been reading and

enjoying *The Magic of Awareness* by Anam Thubten. I bought the book and devoured it. Then I took it everywhere with me for a month or so, like a kind of battery pack that I might need at any moment if my spirit lost its charge.

Anam Thubten is one of the rising Buddhist teachers in the West. He grew up in Tibet and began at an early age to practice in the Nyingma tradition of Tibetan Buddhism.

I underlined my book where Thubten wrote, ". . . everything we want to transcend doesn't really exist in the ultimate sense. It only exists as our own mind's display . . ."

If I'm displaying from my mind a wife who doesn't like me she can say, "You look good today" and my mind will translate it to mean, "You look good for a change."

My answer to her of "What's been wrong with the way I *have been* looking?" confuses her. She doesn't realize that I'm seeing through a faulty lens . . . the lens of my thinking.

I could have lived forever believing that my father didn't believe in me, but when I saw that this was just a projection from my own mind, life got open and bright.

Now the trick would be to find out how to transcend the filters. How to ditch the purple glasses. How to see and hear clearly. How to enjoy the whole of life *right now.*

When I look inside Thubten's *The Magic of Awareness* I see that he prescribes something he calls "crazy love."

"Crazy love is a very ecstatic way of transcending this mind and its ultimate mistake of buying into its own display," he says. "We just see everything as sacred and love everything without having any specific object of love . . . Love without boundaries, crazy love, is sacred perception . . . Crazy love loves everything . . ."

Wow. To me that sounds a little crazy. Maybe he knew it

would sound that way, which is why he gave it the name. But when I read that I was willing to try it. I mean, I'll try anything. Wouldn't you? If it meant transcending the mind's projections?

Okay, so where to start? I looked back at the book and saw that Anam Thubten had anticipated my question.

He says, "The question is how do we, in this very ordinary moment, jump into that realm of crazy love? Instead of holding an answer as a kind of recipe, let's keep asking the question . . ."

He's brilliant. The answer won't be useful. Because his answer might not be mine. Mine might not be yours. So it's the question itself that I want to keep with me. How do I, in this very ordinary moment, jump into the realm of crazy love?

~ RIGHT NOW

145

No idea who Spartacus is

Sometimes I like to quote Werner Erhard to clients (and even friends looking for help). I especially like to pass on his wisdom about choosing to be "cause in the matter" of their lives.

My friend, whom I'll call Tanya, was confused about this idea after we talked about it because she wondered about all the things truly out of her control, like the death of a family member, and learning to accept and love "What Is." It was hard for her to reconcile that with being the cause in all matters of her life.

I asked if she'd ever seen the movie *Spartacus*.

"Yes, ages ago."

We talked about the movie and she remembered the scene where the Roman guards came to take away the galley slave Spartacus for crucifixion, and before he could identify himself many of the other slaves, one at a time, stepped up and said, "I am Spartacus!"

It was a moving moment in the film, but what I wanted Tanya to see was the power of their declaration, "I am Spartacus!" By declaring that, the Romans had no idea who the real Spartacus was.

Well, the slaves who yelled that phrase weren't *really* Spartacus. It wasn't true, what they said. But it was powerful. And it got the job done. Which was my point in asking her to recall that scene. It doesn't have to be *true* that you are the cause of your life for you to gain benefit from saying it. This is a game we're playing here.

Werner Erhard says, "That you are the *cause* of everything in your life is a place to stand from which to view and deal with life—a place that exists solely as a matter of your choice. The stand that one is *cause in the matter* is a declaration, not an assertion of fact."

The key words there are "not an assertion of fact." In other words it's not a fact that you cause everything, and he's clear about that. Tanya had already seen that it wasn't a fact that she was the cause of everything. She was even happy about it. She felt how healthy it was to be at peace with whatever happened and welcome reality in. Some say this awareness grants us "the serenity to accept the things I cannot change." It's healing.

BUT what Werner is saying (and I am saying) is that a declaration (I am CAUSE) can be extremely useful "as a place to stand from." A role you can play. A place you can come from. Out in the game of life, when you're playing that game in society and with other people.

When I first learned this idea of "being cause in the matter" of my life it was a turning point. I had always felt I was merely at the mercy of outside forces. In my mind, everything in the world marketplace was about luck and privilege. And when I heard stories of people working their way up from nothing I believed they had self-motivation in their DNA and I didn't. From an early age I also believed that grownups had all the money and all the power and I knew I would never grow up. I was a poster boy for a victim mindset and a permanent case of arrested development.

And it turns out that I was truly an extreme case. My belief system led to hugely dysfunctional interaction with the real world. Or lack of interaction, depending how you see it. Lack of action, for sure. My being the effect and not the cause resulted in a kind of spiritual atrophy. I was overcome with weakness. In my real world there were huge breakdowns. I ended up dealing with (and feeling like a victim of) bankruptcy, divorce, alcoholism . . . and we could go on.

Dr. Martin Seligman's studies refer to a life like mine as "learned helplessness."

Fortunately the mentoring I got from 12-step sponsors, teachers and then coaches saved me. That and the books I started reading. They led me to the option I never knew I had. This option was that I could declare myself to be cause in the matter of my life. My business consultant and life coach at the time, Steve Hardison, actually had the word CAUSE on his car's license plate. So he was an effective advocate.

Soon I found that by coming from that place, from declaring that I was cause, I could make things happen. And the joy was that it was not my personality doing it. In a funny way, it was not even about me.

It was the stand itself.

The stand was enough. I didn't have to wonder if "I" had what it took. I didn't have to worry about my permanent identity and whether that person could ever make anything happen. The stand itself (coming from a created place inside of me that declared that I was cause) was more than enough to start me on the path of getting my whole life turned around.

It was a way to play the game.

No one I've met since those days has had a case of victim mindset quite as severe as mine was. But almost all people have *some* version of it that keeps them from enjoying the game and playing it wholeheartedly. And it's no wonder that almost everyone has a touch of this. The movies, the media, most parents, most everyone in the culture teach us to get used to being at the mercy of circumstance. All power seems to be *out there* in the hands of events, companies, politicians and other people. We learn that. It's deeply drilled into us.

But when I decide that I want to create a business or make my relationships better this declaration of being cause helps clear my head and gets me connected to the real creative power of life (within me). Standing as cause helps me sort out my day. It shows me what to focus on. It gives me strength and the glory of simplicity.

~ RIGHT NOW

146

Dead leaves in my pockets

D ead leaves. That's how I regard any bad memories I might have blowing through my mind today.

That was not true in the past. With eager encouragement from my psychotherapist I was asked to bring those memories back and give them fresh life and then experience the feelings that came up from that. It was suggested that we would "get it completed and out of your system."

So something you focus on and repeat over and over is going to, as a result, have less of a presence in your life? Looking back on that theory, it's easy to question. But at the time I was willing to do anything.

So I was cheered on and taught to cultivate my rage and give it new life. Sometimes I thought I would die trying to do that. Instead of completing and "getting closure" on my past memories, it only gave them more significance. Instead of giving me new life it gave my rage new life.

My clients come to their life-coaching (and even business-coaching) with a lot of dead leaves in their pockets. Some clients bring them out to try to give them life again and try to understand them as the cause of their current dysfunction. (We've been taught to think we must *fix* anything not immaculate in the memory bin.)

But how could this dead leaf be the *cause* of some current emotional energy? Maybe that whole practice was backwards.

My best experiences with myself and those I try to help happen when we let the wind just blow those leaves through and away. So we can start fresh. In this moment, with this beautiful green tree of life.

~ RIGHT NOW

147

Is there life after high school?

There have been books written on this subject, some with the exact title of this chapter, and the conclusion is . . . basically? No.

In other words we don't change much after that. Who we were in high school is likely to be who we are now.

Unless, of course, we are willing to see through all of this play acting we do. Not making it wrong, because it lets us play on the stage of society with all the other actors. But seeing it (and enjoying it) for what it is.

My suspicion is that high school is where we completed work on the creation of our personalities. No, even deeper than personalities . . . on what we thought were our very identities as separate selves in the world. The goal of each of these character-creations in high school was to avoid embarrassment. In high school there was no pain as great as embarrassment. We'd rather receive a full-on oncological radiation treatment than to blush with embarrassment.

Why? Because that was the time when our teenage hormones were surging. So the mission of being liked and admired, or at least accepted and appreciated, was the most important thing in the whole world. It was foremost in our minds throughout the livelong day.

Who will you be to avoid embarrassment? *Who will you be* in order to be liked? Some of us chose to shrink back and become shy and humble characters. That felt safe. Others needed to pump up the volume and be big and extroverted to cover their insecurity. Whatever seemed to work!

All of that activity was understandable. It was our abrupt entry into the social world and we would have to learn to survive.

But there was a problem with this process of character-creation in those formative years. The problem was that we inevitably believed our own act.

We eventually thought that who we were creating ourselves to be was actually not an invention, but rather a permanent set of pre-existing characteristics and qualities. So as the years went by those characteristics were given more and more significance and permanence.

And then it felt solidified. Not only did we think our characteristics were real and hardwired, we started to believe that they were even causative! They caused our behavior! We started using our characteristics to explain everything! I am not a detail person! I'm an introvert! I'm not good with languages! I'm not good at dating! I'm a cake person!

It's as if we all were assigned parts in the school play and then couldn't stop being that character long after the play was over. Forgetting completely that it was just a play. (A musical comedy if we look back honestly.)

Soon all our actions were based on the characteristics of the person we made up. We didn't see that our actions *could* spring from the opportunity that called to us in the present moment. We missed the beauty of the present moment entirely because our focus was on who we thought we were and what the characteristics of that person were causing to happen.

From that delusion it was hard to create loving, lasting relationships. Because, as Byron Katie says, *"Personalities don't love—they want something."*

But sometimes . . . and not very often . . . sometimes we got glimpses of the truth.

We'd see someone across a crowded room at the prom and our heart would stop. Our thoughts about ourselves would disappear and it felt like we were in heaven. What was happening? Were we falling in love?

Maybe what really stopped at that moment wasn't the heart. What if what stopped was just all those thoughts? All those thoughts that were headed for the future or else going into the past.

What if when the truth (beauty) is glimpsed those thoughts fall away? And love is just the beauty arising out of feeling the here and now.

~ RIGHT NOW

Recovery

148

The pursuit of more

I'm thinking that I'm not enough. No wonder I'm always adding something to me . . . something from the outside world.

Byron Katie talks about being addicted to love and approval. Believing we need it. There are clinics for sex addiction and romantic love addiction.

A man I know says to me, "Yes I have an okay marriage, but I myself am not happy," so he says maybe if he just *added* this one adventurous, romantic love relationship to his life it would feel more like the life he deserved. (Surprise: It turned out badly.)

I read the tabloids to keep up with what addiction can do to people. Famous people in celebrity rehab. Look at all of them. Adding like crazy. Look at Oprah's five beautiful homes! It's a magazine spread.

Ben Affleck has a good marriage to Jennifer Garner (I'm putting my groceries on the conveyor belt slowly now so I can read all of this) and he decides to add to that a romantic relationship with their nanny. In the following weeks and months I read all about custody, betrayal, heartbreak, financial penalties, bitterness . . . in other words a major life hangover. It all comes from adding.

A national politician had a reputation for taking huge speaker's fees from banks and corporations to give her meaningless talks to empty halls. She was searingly described in a magazine as a "tragic bag of appetites."

Business author Jim Collins notes that one of the main reasons great companies collapse and fall apart is what he calls "the undisciplined pursuit of more." What brings down a company will also bring down a human being.

I saw a viral video on the internet during the holidays. It shows a group of hyperactive shoppers shoving and tripping over a stack of vegetable steamers. They were rushing wildly to pick them up. Then the video shows a crazed woman coming up to a boy and his mother, and quite literally ripping a steamer out of the kid's arms. She had to have it. She had to add it. Had to.

~ Death Wish

149

This was already in there all along

The famous beat generation author and drug addict William Burroughs killed his wife playing a William Tell game (I'll shoot the apple off the top of your head, okay, stand still, what could go wrong?) at a drugged-up, drunken party. He was the author of the books *Naked Lunch* and *Junkie*. He was actually a brilliant man, and never so brilliant as he was in his later years when he was clean and sober and said that there wasn't anything, any feeling, any high, that you could get on drugs and alcohol that you couldn't get *without* drugs and alcohol.

And that's because that treasure of good feelings is already in you. The drug (and I always include alcohol as a drug) just temporarily breaks down the brain barriers. It releases what's already there. But only for a quick flash. It shows you what you could feel most all of the time if you were truly free and clear.

It took me awhile, some years clean and sober, to find out that William Burroughs was right. You don't need the drugs to feel that way. Through meditative living, devotional work and helping others, and an ongoing spiritual life you can find out faster than I did that you can have an even happier life than you did at your best drunken, drugged-up moment.

I used to believe I had to add drugs and alcohol to my system to feel the things I wanted to feel. If I wanted to feel more relaxed or more courageous or more confident in a crowd of people, it was never going to happen unless I *added something* powerful to my system. I did get (most of the time, at the beginning, until it turned against me) the feelings I wanted. But they were all-too temporary.

But as Burroughs found out, the drug itself doesn't directly produce the feeling. It just removes the thought-blocks in the brain to the treasure that's already there.

There are other ways to remove those barriers, thank God (and the people who helped me).

~ Death Wish

150

Why demonize your healthiest desire?

In my book *Crazy Good* I tried to explain my theory that it's almost impossible to immediately go all the way from bad to good. To ski-jump the polarities. In one foul swoop.

But that's what people try to do all the time. People including myself.

It always failed.

It is far easier to succeed by going from pretty good to a little better. Progress not perfection. But it means you have to start with pretty good. You have to be happy with doing the best you can do. (Most people are not!)

You have to find a way to feel good about your basic innocence . . . to not berate, condemn or label yourself negatively. Which is why it was so valuable to see an "urge" or "craving" to indulge my habit as a hidden desire to thrive, which was a good desire.

Wanting to thrive, to flourish, to expand upward and outward in a joyful spiral of release is evolutionary. It's the healthiest view we get of the life force that connects us all. Why make it a sickness? Why not just understand it?

Once I understood it I had a chance to direct that desire toward something healthier and more life-sustaining. Like replacing false "spirits" (the old frontier name for alcohol) with true spirit.

~ Death Wish

151

Show me the way to go home

As I was growing up from newborn to two years old to four to six to ten, the feeling of personal warmth and security was gradually leaving me! What the hell?!?!?!

I was becoming an individual. It felt like it was happening against my will.

Some psychologists call this "individuation." It became *extreme* at age eighteen and I took my first drink. *Maybe this will re-connect me to the life force.* (I know young people often experiment with drinking and drugs at earlier ages now, but I was old school. I was eighteen.)

Unfortunately, my first drink led very quickly to an obsession with altering my own consciousness. Some people think I had Peter Pan syndrome, a refusal to grow up. I used drugs and alcohol to stay young and foolish. I never even tried to enjoy life without alcohol. I never even tried to grow up.

But my belief today is weird: I think if you can understand how to recover from addiction into what people call "good sobriety" (a very low risk for drinking or drugging again), you can understand how to enjoy all of life, even if you are not an addict.

I came upon this belief after noticing that my own recovery, after years of meetings and endless hours being mentored by my sponsor, was no longer about alcohol. It was about enjoying life. And what I learned had a major influence on my created profession of teaching and coaching. Spiritual progress can be applied to everything.

By spiritual progress I mean spiraling up beyond the illusion of individual ego. (Others might make it mean other things. Although I think we are all pointing to the same universal life force Einstein talked about, and I'm not afraid of the word God. Not anymore. I gave up that fight soon after I gave up always trying to sound intellectual. These days it has become a shortcut to being perceived as an intellectual to call yourself an atheist. So much easier and quicker than reading and study and reflection.)

When the vicious circle of addiction I was in broke open and upward into a spiritual spiral, I was trucking, as the Grateful Dead would say. I understood Vladimir Nabokov when he exclaimed that "a spiral is a spiritualized circle." I saw the possibility of liberating this vicious circle that was my ego life of short-term desires, so I could spiral up. Into spirit. (Do I sound like I'm from California yet? I'm not. But I can see the risk.)

I later discovered in my coaching and teaching work that even non-addicts had found their own vicious circles. They were making the mistake of taking the game of life too seriously, taking the behavior of others personally and circling around and around between worry and resentment, fear and anger. They had even created their personal sense of identity out of their grievances. They'd meet each other at social events and ask, "What are *you* a victim of?"

Babies don't do that.

There is an oceanic sense one has as a baby. Like feeling that you are a small, jubilant wave in a huge, thriving ocean of life. No name, no separation, no individual ego-hallucination yet.

No separation means I cry and you come feed me. The two things are as connected as my hand and my fingers. I sing out, you come change me. I don't know yet that there's any real difference between you and me, or between me and anything else. I don't yet feel the disconnect. It's awfully warm and secure on this fine, interconnected planet!

Like a wave upon a breathtaking ocean. The wave doesn't know it's a separate wave, or a good wave for surfing, or a bad wave. It feels like it's just an expression of the ocean. Which it is! A gesture! A gesticulation! One hand waving free! Silhouetted by the sea! It is only we, we labelers, who call it a wave. And by labeling it, we make it separate.

So as a baby I was the ocean itself until I grew older and my parents kept insisting that I was a unique wave. And only that. An exception!! A unique, individual wave like no other. A wave with a name. The name was so important. It made my separation final and "the truth" about my life. My identity. In stone.

My first drink took me back home to the ocean.

I was like Quint, the character played by Robert Shaw in the movie *Jaws*. He is out on the ocean in his little boat. Drunkenly he sings, "Show me the way to go home. I'm tired and I want to go to bed. I had a little drink about an hour ago, and it went right to my head."

~ *Death Wish*

152

I have got to HAVE IT!

When I was a little boy, after I was taught that I was separate, I was then taught that some things were mine, and some things were not. I began to learn the difference between being and *having*.

Just the mere fact of *being* used to be blissful and more than enough but now *having* became the thing. All the rage. (In both senses of the word rage.) I saw a toy in a store window and I had to *have* it. I learned the importance of the word *mine*.

If you want to torment a child (and why would you want to do that, really? Maybe just briefly to understand this idea.) . . . point to something the child is holding, a stuffed animal maybe, and say the word "Mine!" Watch the alarm ripple through the child's body as he pulls the soft stuffed puppy away and shouts back at you, "*Mine!*"

And so the fear begins. Security is threatened. Nothing is really safe anymore. Who can you trust? Your parents promise we will all be together forever and then they divorce and one of them moves away! Even Santa Claus turns out to be a deception. (The grown-ups all told you he was real. From now on, you will trust no one.) You've been made a fool. You need to learn to protect yourself from all this deceit delivered by *other people*. (They are not on your side, you now see.)

Given this rude turn of events, can you blame a boy for wanting to get drunk? To find a way back home?

But maybe that boy will learn that this insecurity is all happening in his head. It's all a recurring bad dream happening each day in his imaginary world. And recovery is his chance to finally wake up.

~ Death Wish

153

But how do I live?

Okay, now that I was getting clean and sober, how was I going to *live*?

Well . . . how about I just complicate my life in as big a way as I can and then deal with the complication? That way, I don't have to chart a course for myself, I'll just solve all the problems I've created for myself and fight the dragons I've produced through my own thinking and doing. Like creating your own scary video game to play.

That was my best thinking. When I first got sober.

Besides, I never knew how to live in this world anyway. I never had a "calling" or soul's purpose. Others seemed like they did, but I did not.

I got married and started having children right after I got clean and sober . . . why not stir the pot and up the ante? Call myself forward! See what I'll do with *this*!

And it was a grand distraction. Huge adventure. There was something about those children, as they kept coming, that reminded me of something I couldn't put my finger on. Something about the comic joy of everyday life that I used to know as a child. Something about love.

The children got it and lived it.

I watched it and loved them for it.

I assumed back then that their spirit was a result of their being young. Happiness, joy and adventure came with being young, right? Once you passed through that phase you had to get serious.

It turned out I was wrong about that. And that revelation was what G.K. Chesterton used to refer to as "absurd good news."

154

Children give us clues

I often wondered why I so enjoyed being with my children while raising them. Maybe they had the key to something. What was it? (I would later know. At the time I didn't know, I just knew I had done something right by having them and watching them grow.)

They made up games and songs. Every day. Unprompted. They made up little plays and costumes and put them on for me when I came home from work. They were showing me something I didn't quite understand at the time. They were modeling the way I *could* have lived but wasn't.

But how could that be true, how could I have lived like a happy child, when most of grown-up life was so serious? Like going to work and making money. Like grinding away and working harder and harder.

I mean, really, there was no comic joy in my workdays as I struggled to be a journalist, an advertising agency guy . . . career after career, whatever I could find, and always the daily grind was an ongoing struggle to put food up there on the table and pay the rent. Or so I always thought.

I had not discovered the link between joy and productivity. I had not learned that serenity led to simplicity, power and productivity. Those lessons took me nearly a lifetime to learn. (They didn't have to. You can learn them rather quickly if you're lucky enough to find the right path and mentors.)

I struggled with the grind of life and work. Then, as if life wasn't hard and serious enough, the children's mother suffered a brain disorder and was institutionalized for a long time. Now it was just the four children and me. Stumbling unconsciously toward a daily love of life by watching Bill Murray movies and singing together in the car.

Oh the long car rides. Going to a faraway city to visit their mother. We'd stop along the highway and put pennies on the railroad tracks. It gave us flattened copper memories of the good times.

We drove through pecan groves that bloomed each year right around little Margie's birthday so we started calling the trees "Margie's birthday trees!" Then her younger brother Bobby got jealous and one day pointed to a big rock as we drove through Red Rock, Arizona, singing along with the "Garden Song" by Paul Stookey, and Bobby said, "That's my rock! I want that to be my birthday rock!"

Margie began laughing at him. "A birthday rock??? That's SO stupid, Bobby. A rock never changes. My trees change on my birthday, that's why they are my birthday trees."

Bobby's response was to start beating on her in the back seat of the car as she screamed for my help. I didn't want to take my eyes off the road so I reached into my box of cassettes and began throwing cassettes at both of them over my shoulder while shouting at them to stop. I went out of control. Now the whole car was yelling and ducking for cover. You can see that I was an excellent parent. If you want my coaching, I'll help you find things to throw. I know cassettes aren't around anymore. (Who knows how to parent, really?)

I just didn't always realize these kids were teaching me how to live. But I can see it now.   *~ Death Wish*

155

The energy we call heaven

S o what could I have learned from my children that I did not
learn back then?

This is it: Life is fun.

All of it.

And there is a humor behind things. But we don't see it
because we take our thinking so seriously.

This is what the suicide does not see, as he ushers himself out
of life, lost in the drama of his thoughts (mistaken for reality). He
is only thinking about the thoughts he's been thinking. But not
knowing that he's only thinking . . . to him, the dark thoughts are
a direct line to "reality" itself! And, as his thoughts tell him: there
is a lot that is hopeless and "wrong" about reality.

But that's his illusion.

The laughter that created the universe is not *against* anyone.
That creation of the universe is sometimes called "the big bang"
which is endearingly primitive language developed by overly
serious people in the world of physics. Big bang is a very childish
and clumsy way of describing a laugh. I'm sitting here watching
a child try to put a baseball cap on a dog and what happens inside
of me? A big bang! A big bang inside of me! Ha! And then, Ha
Ha Ha!

I used to view the comic adventures of our home life as a

welcome diversion from serious reality. I didn't see at the time that it was better than that . . . it was a deeper experience of our true nature as living beings! It was not an isolated frivolous experience that occurs during time out from reality.

There is a poem by A.S. Wilson, set to music by Phil Keaggy, whose words have had a lasting effect on me:

> Is it a beatific smile,
> . . . a holy light upon your brow
> Oh no, I felt His presence when
> you laughed just now.

~ Death Wish

156

Flying too close to the ground

I give a lot of credit to Willie Nelson for writing the song I so love to listen to: "Angel Flying Too Close to the Ground."

> I knew someday that you would fly away
> for love's the greatest healer to be found
> so leave me if you need to, I will still remember
> angel flying too close to the ground

It reminds me that G.K. Chesterton said that the angels can fly *only because* they take themselves lightly.

I think we were designed to be like these angels. It's already in us to be that way. But then we get heavy-minded. Soon we are flying too close to the ground. Because of the heaviness. Because we weigh ourselves down with such deep, serious thoughts and beliefs. Soon life looks unfair. We are victims.

Poor me! Poor me, poor me, pour me another.

One time my friend Dicken Bettinger was giving me a mentoring session via Skype as I told him about a very serious problem in my professional life that I had been trying to solve for months. He listened patiently as I explained the seriousness and complexity of it and when I was finished venting I waited for his analysis and possible solution.

He said, "You look so serious."

I was a little unnerved by that. Was he not listening to my

words? Was he just looking at my face? Of course I looked serious. This was a real problem I was describing.

Both of us sat in silence for a minute and I said, "And . . . ???"

"Well," he said. "You don't have much of a chance solving this thing from the mood you're in right now. This may be an important decision in the context of your business, but you yourself don't have to feel so serious about it."

It took me a minute to get what he was saying. Soon I snapped out of my dark mood and started shaking my head and chuckling and he saw me do this and he started laughing. In less than three minutes the "solution" to this heavy problem just appeared to me. It just occurred to me. I was amazed. I have never forgotten that exchange, and Dicken's suggestion that a lighthearted mood is better suited to the "problems" of life than a weighed-down, heavy-hearted mood.

But this had always sounded too good to be true.

That we do better when we are lighthearted and happy. That we perform at a higher level of effectiveness. When we're smiling. What if we didn't have to take *anything* seriously? Would we still be grown-ups?

It feels funny that I had taught the creative value of humor to seminar students and coaching clients. For years. You are more creative when you're happy than when you are feeling like a victim. A lot of research backs that up. But teaching it is so different than the actual experience of it.

Getting it intellectually was not wrong or bad. It was a good place to start. Because at least I was awake to the possibility that what I was teaching could actually show up somewhere in real life! At least I was not *opposed* to the idea that happiness was more powerful and productive than seriousness. But wow when I experienced it deeply? Like in that moment with Dicken? I never lost the awareness after that. Heavy thoughts don't solve problems.

In the past, my intellect may have told me to put on a happy face. Or a beatific smile. But I always thought I had to try to take a long hero's journey toward joy and spirit. A treacherous pilgrimage! But why go on a long journey to experience something that I already felt when I laughed just now? Why travel if I'm already there?

~ Death Wish

157

The most widespread addiction of all

Although my personal path was through alcohol, I want to acknowledge all the addictions, both life-threatening and not, to sugar, shopping, gambling, gaming, porn, the internet, and the most popular addiction of all: **love and approval from others.**

What I do to win your approval! It can be so heavy and embarrassing. Then I have to do it all over again because approval doesn't last. It can't really be trusted to hold.

And there's a clue in that.

Someone else's love and approval is as fleeting and ethereal as a champagne high or a hit of cocaine. Wow! It feels good. Then it's gone. Then it's doubted. Then it's turned to fear. I better start winning you over all over again.

Approval-seeking sounds almost benign compared to drugs or booze but it's pretty clear (to those of you who have seen it for what it is) that this addiction may be the most common of all and that it ruins the enjoyment of life.

I credit my own business and life coach Steve Hardison with teaching me that loving service is its own reward and doesn't need praise or approval. It feels so good just to serve someone without needing or wanting anything back.

Approval-seeking and love-seeking are actually a lot like

drugs or alcohol. The same illusion is underneath it all. That something, some substance outside of me must be sought, found and ingested for me to feel good. Approval is a finite substance. It's a metaphorical powder up the nose into the brain stem. (The heart is ignored.)

What's the solution to this lifelong seeking? This lifelong craving, to be impressive . . . to be liked and admired?

The solution is to *already feel good*. To come out of the gate that way. Without negative thinking clouding the day, it feels good to be alive. It feels alive to be alive.

My three-year-old grandson will burst into my house, already loving the feeling of being alive. His eyes are sparkling like there is possible magic afoot. He does not think he needs to win friends or influence people right now. He already feels his life. He is happy to share that feeling.

~ Death Wish

158

Alone, as a concept

I think I'm alone.

Yet:

If the sun goes out I die.

If all the plants disappear, I die.

They keep me alive.

So. Am I separate from them?

When I help new people in the meeting get sober

am I separate from them?

I am alone.

How could that be true?

~ Death Wish

159

All the king's horses, all the king's men

For years my books and blogs have talked about my own recovery from drugs and alcohol, and the long and horrible time I spent drinking and drugging. So people often ask for my help and advice.

Family members of addicts and alcoholics are in such distress, and who can blame them? Addiction creates so much collateral damage. Addicts themselves also contact me and tell me they can't seem to stop.

I don't want to be an expert on this. I just want to talk about my own experience. I don't even want this book to try to be an expression of expertise. It's just an outpouring of my own experience and (especially) a lot of possibility.

Because there is hope. That's my message: hope for a full and total recovery. For anyone. Everyone. No exceptions (despite what you might be thinking).

There's even more than that. But that might be too good to talk about. Too unreal sounding. Most people are really suffering and just want some immediate relief. I don't want to confuse them by rambling on about the unexpected benefits of this path. It might just confuse the issue.

Let's just get your person back to square one! How about a return to normal! Stop the bleeding. There might be too much brokenness here to talk about a glorious life ahead.

Brokenness: a major, inevitable consequence of alcohol and drug addiction. Broken homes. Broken hearts. Broken windows. Broken bones. Broken vows. Broken dishes. Broken cars. Broken promises. Broken lives.

Please put him back together again. Bring him home. He was never like this before. Will you reach out to him?

But how can mere sobriety repair all that was broken? How can it erase the wreckage of the past?

Maybe it can't. But maybe it can do something better than that. It can create a fresh start. It can give a person hope. A new beginning. A bright future. Unlimited possibilities for creating a good life!

Every year during spring training baseball teams and their fans feel the optimism that seems to flow eternally. "We could go all the way! We could be a force this year. We have so much promise! Look at these young arms up from the minors fighting for a place on the roster! Listen to the crack of the bats as the youngsters flash their strength!"

That's what new sobriety is like. And then it gets better. If you stay with it.

~ Death Wish

160

A blank slate called the human

If individual human personality was real, you wouldn't have so many people trying to "find out who they are." That's what my sponsor LC used to say to me.

I said, "I guess, now that I am learning to live a clean and sober life, I am kind of a blank slate." We were talking one night when we went to coffee after a meeting.

"Welcome to the human race," he said. "We are all blank slates. We start each day empty and new. We're just not always clear-minded enough to see it."

I said, "But I mean . . . I think I need to find out who I am."

He would joke with me. He would say, "Look in your wallet. Won't it tell you who you are? Look at your driver's license. It will tell you who you are and even where you live."

"That's not helpful. That's just a name."

Which was his sarcastic point exactly. There was much more to this life than a made-up personality. And when I was in these meetings, liking and identifying so totally with other people who I used to think were not like me at all, this whole new experience . . . this unfolding world . . . felt bigger than before. I no longer felt like a narrow, trapped, gripped, clasped, clotted, balled-up, tightly-wound, compact little individual.

That former individual used to feel separate and isolated from the dancing world of being. I was a piece of driftwood. You could have called me Steve Driftwood. A singer's name. One who carried a sad sack of blues. No rhythm. Just blues.

But this new feeling, this was different. This was connection. This was dancing by the light of the moon. This was the light itself . . . like a long lost lamp that finally got plugged in.

~ Death Wish

161

You are not my God

One of my daughters gave me a gift over the holiday season of two CDs (I'm old school tech) of death wish songs . . . songs about addiction, suicide and recovery. This would, under most decorated trees in December, be a strange, ominous gift.

But for me it was fascinating and uplifting.

On the CD Keith Urban sings "You're Not My God," and there is a fierce joyful anger in it that rocks me when I listen. He has found free will. He is singing to his drug of choice:

> But you're not my god
> And you're not my friend
> You're not the one that I will walk with in the end
> You're not the truth
> You're a temporary shot
> You ruin people's lives and you don't give a second thought

I remember when drugs and alcohol were felt to be my only real friends. They were my gods. My fear of losing them overrode everything, even though they were ruining and wasting my life. I remember that fear.

Keith Urban checked himself into a residential rehab center four months after marrying Nicole Kidman. This was after she and some friends staged an intervention on him. His drinking and drug use were ruining his life and career.

370 | The Very Best of Steve Chandler

Fortunately, for those of us who like his music, the drug is not his God anymore. It is not even his friend.

162

A brain like Hitchcock's *Birds*

Sitting in the meetings (some of them bright and early in a sunlit Tucson morning) I notice something weird and hopeful. I notice that a bad feeling (of shame or anger or fear) doesn't need to be actively gotten rid of by me.

This was a huge breakthrough, a major epiphany. Because I'd always actively *dealt with* any bad feeling. I'd often medicate against it. Nervous? Take a drink or a drug! Scared? Bottoms up! Depressed? Go to a bar! Maybe even a biker bar where it's macho to drink early in the day! Change the feeling. Always change the feeling. You have to deal with it *now*!

But I noticed in meetings and at home between meetings when I was not drinking that a bad feeling would often just mysteriously disappear.

(Hey, where did it go? I haven't dealt with it yet!)

I forgot to take it seriously. So maybe the feeling itself pouted for a while and then stormed out of the building. Took its ball and went home. Who knows? Where is it now?

Later, after quite a bit of sobriety, I understood what was going on.

These "bad feelings" were only and always caused by thoughts. Fleeting thoughts at that. Never were they caused by other people or circumstances.

So if I stopped clinging to a fleeting negative thought, it would just fly right away along with the feeling it had produced. Its very nature is to fly through. Like a blackbird. Take these broken wings and learn to fly.

Bye bye blackbird, but oh look now there's a bluebird: here it is and there it goes! Another blue bird. Another blue mood. Another blue song. Put on Miles Davis. Feel the music behind all the fleeting birds.

But at first I misunderstood this phenomenon. I thought the meeting itself changed my emotion from depressed to happy. Or I'd think a visit with my sponsor had me feeling more relaxed. Or a talk with a friend. I still thought it was external. **Circumstances** were causing my feelings, so when I felt bad I'd try to change my circumstance.

This was a step up from drinking as a way to control feelings. Because now I would go to a meeting, or stop talking to a person who "made me" crazy. Now I could call my sponsor or go to a meeting or get a new job.

Rearranging circumstance until I felt a little better!

I couldn't see yet that all circumstances were like the deck chairs on the Titanic. Rearrange them all you want . . . *we're still going down.*

I was not seeing the role of thought at all.

I was not really understanding some of my favorite words from Shakespeare. Up until now they had just been lovely words: "There is nothing good nor bad but thinking makes it so."

~ Death Wish

163

Back to the fundamentals

One of the heaviest wet blankets in my personal belief system is the recurring thought that I constantly need to win friends and influence people. Don't people tell you that? To be really successful and happy I need love and approval. From people outside of me.

When I was still drinking I started to become convinced that I couldn't talk to people without drinking or taking a pill, or that I could not be interesting or entertaining without it. And it was so obviously important to be able to win people over and get their approval. I was just totally lost in a belief system around drugs and alcohol and socializing that was completely wrong.

I mean it was just not correct.

But it sure felt true at the time. And even when the drinking habit got me into all kinds of trouble, legally, physically, with my family, with *everything*, it still felt like, well, it's the only thing I know. It's all I know how to do. I don't know what else to do.

Thank God so many people were willing to help me get out from under my beliefs.

So good to see now, through prayer and meditation and simple relaxation, that a thought is just a thought.

(Just as a kiss is just a kiss, a sigh is just a sigh and the fundamental things apply, as time goes by. My recovery came from getting back to the fundamentals of life . . . those fundamentals that came naturally to us as children.)

~ Death Wish

164

Pour me a way to fly home

Roxann Burroughs taught me something. She is a masterful practitioner and teacher of Byron Katie's work. She taught me that the idea that something is true *just because I'm thinking it* is the ultimate in self-deceiving narcissism.

Negative thoughts are impersonal and unoriginal and can't claim ownership of any kind. They don't "belong" to the thinker. And they don't come from a place anyone can claim is protected by copyright. They're homeless and ownerless snow flurries in the wind, mischievously looking for someone to give them meaning. When that doesn't happen they evaporate.

But . . . but . . . it must be *true* because I just thought it!

Look at "my" thoughts here: 1) He's out to get me! 2) She doesn't appreciate me. 3) I don't know how to succeed. 4) I need a drink.

When I realized that these thoughts were just coming out of nowhere and needed not to be given such actionable attention, I found something new. I found a path back to the freedom I was born with. Many spiritual teachers call this coming home.

That's what I was unconsciously looking for when I was drinking. In fact one of the songs I wrote (with my songwriting partner, Fred Knipe) had the line in it, "Pour me a glass of Canadian whiskey, pour me a way to fly home."

~ Death Wish

165

Dying to believe unbelievable beliefs

My recovery group's literature said we "came to believe" that a power greater than ourselves would restore us to sanity. And that we could recover forever from being drunks and drug addicts.

"Came to believe" is in quotes because I had decided to give the program the benefit of the doubt. Even though I thought they were using those gentle, passive words to try to do an end around and lure me into a religion.

I had been taken to Methodist, Presbyterian and Congregational churches at various stages of my youth, and it wasn't long before I'd become so disbelieving of all their contradictory stories about supernatural beings who looked down on us like Heidi's grandfather would were he God . . . well . . . it was confusing for me. (And therefore the voice of the addict in me was an eloquent debater on religious issues.)

I remember once writing a song with Fred Knipe called "Dying to Believe." We had read in a songwriter's magazine that you could never write a hit country song with the words "death" or "dying" in the song title. We always liked breaking the rules. We wrote a cheating song:

> I'm dying . . .
> dying . . . to believe your lies

> Because it was loving you
> that made me feel alive.

I was dying to believe in a higher power. Fortunately, after awhile, I was able to drop all of that effort. I just kept joining the group of drunks and listening to their wisdom. Anyone who used to be hopelessly drunk or addicted all the time who was now sober all the time was worth listening to. And for me, and for now, they were more worth listening to than the religious scholars of old. Because this was real-world street wisdom I could use. This was hard-won experience. This was more fun than metaphysics or theology.

And then surprise, surprise. After awhile I didn't have to try to believe it. Because I could feel it. I could see it. I could hear it. I was experiencing it. It became simple reality. There was more to me than my thought-created ego. My made-up personality. (Personality is from the Greek, *persona*, which means mask.)

Whatever anyone called this higher power it connected us all and gave us life and energy.

And finally I knew, as an experience, what people were calling God, or infinite intelligence, or the Tao, or Buddha-nature, or divine mind, or Jehovah, or the universe . . . and the list goes on.

My sponsor said this would happen.

That if I kept coming back to meetings and letting myself surrender to the reality that the universe held me in its arms, then the whole believing thing would not be an issue. And he was right.

~ Death Wish

166

The best ideas come out of the blue

Sometimes, as years went on, I caught myself referring to this higher power (this life force) as "the blue." Things came out of the blue.

All my best ideas came out of the blue. The best song lyrics. The most inspired thoughts. All the epiphanies and realizations. Out of the blue!

Even though, at first, they only came "once in a blue moon." Because I was so stressed by life. And all the circumstances I had to deal with. Or, at least, at that time, I *thought* I was dealing directly with life and circumstances. I assumed I was feeling their impact directly.

But then I was set free even from that. My first freedom was freedom from addiction. My second freedom was equally liberating and exciting. It was freedom from thinking that circumstances and other people had direct causative power over the way I was feeling.

Now I could see that all creative power comes out of the blue into my heart and soul. Worries about outer life mean nothing. They are projections of my imagination.

Writers, artists and poets in the old times used to call this sense of creative power "the muse." The muse was thought to be either an actual person or a goddess or an angel who inspired the poet's most creative work. One thing that made her so elusive and mysterious was that she only made rare appearances. She could disappear for a long time.

Or so it seemed. Or so they thought. The truth I found is that the muse is always there. The muse is inspiring everything good. Usually I'm just too busy-minded to hear her message.

~ Death Wish

167

Serenity is the way back home

People in 12-step meetings love the serenity prayer, and I say it with them, and I even like most parts of it, but . . .

Well, you know it. It goes like this: "God grant me the serenity to **accept the things I cannot change**, the courage to change the things I can, and the wisdom to know the difference."

And then sometimes we have whole meetings on the subject of acceptance. I need to accept the things I cannot change. Those damn things. Those damn people, places and things. Because they can be pretty awful. Or at best, stressful.

And for years, in my first experience of recovery, that strategy was fine and worthy. And even, in my mind, the best I could hope for.

But today? Today I have no more use for the word "acceptance."

I don't like the defeated, fatalistic feeling in it. How it feels like a sad reconciliation with unpleasant reality. What a buzzkill it is. In a way it's even condescending. Hey, Reality, are you listening to me? I've got good news for you! I've decided I will finally and reluctantly *accept* you. I hope you appreciate that.

Today, it would not be a good enough life for me if I were to settle for merely *accepting* things. Tolerating them. Learning to cope with them. (My psychologist used to say to me that our work together was for the purpose of helping me *cope with* life.)

If someone gives me a trip to the south of France, I want to *explore* France! I want to *enjoy* France! I don't want to learn to accept France.

Acceptance has its hands on its hips, and a slight pout on its face. There are better ways to do life than that.

God, grant me the serenity to explore (and enjoy) the things I cannot change. The courage to change the things I can, and the wisdom to love the difference.

~ Death Wish

168

Out from under the volcano

In my last year of heavy alcoholic drinking and sporadic drug use I was exchanging letters with the author Art Hill.

Art was also the father of my childhood friend Terry Hill. So I knew him well. I may have spent more time growing up at his house than I did at my own.

Art was a former alcoholic who had found sobriety and a whole new life. He was now writing books and newspaper columns and using his creativity and talent in positive, rewarding ways. I admired him for that. I did a thesis paper in college on his unpublished poetry, which was marvelous.

One day I wrote him a letter congratulating myself for going two weeks without drinking. I was having a little contest with a drinking buddy to see who could go the longest without booze. (I lost.) But what was gratifying to me was finding out that I wasn't an alcoholic or even a problem drinker because those kinds of people just can't go two weeks without drinking.

Art disagreed.

Art disagreed quite strongly. He said that the letter confirmed for him what he had long suspected . . . that I was a classic alcoholic. Even though I had always tried to spin my drinking and drug use as being the result of having a wilder, freer spirit than most people. I said I was merely a rebel. I didn't play by the rules.

I was like Cool Hand Luke. Just like him.

Art didn't buy it.

In fact, Art said I was the opposite. Not a rebel, not a free spirit at all. But just a commonplace drunk. Like any other banal, boring, disgusting drunk. I was no different than the guy who sleeps in the city park wrapped around a blanket and a bottle.

Whoa! Hold on! Say what? Back off. That's a *judgment*!

I was really floored that a formerly kind and graceful person could lose his bearings and lash out at me like that. I walked around my house angrily holding the letter in one hand and a bottle of beer in another. Well, actually it was not my house, it was my mother's. I was living in my mother's house at the age of thirty-four. (That should have told us something.)

In the letter, he told me to get to a meeting. He said he himself did that, and it saved his life.

Well! This was a lot to think about. Could he be right? What if he was right?

For some strange reason my anger turned immediately to a fleeting feeling of joy. What if this explains everything, and there's hope for me? What if I could be free and creative like he was?

The following week I talked to a person at the newspaper where I was working. He was a known sober alcoholic who went to meetings. I asked if he might take me to a meeting with him. I told him I didn't know if I was an alcoholic or an addict, but I was willing to find out.

Best request I ever made.

Art Hill's letter had been the exact wake-up call I needed at just the right time. Without his bold honesty, I wouldn't be sitting here today. I wouldn't be sitting anywhere. I know that.

In his book *Booze, Books and The Big Deuce* Art writes

beautifully and lucidly about his alcoholism and that of the author Malcom Lowry. Art dissects Lowry's novel, *Under the Volcano*. He points out that the literary critics who reviewed that novel all made a vital mistake. They mistranslated a key Spanish phrase that the book's hero is mesmerized by.

The phrase is, "No se puede vivir sin amar," which the critics said meant "You cannot live without love." It actually means, "You cannot live without loving."

Quite a difference. That difference is everything.

Love is that thing you look for, thinking it's always outside you, thinking you need someone else to give it to you. It's what you look for in all the wrong places.

But *loving* is what you already have inside you. Ready to give others at a moment's notice. It's what you begin to feel emerging when you attend meetings like the ones Art Hill recommended to me.

It's what has you reach out to someone still suffering from all this.

It's what holds the stars in the sky at night. It's what puts the music in the birds during the day.

It's you.

~ *Death Wish*

Creativity

169

Something better than heaven?

There is something better than heaven. It is the eternal,
meaningless, infinitely creative mind. It can't stop for time or
space or even joy. It is so brilliant that it will shake what's left of
you to the depths of all-consuming wonder.

~ Byron Katie

You read that quote and wonder. What is she saying? Does she mean *my* mind? Or does she mean some kind of universal mind? The bottomless well of creativity that Napoleon Hill called "infinite intelligence"? Or is it all the same?

Wouldn't that be exciting, though, to discover something better than heaven and to have that discovery shake me to the depths?

So I wondered how she could say that with such relaxed certainty. Would she be trying to sell us some new-age product or course? That would be a cynic's view, which is to say it would be *my* view when first I encountered this claim of hers that there was something better than heaven.

A cynic will hear something like this and start to get excited, but then will stop himself. His conditioning has kicked in. What about these bills and these kids to care for? What about all the books and essays I have read by the highly intelligent philosophers of existential despair? Didn't they convince me that the "human condition" was essentially negative?

Yes they did, and it matched up nicely with how I perceived my own condition.

But then things changed, and I began to see that my "condition" was actually only my conditioning.

But what's the difference? Seems like there's no difference.

Here it is: When people like me talk about their "conditioning" they speak of it as if it stopped somewhere. Usually in childhood. That's where conditioning solidifies into the human condition. Or so we're told.

There was conditioning that was caused by what I was taught and how I was raised, and then the conditioning came to completion. After that, for the rest of my life I would be stuck with how I was conditioned. I would refer to it as "my conditioning." It would never change. How could it? It was over and complete.

Inside that story, I had been conditioned just as a piece of meat gets marinated. I'd be sitting in a Polynesian restaurant eating marinated chunks of steak telling you about my childhood and my conditioning as if they were one and the same.

What could be wrong with that story? What is it I didn't know, that if I knew it, might change the game of life forever?

This is what it was:

Conditioning never stops.

Conditioning is ongoing. I'm not marinated meat. I am literally always like a culinary work in progress. Each day is full of possibility. The menu is always new.

Conditioning is continuous. What I did and saw and learned this morning is as vital a part of my ongoing conditioning as the conditioning that occurred in childhood. In fact, today's conditioning is even more vital than my childhood conditioning, especially if it takes me in new directions. Especially when it counters and replaces earlier conditioning.

When I looked back on my life there was more than enough evidence of this. I had been conditioned to believe that drinking alcohol made life better. Then I was conditioned to believe, after I descended into alcoholism, that the only way I could get relief from the pain of living was through drinking and drugs.

But then I joined a program and got a sponsor and created the mental space and spiritual openness for an entirely new conditioning to drop in. This resulted in a total transformation of my relationship to life and people.

And this wasn't childhood. This was my access to ongoing conditioning. Something I didn't know I had. I didn't realize that when it came to conditioning I was now able to assume my rightful role as *creator*. I was now in charge of it. And that wasn't the case in childhood.

So this morning I read the words of Byron Katie and reflect on them. I relax enough to see the truth in them. And I think of my first response to her teaching years ago and understand why it was so pessimistic and dismissive.

People don't change was my core belief. I was stuck with my weaknesses and faults. My job was to try to hide them if I was to have a life. I had to hide—or distract you from—my traits and characteristics. My identity worked against me. And because this was true for me, my first response to Katie was that her words were unreal. (It was a conditioned response.)

But then through a spiritual program of recovery I saw that I could respond differently. I decided to explore. Byron Katie had devised a little meditative system for the deletion of negative conditioning. She explains it in her first book, *Loving What Is*. She called her system "The Work."

Before I bought her book, I noticed on the cover that Eckhart Tolle had said, "Byron Katie's Work acts like a razor-sharp sword that cuts through . . . illusion and enables you to know for yourself the timeless essence of your being. Joy, peace, and love emanate from it as your natural state. In *Loving What Is*, you have the key. Now use it."

That quote hit me hard because I'd already become a fan of Tolle's book *The Power of Now*. Why would he make that kind of statement? It seemed to go beyond praise for a book. It was as if he was describing a magical garden tool. He wasn't saying how much he enjoyed the book. He was telling me to *use it*.

What would I be digging up?

Well, it turned out to be just about everything. All my old conditioning. All the defeated and pessimistic neural pathways. All the old thoughts mistakenly assumed to be the truth about life.

And why did it work for me? Because I did it. I followed the simple directions. The Work worked just the same way it worked for Katie, as she writes and talks about. She was just sharing what worked for her. She was not putting out some new thing to try to believe in. It will work for you too. And it's not the only path.

Byron Katie had a flash of revelation one morning and saw what so many "enlightened" people have seen (all the great religious figures in the past, on up to Ramana Maharshi, Sydney Banks, Douglas Harding, Werner Erhard, Mooji, Eckhart Tolle, Rupert Spira, Francis Lucille and on and on). She saw life as pure love and light.

But then her thoughts started coming back in. All the old conditioning. So she *created* her system she called The Work. It worked for her. It revealed thought to be what it was, and so thought was no longer the great truth about life. And she promised everyone she worked with and taught her system to that if they were courageous enough to stay with it to the very end, they too would see clearly that "There is something better than heaven. It is the eternal, meaningless, infinitely creative mind."

Hers is but one path back to the realization and occupation of the infinitely creative mind. There are many others, both spiritual and psychological.

My clients want to believe in what Katie sees and what Syd Banks and Ramana Maharshi and other spiritual philosophers saw. But their conditioning keeps chattering the old pessimistic mantras. And I can relate to them completely. I wanted to believe, too. I would listen to Alan Watts say, "No valid plans for the *future* can be made by those who have no *capacity* for living now," and I would think, "Okay there go my plans for the future. And I thought the future was going to save me."

I was wanting to believe I could experience joy and creativity in living now, but I wasn't seeing that it was not a matter of belief. It was a matter of experience.

When I was a little boy I wanted to believe the deep end of the pool water would hold me up, but my conditioned thought chatter said, "Don't go there, you're heavier than water."

My mistake was staying stuck inside wanting to believe deep water would hold me up. I didn't realize that belief had nothing to do with it. In fact, belief and disbelief were the things that were holding me back. Stalling things out. Familiarity with the water was all I needed in order to reveal the truth of it.

Both believers and non-believers (in my head) can step aside as I jump in. They are only in the way.

~ CREATOR

170

And a hero comes along

Throughout my boyhood I loved comic book superheroes, as so many children do. Mighty Mouse, Superman, and Captain Marvel filled my dreams. I had the comic books and watched the TV episodes and always felt a surge of excitement picturing myself with their powers.

When I began growing into adulthood the superheroes lost their pull. Adulthood was getting harder and harder for me to navigate, and those old heroes were just fantasies, right? I needed to get into reality. (One thesaurus I looked at recently had a lot of synonyms for the word *creativity* but only one antonym. The antonym they listed was "*reality*.")

I needed to deal with my lack of power that seemed to accompany growing up.

That was the thinking that was circulating inside me back then. And when my not-so-super life of bad choices got too heavy to hold up, I finally hit bottom. I found myself in recovery meetings for alcoholics where we admitted we were powerless over alcohol and that our lives had become unmanageable. I had become Powerless Man. A long way from Superman.

Or so I thought at the time.

But then, little by little, with recovery adding more light each day, I began to wake up. I was free of addiction for the first time and the world began to open up in front of me. More and more often I found myself in good spirits. I was attending meetings about spiritual recovery in which we explored and practiced "conscious contact with a higher power." It was all new to me. But it was real, practical experience. Not just something one hopes for.

It was truly recovery . . . not just from alcohol but from what my meetings called "self-will run riot." It felt like the ego was fading out while the light of recovery unfolded like a blanket of stars.

It wasn't until much later that I saw that my (and our) higher power (the God of our understanding) was creativity itself.

Before it made its real appearance, I had always liked the *word* "creativity," and I had bought into the prevailing belief that it was a rare and precious thing. I also noticed that my ego really liked it when people said I, as an individual personality, was creative. Really? You mean that? I took it very personally. I remember being extremely proud of myself when I was named "Creative Director" of an advertising agency. How special it felt to be seen as creative! And not just creative, but so creative that they want you to be the *Director* of creativity! I was captivated by how *unique* I was becoming and—really—how exceptional I must be! I guess I'll just have to learn to accept that I'm *one of the rare few* who have access to this form of magic we all call creativity!

But my thoughts weren't really matching up with reality. Deep down I knew it. My belief (and the belief of those around me) that creativity was an uncommon personal gift began to lose its credibility. I could soon see that it was a story, like so many of my other stories, designed to keep the ego feeling unique. But it had nothing to do with real creativity. Or real and true reality—no matter what my thesaurus and my culture said.

The more spiritual work and study I did the more I saw that

creativity and the life force were one and the same. And it was a force running through everybody, not just the chosen creative few. In our recovery meetings we all had a higher power, higher than the ego, and higher than human thought.

Here we were, a group of alcoholics and drug addicts sitting together trying to learn to live a normal, clean and sober life . . . and one sign on the meeting hall wall said, "Your best thinking got you here."

We weren't sages; we were drunks. But we were experiencing the same kind of higher power that the sages wrote about. A power without upper limits. You could call it a superpower—just what I longed for as a kid. Maybe my yearning and longing and reaching out for Superman as a boy was not a total delusion.

If I wrote an adventure comic book today I would see if I could introduce a new superhero—which would be no small thing given how many superheroes there already are: Wonder Woman, Iron Man, Supergirl, Daredevil, Batman, and you know we could go on.

My comic book's superhero would be you.

I know that's not a really exciting or marketable name for a superhero. "You!"

No, so let's call you something else. How about this. Do you know how movies always acknowledge the "creator" of various superhero characters? For example, Wonder Woman's creator was William Marston. Imagine how powerful he must have been. It's one thing to be Wonder Woman, but it's quite another to be able to *create* Wonder Woman.

If these characters like Wonder Woman and Superman and Mighty Mouse are so powerful, just imagine how much more powerful their creators must be. That's the ultimate superpower right there: the ability to create.

I'd call that hero "Creator."

And the adventures I'd present would show you that it's all based on a true story: the story of you.

~ *CREATOR*

171

Are you really not creative?

People who tell me they are "not creative" cause me to wonder. Could that ever be true?

Perhaps they have not found a consistent expression of creativity. But there is no shortage on the inside. Not in my experience.

It would be like going to a doctor because of shortness of breath and having the doctor say, "I'm sorry to have to tell you that you have no lungs."

If you are alive enough to hear the doctor, you are breathing, and you do have lungs. In the same way, if you are alive enough to be reading this and wondering, you are creative.

In fact, it goes even deeper than that. You're not just a person who has this characteristic called "creative" among your many other qualities, such as "affectionate" or "sensitive." Because it's *not* just a quality that you may or may not have.

What you think of as "you" is creativity itself.

Creativity! Prior to, and way beyond thought. And driving and dwarfing all those things we see as qualities.

Is it hard to accept? Hard to let in? The fact that creativity is who you are and all you are?

If you can see that people are noticing you are "affectionate" and "sensitive," well, maybe you can know it's because the spirit that is you is *creating* those things.

So don't let anyone tell you that you can't create. Especially don't let your inner voices tell you that.

When they say that, they are speaking to creativity itself! They are speaking into the very whirlwind their words claim is absent. They point out a lack of water in you while being drenched by your firehose. They are crying wolf at you! They are shouting "FIRE!" into your crowded theater. They are pissing into the wind. They are trying to nail Jell-O to the wall. They are trying to shovel mercury with a pitchfork.

They are saying you are not creative!

Forgive them! They know not what they do. They don't get who you are.

Every breath you breathe is an act of creation. Every thought you think. And you can take it from there. Expand it and express it. Paint it all on the ceiling of your cathedral and into the calendar of your life.

Or you can turn your back on it forever and call that adulthood.

But even if you do that, I know who you are, so I'll not call you by the name your parents chose for you and filed with the government. The name *I'll* use for you is creator. I hope you're uncomfortable with that. At least for a while.

Can you see the possibility here? Can you see that in relationship to all your wins, losses, situations, trials, celebrations and sorrows you are creator? That's who you are. That's what you are.

~ CREATOR

172

A quick peek behind the curtain

People who have near-death experiences come back to tell us that this whole universe is a beautiful field made up entirely of love. And it's one love . . . all just one love.

Bob Marley sang us the same message with the words, "One love, one heart, let's get together and feel alright." No wonder his songs had names like "Natural Mystic" and "Wake Up and Live."

Many others have had direct, experiential encounters with this energy field, even without the body's dying first. Some call it "God" or "The Great Spirit," and some said it was enlightenment or Nirvana. It has had many names—reflecting the powerlessness of human vocabularies to nail it down.

Some received their experience by way of devotional religious practices and others through years of deep meditation. But sometimes people got it by receiving some kind of whack upside the soul.

However people find it out, the experience is no longer just found in the writings of ancient sages and saints. It seems to be happening more often to "ordinary" people we can relate to, like Sydney Banks, Eckhart Tolle, Dicken Bettinger, Jean Klein, Ramana Maharshi, Byron Katie, Rupert Spira, Werner Erhard. . . The list of the "enlightened" few is rapidly becoming the "enlightened" many.

The near-death reports back from the other side are remarkably similar. People saw the light and then saw that we *are* the light. Their experiences seem to suggest that we are created by the Creator in the image of the Creator, and therefore we were born to create.

What if you and I, just average people having an average day, truly saw, moment to moment, that that was true?

What would be left to sing but "Hallelujah!"? (We could sing that with Handel or Leonard Cohen or everyone in between.)

It seems to be easier for people returning from physical death to wake up to the creative joy of life, but what about the rest of us? Do we just turn green with enlightenment envy? It's not that easy being green, feeling like we're in exile from that far off spiritual energy field. I can sure feel like that—I'm green with spiritual envy and in the dark out here, a million miles from the joyful in-crowd.

But to realize my creative power I have to let the feeling that I'm in the dark just pass through. I have to consider the possibility that I'm not all that separate and isolated from spiritual teachers, saints and gurus. Maybe that separation is just a story I've heard and bought into and, through repetition, converted into an entire felt sense of how the world is.

Me? The creative source itself?

Come on, let's get real.

The story of my separate, dull, egoic self disconnected from divine creativity gets continually supported by the collective belief system of the culture. It's approved continuously by acclamation and then fed back to us through the virtual reality of the media, the schools and the entertainment channels.

The truth is—rather, I should say, my experience tells me— that we non-saints see the light too. We all do. Sometimes it's just now and then, here and there, but divine light shines through and we see it.

But then most of us don't know what to make of it! We think it's just a momentary flash of happiness. Out of nowhere, a lucky, accidental moment worth treasuring. These are simply moments to remember! And just as we believe our own story of separation, we also think those flashing moments of joy and light are also separate. Contained. Isolated. Independent. Safely sealed off like a biohazard would be.

We don't even consider that that the flashing light we see might be trying to tell us something. In those moments when we feel something true or beautiful, the light of creativity might well be trying to peek through our web of beliefs to show us the source of everything . . . and to let us know that it's always there for us. And if that's so, then maybe creativity itself may be the very energy that words like "eternal" and "infinite" were made up to describe.

The light of creativity can appear in ordinary moments. It can happen when you're writing a note or listening to music or singing a song or laughing at your bad, little dog. For that brief, shining moment it can even feel like the old song that says, "When you're laughing, the sun comes shining through."

If enough of those moments were seen truly and clearly it would become obvious to you that the entire universe was set up to correct you from—and talk you out of—thinking and believing this single thought: "I am not creative."

~ CREATOR

173

You say you want a revelation

One of my flashes of light occurred while sitting in a circle of people in group therapy around thirty years ago. And this wasn't a little flash.

This was the sun.

I had joined the talk therapy group to receive support for something upsetting I was going through in my family. I thought the group could help me not feel so all alone with my trouble. And it did. It was a wonderful experience of togetherness, as in Bob Marley's "Let's get together and feel alright."

The trouble in my life revolved around my late wife, the mother of my children. She suffered from a dissociative disorder then called "multiple personality." None of us knew she had this condition until an incident occurred at a treatment center where she was attending a workshop on "codependency." The facilitators told me she broke down completely and demonstrated psychotic trauma and dangerous behavior, and if I waited a few days I might be able to visit her in the intensive care ward of the mental institution they had put her in.

This was a rather big "Say what?" for me and the four children. It was a shock to our lives and a deeply painful and terrifying experience for *her*. She spent the next year and a half in and out of the institution and in and out of therapy. The children and I were perpetually scared and worried. All the various personalities who were "not our mom" tried to interact with us and deal with the painful strangeness of it all. Sometimes she would disappear for days and none of us, including her, knew where she had been.

I wasn't sleeping. My sense of safety and well-being was gone. I still had my sobriety, thank God (I mean that), and those brave little children under my care, but I was a neurotic mess, and so I joined the therapy group.

As the months went by, I learned more and more from my wife's psychiatric doctors that she had been badly abused as a little girl and taken into a Satanic cult where the abuse intensified. They explained to me that the brain has the capacity to create subpersonalities when the primary personality suffers from memories that are unbearable. Those subpersonalities, or "alters," now live in separate realities with separate memory systems. So they will have no recollection of the abuse.

The problem comes in (and becomes an official "disorder") when the brain starts creating more and more personalities once it knows it can. Soon it's creating new "people" to deal with every little discomfort the other "people" can't handle.

I don't mean to make light of any of this or not acknowledge the pain that came with the confusion and chaos. Although sometimes, to save my sanity, I'd try to show humor . . . I said to a friend once that I kept the TV channel changer at my side, and if a difficult personality appeared I'd reach for it, point it her way, and start clicking.

(I get that that's not funny. You don't have to reach out to me on social media about it.)

But if the whole situation wasn't funny, it was certainly amazing. That began to really sink in for me. Especially after the year and a half of chaos and upset passed and she began to get better and better. (To hold inside a single created self.) I began to be able to reflect on the whole experience and what it might have revealed.

Because somehow, through her therapy and her own strong will to live and "heal," the disorderly aspect of the disorder faded away, and she was able to see the children on a part-time basis and they were able to get the mom back that they loved.

And one day, as I sat in my group therapy circle feeling love and gratitude for all these compassionate people who had helped me through these troubled times, I had a vision. It just descended out of nowhere as a silent voice that came inside my own voice as I looked out at the people in the circle who were looking back at me. My voice then said, "We are the multiple personalities of God."

Some of the people laughed and some looked startled, and I was trying to understand what I had just said to them. They wanted me to say more, and all I could say was that it was something I could just feel and see in that moment of love and gratitude for them, that it was *one spirit* simultaneously appearing as each of us, playing all the parts.

Most of them felt sorry for me. They didn't see what I was saying, and one older guy said, "You've had a rough go of it with this whole multiple personality thing so I can see why you have it on the brain right now. Get some rest. You'll be fine."

But I never forgot that moment.

And I never forgot the clarity of that vision. I've told almost no one about that day until now. And I never thought I'd be telling you or anyone else about it until the thing that happened two days ago happened.

~ CREATOR

174

It could happen to you

"Hide your heart from sight.
Lock your dreams at night.
It could happen to you."

(I hear Jo Stafford singing those words as I type.)

What happened to me two days ago was this: I was casually looking through *Scientific American* magazine to see if they had an article by a writer I like. When I found that they did, I looked at the article's headline and saw this:

"Could Multiple Personality Disorder Explain Life,
the Universe and Everything?"

I had to turn away from that headline and then look twice. Really?

Yes indeed. It did say that.

And it was an article by one of my favorite contemporary authors, Bernardo Kastrup. He was both a scientist and a philosopher, and his books about culture, neuroscience and consciousness had become my latest reading obsessions.

As I looked at that headline again, and the question it asked, I immediately thought back to the flash of vision I'd had decades ago in my therapy group. And that unexpected thing I saw and said: that we are the multiple personalities of God.

Kastrup and the article's co-authors, Adam Crabtree and

Edward F. Kelly, cited extensive studies of patients with this disorder (now called Dissociative Identity Disorder, or DID) in which functional brain scans are used to show that subpersonalities have their own separate areas in the brain—and are therefore not just "acting as if" they were different people.

Kastrup and his co-authors write:

> Although we may be at a loss to explain precisely how this creative process occurs (because it unfolds almost totally beyond the reach of self-reflective introspection) the clinical evidence nevertheless forces us to acknowledge something is happening that has important implications for our views about what is and is not possible in nature.

As disorienting and shocking an experience as it was in real life for me to be talking to different people occupying the same body, it might even be more amazing to look back dispassionately and realize the power of what the researchers call "this creative process."

The *Scientific American* writers conclude:

> We know empirically from DID that consciousness can give rise to many operationally distinct centers of concurrent experience, each with its own personality and sense of identity. Therefore, if something analogous to DID happens at a universal level, the one universal consciousness could, as a result, give rise to many alters with private inner lives like yours and ours. *As such, we may all be alters—dissociated personalities—of universal consciousness.*

Knock me over with a feather. *Scientific American* has just said, in their own way, that we're all the multiple personalities of God. They may call it "universal consciousness creating subpersonalities of itself," but I don't want to split hairs.

Whatever words we choose, it's becoming as clear to science as it has been for millennia to spiritual philosophers that divine, universal creativity is the source and substance of everything, including and especially who we think we are.

It gives me greater understanding of why my friend and life coach Steve Hardison used to ask me two questions, over and over in the course of our work together. When I described a problematic situation in my life, he would listen carefully and then say, "Okay, given that that's the situation, what would you like to create?"

Notice that it was not "How do you want to solve it?" As if the problem itself had all the power. As if the problem were a bomb we had to carefully disarm. He never saw the problem as having the power in the situation. He always saw creativity as having all the power. And together we didn't really have to "solve" anything. We didn't need to. What we created made the problems fade from all relevance.

And the second question he'd always ask me would appear whenever it didn't look like I could do some scary thing I needed to do. Instead of telling me what I needed to do, he would always ask me, "Who do you need to be?" Because he always knew, and I learned through practice, that I could create that being. I could create who I needed to be.

(It's all we ever do anyway.)

~ *CREATOR*

175

Who's doing the creating?

Most people I know who struggle with performing well in business or personal life think the answer lies somewhere inside the question of "Who am I?" They don't see that the real answer lies in the question, "What am I?"

Because when the answer to the "what" question arises as "pure, loving, creative energy," you only need to choose where you want to direct that.

If, however, as is the case for most people, you keep going to "Who am I?" you'll get lost in trying to decide how you should judge and label yourself today. Are you an introvert, a lazy person, a "3" on the enneagram, a Pisces, a coward, a detail person, a daydreamer, a fool, a . . . who in the hell?

You keep doing that and meanwhile the plant you wanted to grow dies. Your good work dies. What you want to create never gets created.

But only because you're looking in the wrong place. You're going personal with everything. Shrinking everything down to the ego. Where there's no light at all.

And why do you do that?

You do it because everyone else does it. We all do it because we have agreed that we are each very personal entities . . . and covered with labels.

Actually these mistaken identities may even start out as fun! It can feel like fun when we're gossiping, judging and labeling and praising and criticizing others and, eventually, ourselves. But if you're like me you will end up (in the words of the novelist John Barth) lost in the funhouse.

The alternative to being lost in the funhouse is to actually live as creativity itself. Divine, loving creative energy. The light. To be it. Not to try to figure out whether you are creative, or how creative you are, or to compare yourself to people who seem to be more creative than you, but to be it and live it. Knowing that it's what you are and all you are.

It's all anybody is.

There is no ranking system. No leaderboard.

When we're all swimming in the ocean, no one asks, "Who's more in the ocean?"

~ CREATOR

176

The light of time and attention

Once I was writing a book whose basic subject was fear. It was an unusual challenge for someone like me whose early life story seemed to have been jerked along by one act of cowardice after another.

So I called the most creative person I knew for advice. And, yes, I know we are all wellsprings of infinite creativity, but some of us have been able to create more beautifully and powerfully than others, for whatever reason. And my friend Fred Knipe was one of those people.

I'd had the great fortune and fun to write songs for a living for a number of years and the only reason that worked out was the fact that Fred was my co-writer. He also wrote many songs on his own, and he'd won Emmys for his TV screenwriting and made a good living as a comedian as well. No one in my life had such a great track record of converting his innate creativity into amazing creations for people to enjoy.

So getting his advice on how to write that book was an obvious move on my part.

I asked him, "What's the most important factor in making sure this book is all it can be? I really want this to be a great book. What's the one thing that will make it great?"

His answer surprised me.

I'd expected him to give me some kind of magical algorithm or secret sauce that only a creative genius would know about. I was prepared to take notes on it and ask him questions about it so that I wouldn't misunderstand the nuances of it. I wanted to learn this most important factor and apply it to my book.

So what was it? His simple answer was, "Time spent with the book."

What?

That sounded so simple and ordinary. Blue collar, even. Where was the magic in that? Where were the magical nuances I longed for?

I immediately thought about all those stories about creative flashes of genius arriving to artists, writers and inventors in mere seconds. Didn't Bob Dylan tell Ed Bradley that "Blowin' in the Wind" was written in a matter of minutes? Don't we all have infinite, loving creative energy at our fingertips?

But the longer I reflected on his answer, the more I saw it. We do have access to infinite creativity. All of us do. But when it comes to creating something big and exciting, there's more to it.

So Fred's advice—"time spent with the book"—hit me like a silver hammer and has stayed with me ever since.

I've since learned that most great creative work usually depends deeply on **time and attention**. And time and attention are usually overlooked. Nobody seems to realize that time and attention are the true secret sauces.

For creating anything.

Because even Dylan's song, which seemed to come so quickly, was preceded by the years of time and attention he gave to writing his earlier songs, and to the deep study of poetry, blues, popular ballads and folk music that he had done. Not just casually, but thoroughly and obsessively.

The artist Pablo Picasso is best known for the wildly unconventional paintings he did late in his life. We might assume he just opened his channel to the infinite and let the shapes and colors fly! And perhaps he did. But the younger Picasso also received great discipline and training from his father, and then later from the more traditional academies of art in which he trained.

When writing about Picasso in *The Zen of Creativity*, American Zen master John Daido Loori pointed out, "Originality is born of craftsmanship, skill and diligent practice, not from trying to stand out in a crowd."

So creativity is our infinite nature, and extraordinary creative works thrive on the gift of time and attention.

~ CREATOR

177

Just find your path

Personalizing my explanation for why I'm not creating what I want to create has always turned out to be the wrong way to go for me.

Anytime I collapsed into "What is it about me?" creativity would disappear.

That was my hardest lesson: learning that creativity isn't personal. The creative flow is not related to the ego. No matter how much the ego tries to get involved and take credit.

I also used to think I had to force creativity to happen. When I was writing song lyrics for a living I used to sit over my typewriter and bang my head with my fist, trying to force creativity.

It was only after I gave up, pushed my chair back, and heaved a big self-pitying sigh that the words would start to appear . . . they would appear like fireflies in the dark night . . . and soon I could begin to see them.

A friend recently asked me for help. She said, "I find myself switching back and forth between things and not really creating my career. Once I hit a snag I am tempted to stop or switch to something else. How did you solve this?"

I thought for a long time. Then it hit me. This isn't about some personal problem that has to be solved. It's more about a direction. In other words:

There is a path.

A path to the completion of what you want to create.

A new song? A freshly painted bedroom? The ability to play "Over the Rainbow" on the ukulele? The creation of a prosperous career? Whatever you want to create!

There is a path.

And when you're not on that path you're not creating, and when you are on the path you're making progress.

Sometimes I hit a snag and am tempted to leave the path for a while. Sometimes I do leave and walk down a side road.

But the path is always there. It waits for me. It has no judgment. It will wait days, months and even years for me.

You asked, "How did you solve this?"

There was nothing to solve. Because there was no real problem. There was only (but always) a path. A path you were not on. And the good news is that a path is not a problem.

It's something you're on or you're not.

If I see that I've left the path for too long to do something else, I can just go back to the path. If I want to create what the path leads to, I know to go back to the path.

~ CREATOR

178

How I block creativity's flow

The fastest way I block creativity from flowing through me and into the world is with a characteristic.

In the game of life, if I want to block my own creativity, I place a piece on the board called a characteristic. In other words, a label. For example, if I'm about to reach out to someone I want to do business with, I might put a piece on the board to block myself, saying, "INTROVERT to block."

That's because I think I'm an introvert. It's a label that means I'm inherently shy, so I don't reach out. The ability to reach out remains on the side of the game board. An option? Not a direct option, because I've blocked it with "INTROVERT." So far, anyway. Maybe I can do some more generalized marketing and advertising that my prospective client might accidentally see. Sure, it will cost a lot of money. And whether my prospect will even see it is a long shot.

I'm not able to see that I could have used another "option" piece: I could have created a conversation with the person. If I hadn't blocked it with a characteristic . . . some label I put on myself.

What's ironic and even amusing once I see it is that this permanent individual person, the player, me, made up of characteristics and labels, was a creation. It was made up. It was created so devotedly and thoroughly that it was made to look real.

The irony is that I used unlimited creativity to create a permanent identity that now limits creativity. Like the story of God dreaming up Satan. Like "the good book" filled with "good news" dreaming up the anti-Christ.

Today I have clients who have done the same thing as I did. They tell me what they are not good at. I ask them why they think they're not good at it, and they say, in effect, that it's simply because they're not good at it.

I pressed a business leader recently who'd just been promoted to his first leadership position about why he thought he wasn't good at leading meetings.

"I'm not wired that way," he said.

I asked him if he'd asked for help. Maybe there was someone in the company who he thought was good at leading meetings. Maybe they could help him learn.

He said, "I'm not good at asking for help."

Characteristic to block, characteristic to block. (Permanent self to imprison.)

Then I asked him if he spoke French.

"No."

"Why not?"

"Well, I don't speak French."

"Why do you think that is?"

He was puzzled. He said, "Well I don't speak French because I haven't taken the time to learn French and practice French."

Oh, good! Somewhere, deep down, he gets it. I was afraid he was going to say he was hardwired to speak English. But with something simple, impersonal and non-threatening like a language, he sees how it all works.

I asked him to consider the possibility that he was not good at leading meetings because, like French, he hasn't taken the time to learn and practice leading meetings. And the reason he thought he wasn't good at asking for help was simply because, over the years, he has not yet practiced asking for help.

The permanent, characteristic-bound personality he has created blocks the creation of new skills, new powers, new possibilities.

It does that for him, and it does that for all of us whenever we fall for the illusion of personal permanence.

Therefore, to reactivate our awareness of infinite creativity, we might want to replace every "I'm not good at" with "I have not given time and attention to the practice of that."

With that awareness, we can create almost anything.

~ CREATOR

179

How I flunked journaling class

So many people told me over the years that keeping a gratitude journal was a great and useful thing to do that I thought I needed to give it a try.

That was back in the day when I believed my happiness and sense of fulfillment were dependent on lots of stuff out there in the world, outside of me. Things! Things like cars, houses, musical instruments, books, sound systems, jobs, money, friends and lovers. Just to get started.

So the chase for accumulation was always on. My feelings of unhappiness and anxiety drove me to try to add more objects of desire. For most of them the pleasure charge didn't last, so they'd always have to be upgraded or replaced.

The continuous seeking became a dangerous, high-speed chase, because it seemed like I never could go fast enough and obtain enough things or relationships to make me feel at peace. I knew I needed more, and I always hoped that certainly someday, if I chased hard enough, I'd *have it.*

Therefore I was always looking for something that would help me go faster toward this eventual fulfillment. Any self-improvement trick or technique you might suggest would be worth a try.

One day a friend recommended I keep a gratitude journal.

When I questioned the practical value of that he sent me a quote from Deepak Chopra, who said, "Gratitude opens the door to . . . the power, the wisdom, the creativity of the universe."

Power, wisdom and creativity? Really? That would make it worth a try. Those three things would certainly help me get what I wanted faster. So I was in. I'd see if keeping this journal would give my mission for acquisition a measurable boost.

So I began to keep a gratitude journal. I would wake up in the morning and list the things I was grateful for. It was hard to think of things at first, but I finally was able to find things to put on my list. As the days went by, I wasn't noticing any increases in power, wisdom and creativity, but I was willing to hang in there. Maybe it would take a while.

But then something discouraging began to happen. As the weeks went by I noticed that my gratitude list was getting smaller! That was weird. Was this supposed to happen?

Some of the people I'd had on the list had let me down so I took them off. The car I'd been listing was falling apart so it came off. My sound system didn't work right any more so it came off the list, too. My family didn't appreciate me at a gathering I went to so I took the lot of them off. One day both of my dogs wouldn't stop barking so they came off the list.

The smaller my list got, the more useless the whole thing felt.

So I stopped keeping the journal. I even threw the little notebook itself away so I wouldn't have to see it and have it remind me of the latest failed project.

Looking back from this vantage point now, I can see what my problem was. I was only trying to find gratitude for *things*. They were all things that come and go. And even when they seemed to stay, their ability to "make me happy" always wore down. So they went off the list. How can you be grateful for something that no longer makes you happy?

If you had asked me back then why the things on my list were not making me happy I would have said, "Because they're not enough!"

So what, then, did I actually want? Back then I might have said, "I want it all."

Even though I had no idea what that meant. But it sounded like it would do the trick. It sounded like a bold mission. And I noticed that people were often admired for raising a fist and saying, "I want it all!"

Salespeople and self-improvement marketers seemed to love people who said that. They encouraged that goal and said things like, "Yeah, baby, say yes to your badass self! We're gonna help you go out there and crush it! You deserve to have it all!"

I tried to get myself to believe my badass self deserved to have it all, but it was never something I could take seriously.

Today I see many badass people keeping gratitude journals that contain the same kinds of lists of shiny objects that I tried to accumulate. They list all the people, places and things they hope someday will reach critical mass, that final tipping point that replaces "I'm not enough" with "Now I have it all."

If these people are anything like I was, their journals have the wrong stuff in them. Yes, it's unfairly judgmental to use the word "wrong." But it's in the same spirit that I would tell you that your flashlight had the wrong kind of battery in it and that's why it gives no light.

What should I put in my journal?

If you want it to give light, why not look to the source of all creativity and put *that* in your gratitude journal. Instead of all those outside things that have already been created by others.

And if you really opened up to that source, you probably

wouldn't need a whole journal for it. You could use a post-it note or a drink coaster at the bar. You could just write the word "consciousness," and there's your whole gratitude list right there.

But who would really do that? Who would wake up and put "consciousness" as the only thing in their gratitude journal? Who today even puts it in as *one* of the things? If we could seize and read all the gratitude journals being kept in the world today we probably wouldn't find it listed anywhere. Too bad we don't yet have Gratitude Police to do that.

Who among the keepers of journals realizes at the deepest level of appreciation that without consciousness there would be nothing, not even their little journal? No journal and certainly nothing to put in it.

But if that were to change for you and me?

What if consciousness itself were deeply appreciated first thing each day? What if that overwhelming feeling of gratitude had us waking up and "falling in love with awareness," as the spiritual philosopher Greg Goode puts it?

I bet that would have us hearing the words differently when Deepak Chopra says, "Gratitude opens the door to . . . the power, the wisdom, the creativity of the universe." My guess is that Chopra himself, when recommending gratitude, was not referring to the little material things we are putting into our gratitude journals. As his book *You Are the Universe* suggests, we can go bigger than that.

Once my primary gratitude at the deepest level of the heart became gratitude for life itself and the conscious awareness that is behind it all, it no longer became necessary to use a journal to jump-start that feeling.

But there's a big "however" here. An important counterpoint. Because even though it helped me make a point to say that most people put the "wrong" stuff in their journals, I do know many people who keep these kinds of journals and benefit greatly from them. It helps them develop their feeling and expression of gratitude.

As those feelings grow through cultivation, they find themselves adding more and more things to the journal. Even formerly inconsequential and problematic things start to get added. Even people they see as difficult people start to get added to the journal!

These kinds of journal-keepers are different than I was. They see more than I did. Their hearts are more open than mine was. Their judgments fall away, and their appreciation for impermanence and the transparency of things grows each day. Soon their journals are open to including everything. Everything they are conscious of.

That's when they see that they no longer need to "want it all." Because as one look at their gratitude list tells them—they already have it all.

~ CREATOR

180

Every breath we drew was Hallelujah

Even though creative energy is who we are and always there, it's difficult for adults in this culture to give it expression. Certainly not like we did as children.

The same creativity we had as children is still there, ready to sing out, or build out, or dance out, but our ego's worries and fears about survival have boarded up the process.

Like putting boards on our windows and doors that ended up with keeping the hurricane *inside.*

But as we saw, there are those who do allow creativity to break through and channel out. Those people create great things, and we can take inspiration from them.

One of my many inspirations is obviously Leonard Cohen. He has lit me up since I first heard Judy Collins sing his song "Suzanne" decades ago. People are most familiar with his famous song, "Hallelujah." It has been recorded by over a hundred different artists, and it keeps appearing in movies and on TV series and was even a big musical moment in the Olympics when K.D. Lang sang it in the closing ceremony. Few songs have ever had that kind of widespread impact.

One might wonder what kind of dramatic visitation Leonard Cohen's muse must have made. Some stormy night with flashes of light and inspiration coming in through the bedroom curtains making him sit bolt upright in bed groping frantically for his paper and pen.

Actually it didn't happen that way. That song took Cohen two years to write. He had written more than eighty finished verses to it before he selected the final few.

So much for the myth that a creative masterpiece has to happen in a single *flash* of inspiration downloaded from infinite intelligence into a single human unit's brain. Of course that happens sometimes. And the myth might even be accurate about the source. But if what I'm pointing to here is true, that creativity is *always* there for you, then there's no reason why it can't also flow in gently, during the day . . . Moderately but always reliably for those who've learned to open to it.

And not just open to it. But also willing to participate in its arrival.

It doesn't have to be a special esoteric welcoming ceremony. It can be a blue-collar project. It can appear as a craft or a task or a random act of kindness.

Cohen's workmanlike process for writing songs like "Hallelujah" offered its own form of inspiration to me! I don't have to write the perfect verse or be exceptional in every moment. He wrote eighty verses! Wow. That's blue collar taken to the glorious.

I'll tell myself to put on my famous blue work shirt and get moving.

Natalie Goldberg, Zen teacher of creative writing, had some memorable advice for writers that might be something all of us can use, whether we are writers or not.

Her advice was, "Keep your hands moving."

That's it? Yes it is, yet it's usually the last thing I remember to do.

When I own up to my immobile hands, not only do I remember my grandmother singing in the kitchen and telling me "busy hands are happy hands," but I also start to realize that the actual *doing* of creative things really isn't the problem for me. *Thinking about* doing those things is the only thing in my way. It's always harder to do things ahead of time in my mind than it is right now in the real world.

~ *CREATOR*

181

Money in her guitar case

My old habits of thought continue to produce the dread and worry that whatever I create won't *compare* well. Not realizing that none of that is important. Comparing is gratuitous. It's a random act of unkindness to myself.

But what if what I create inspires? Who cares about comparison then?

I was inspired by a street singer the other day. I put money in her guitar case and came away glowing with inspiration. She got to me. She sang, "I Will Always Love You."

Did I think, "She doesn't compare to Whitney Houston." No. And the way she sang from the heart, in the moment, I would bet that she wasn't comparing either.

I have a friend who is part of a small mastermind group I meet with quarterly. We all share ideas and experiences and strength and hope about our profession. My friend is a powerful, successful consultant, speaker and author who changes lives with her work on a daily basis. We are inspired by her.

But she compares.

There are people in the group she compares herself to and she begins feeling a little sad and discouraged. Her creativity starts to go into hiding.

She doesn't see yet that when it comes to knowing you are

creating a life of profound service to others (which she is), there's no comparison. No need for it. No sense to it. And those rare (but increasing) times when she's in touch with who she really is? Her face lights up. She knows herself as love and beauty and the divine energy of creativity. And inside that *knowing* there is no possibility of comparison.

But creating to serve others is just one aspect of creating. And not even a necessary one for creativity to bestow its gifts upon you. The more you inhabit your creative energy the more you receive the benefits of creating. You can't keep it from getting better and better. And creating can be wonderful even when it doesn't touch or inspire anyone other than you. Don't trust this to be true. You'll know this by testing it. You won't have to try to believe some belief about it based on nothing.

The more good feelings you experience in creation, the more it will occur to you that joyful expression is what the human system was designed to do. It's set up to do that. All ready to go. The natural you will actually proceed to do that.

Unless you mess with it.

Unless you tinker with the natural process and put stuff into it that doesn't belong there. Extraneous stuff like beliefs of limitation and feelings of permanent personal shortcomings. For full-on celebratory expression of creativity you'll want to investigate those beliefs and feelings and send them back into the emptiness from which they came.

Walt Whitman wrote:

I celebrate myself, and sing myself,
And what I assume you shall assume,
For every atom belonging to me as good
  belongs to you.

And clearly he wasn't singing and celebrating some belief-bound, isolated entity called "Walt Whitman." His flow of creative poetry and joyful living came from being awake to, and participating in, a much higher, more inclusive "self"—one whose "every atom" is shared by you, and shared by me.

In 1888 Whitman gave an interview to a college newspaper in New Jersey. They asked him for his advice to young writers, and he told them, among other workaday things, to carry a notebook everywhere and engage in writing like it was a long-term work project.

"Whack away at everything pertaining to literary life," he said. "The mechanical part as well as the rest."

Today, if I'm stuck with what I'm creating, I'll look down at the notebook I now carry everywhere and turn to the page where I've written Natalie Goldberg's words:

"Keep your hands moving."

~ CREATOR

182

Just show up for work how about?

But it's not just about writing. Creativity wants to play everywhere. Especially in our day-to-day work. My own work as a business and life coach is an example.

Today I have been doing my consulting work with a young man whose website says he's a "success coach." That means if you want to succeed at something you're not succeeding at, you hire him and he'll help you succeed.

He tells me how badly he is struggling. His wife wants him to go back to work in the big corporation he left (because he hated it) because she worries about the fact that he's not getting many clients and not making much income.

I always used to think the idea of an unsuccessful success coach was funny.

But there's some pain in there, too. Actually a lot of it, I'm noticing. I've decided to give him a scholarship to a school I run. He is almost too grateful. He says that for him, it's "the last house on the block."

So he'll be attending my practice-building school for coaches and consultants. He won't feel so alone anymore. He'll meet a lot of coaches who don't understand why they aren't financially successful yet as coaches, why they haven't "created abundance" in their profession.

Usually the answer to that question is very simple. And the solution to the problem isn't mysterious or even very difficult to bring about. The solution reminds me of Leonard Cohen's blue-collar approach to his songwriting craft.

Just as in the arts there is a myth about creativity arriving in huge, unplanned flashes, in coaching there is a myth that says creating a prosperous practice requires flashes of extraordinary personal courage, that succeeding as a coach takes massive amounts of bravado, self-esteem and bold action. You have to jump waaaay out of your comfort zone every week, dream big and hold your breath and holy freaking GO FOR IT!

Okay . . . but why?

What other profession requires that? If you were to tell a friend that you've chosen to be a certified public accountant would your friend say to you, "Wow! Really? OMG, I hope you have the courage!!!"

Of course not, so why is that necessary with coaching? (Almost every starting coach thinks it is.) Especially when the truth is that coaching is an honorable and useful profession in our society today. That's why it is growing so fast. Each year there are more and more coaches making more and more well-earned money. That doesn't happen if the profession is not useful and legit.

So why all the heart-pounding courage being called upon?

Why do people approach it at the coaching pep rallies like it's some huge, IMPOSSIBLE dream that you have to dig down deep into your soul to make manifest?

I have known of new coaches who start their panicky day with meridian tapping for abundance, deep yogic bellows-breathing for elevated mental states, aroma therapy for valor, and petitionary prayers to the supernatural so that they might be blessed with the exceptional, extraordinary powers they will need to make this impossible dream job work.

Hey, just slow down. See if you can get a hold of yourself.

Do you need to scare yourself to make this profession work out financially? Why would that be true?

My experience says it's not true at all. The coaches I've seen succeed just relax and do their jobs. They do the doable. They learn the simple systems used by other successful coaches. They show up for work each day, just like other people do, and they practice their profession, just like an accountant or a lawyer would do.

Or a tinker or a tailor or a soldier would do.

They are okay feeling like average people having an average day making an average amount of progress each day toward professional strength and prosperity.

Rather than taking a daring leap, they just settle in. From there, the good career gets *created*.

The system is that simple: settle in.

Just like you see the pilot on your commercial airline flight settling in prior to the flight. He or she smiles at you, settles in, shares some easy conversation with the attendants and the co-pilot and then goes through the routine instrument check.

The pilot doesn't walk through the jetway hyperventilating, fingering rosary beads and yelling, "Oh My Dear Lord, I hope I'm up to this! God help me and my family!"

At least we hope not.

So why does the coaching profession seem to require that approach—a superhuman victory over the insurmountable?

Maybe it's because this profession often draws inspiration from motivational speakers and authors who tell inspiring stories of humans who achieve things against all odds. My own books and talks often focus on amazing transformations that people make.

Coaches are drawn to this kind of thing, which is great until they start to believe their own profession requires the same kind of unusual and amazing achievements.

Becoming a well-paid professional coach simply doesn't require that.

When a new coach believes that success in this field demands some kind of bravery and extreme daring they have a hard time getting their career off the ground. In fact, they have a hard time looking forward to the next day's work.

How could you consistently look forward to a day of you trying to overcome your fears?

Soon there's no enthusiasm in that coach's day. And that leads to low energy and dwindling access to creativity. Coaches in this mindset soon start telling me that they have a feeling that they're "hiding out."

Hiding out? No . . . not a good activity. What if the airline pilot we were talking about did that? The flight attendant running down the aisle asking everyone, "Have you seen our pilot?" Not a situation you hope for if you're a passenger.

The lack of enthusiasm that leads to hiding out soon leads to all kinds of problems like procrastination, poor business decisions, low productivity and all the dysfunctions that come with not being able to create what you want.

So how about we just set that whole depressing cycle aside and do this profession like any other? We'll just do blue-collar work, maybe carry a notebook everywhere, learn the mechanics of the profession and have fun whacking away at it.

Maybe we can even be okay working from *inside* our comfort zone, doing what's *doable*, and being happy with having a very enjoyable, average day.

From there you can serve a lot of people well. It works for me and all the successful success coaches I know and work with.

There's a quiet power inside that approach.

And it's from that relaxed, enjoyable, doable experience of my workday that the most creative ideas arise.

~ *CREATOR*

183

Who have you created?

My work in the world of corporate training took off when I created a course that taught employees various thinking tools that were designed to inspire them to take personal responsibility for their own spirit and morale.

Obviously companies liked that training because anything that improved morale ultimately benefitted productivity, performance and the bottom line. When people are upbeat they are more innovative, more collaborative and more energetic.

What companies didn't know was that what inspired me to create the course was my own study of the work of the spiritual teachers Alan Watts, Yogananda and Krishnamurti, and the philosophy of Colin Wilson. Reading and listening to their works deepened a "spiritual awakening" that occurred for me during my recovery from alcoholism (about which I've written more extensively in my cheerfully-titled book, *Death Wish*).

The corporate course I taught was about the power we have to create who we are—at least at the social level, where we create what we call "personality." I talked about creating how you're going to show up in the world. I talked about Shakespeare's stage.

Shakespeare's character Jacques in *As You Like It* says,

"All the world's a stage,
And all the men and women merely Players;

They have their exits and their entrances . . ."

If they didn't resonate with Shakespeare, I'd remind them of Elvis Presley's hit song "Are You Lonesome Tonight?" It has a spoken part in the middle of the song that begins with Elvis saying, "Someone said the world's a stage, and you must play a part . . ."

So the idea has been out there!

We are all playing a part. Which means there is nothing inevitable or permanent about "who we are being." Remember when you were little kids at play and yelling out, "I'll be Batman, you're Robin!"

Most people would agree that when we're in community theater or at a Halloween party we play parts. They'd even concede that they've done some serious play-acting pretending to be themselves when they're trying to impress someone or get something. I remember doing a great impression of a grateful, sincere, apologetic boy while being scolded and disciplined by my father or a schoolteacher.

People relate to and accept that kind of play-acting. But they also assume that they're just putting that act *on top of* who they really are. The real, true personality—who they think they are when they think they're being "authentic."

And the people who took my courses would usually take it on that level. They learned new ways of being like they were acting "as if." So they learned the benefits of acting and speaking "as if" they were owners of their own spirit and morale instead of victims of other people and circumstances. It worked for them. They felt better. They got along with people better. And by communicating in ways that took more responsibility for their own lives and happiness, they were able to see better relationships emerge in the workplace.

They also learned, in those courses, about the research work of positive psychology and especially the books on optimism by Dr. Martin Seligman, who has demonstrated that optimism and pessimism are not permanent personality characteristics. Optimism was proven to be a skill that could be developed over time with practice and study and insight.

Sharing the news of that research sealed the deal. People in my courses couldn't argue with it. It wasn't just a theory. So they became excited about changing themselves for the better. They were able to see that the changes would be a benefit to them personally and not just some new training the company wanted them to take to benefit the company's bottom line.

Excited by the widespread success of that training, I wrote a book version of the course, and I called it *Reinventing Yourself*. The book went on to become a bestseller and just recently the publisher put out a "20th Anniversary" revised edition that for some reason left out the book's most important quote:

> Why are you unhappy?
> Because 99.9 percent
> Of everything you think
> And of everything you do,
> Is for yourself—
> And there isn't one.
>
> ~ Wei Wu Wei

That quote, when I first saw it, almost knocked me over. It expressed my own deep spiritual realization (for lack of a better term) that happened during addiction recovery. The wakeup call went something like this: As far as who you are, it's all a creation. Even your seemingly "authentic" personality, the one you think you're improving or adding play-acting on top of—that first personality, the real you, was just made up.

Talk about basic creativity!

Now I don't mean that at the level of spirit and soul, at the level of God-given awareness and *being*, some individual human called me created that. I'm referring to what Alan Watts called our "skin-encapsulated ego." That ego with a birth certificate with a random name on it (a name some partially drunk parent might have chuckled about)—that's what I'm referring to. That's made up.

We make the permanence of that person's identity up. Then we believe our own story about ourselves. And that story, like any lie repeated enough times or believed deeply enough, sooner or later feels really true. No question. Right down to the depths of our understanding of the word "true."

You see this guy? This guy's in love with his story. Pull the string coming out of his back and he'll say, "This is what I'm like."

This kind of capacity the brain has to believe stories that are not true is how and why certain people who are "skilled" at this can beat lie detector tests. To them, what they are saying is not a lie.

That's how they beat the test.

But here's the problem with talking or writing about this kind of spiritual awakening or neurological insight: people will think you are crazytown.

So in my course I had to make a concession to that, to the prevailing beliefs of the culture and society that we are all permanent, disconnected, individual personalities with permanent traits and characteristics. I had to have it be okay with me that most people thought they were only learning to be more creative about how they showed up in the world to their families and co-workers and leaders. I rationalized it by thinking it would be a good start. And in a sense, it really was, so I have no regrets.

Deep down I wanted them to get it at a more spiritual level. Sometimes I even said things in front of the room like, ". . . and one of the reasons you *have* this ability to reinvent yourself is that you invented yourself to begin with. You just didn't realize it."

Hmmm . . . Puzzled looks. Sometimes occasional smiles. But never mind you guys, back to work, on to strategies and communication systems! Self-improvement!

I'm not assuming you'll take my word for any of this "you are made up" stuff being true. I mean, it can't be true yet if it's not true for you. I'm just taking the risk of relating my own experience with it and justifying that by pointing out how it has influenced my understanding of the nature and power of creativity.

There are wiser and braver people than I am who write and teach exclusively about this kind of spiritual awakening. I urge you to read them and discover for yourself how exciting and real the awakenings can be.

I certainly don't recommend the path I took. There was blind luck that had to occur. Even for me to be alive today. The path took me from bottomed-out alcoholism and addiction, bankruptcy and divorce into a program of spiritual recovery. The realization that I was not just my ego gave me the strange and beautiful feeling that the mystic Catholic philosopher G.K. Chesterton called "absurd good news."

Part of that good news is that no matter what level you look at this, from a game-of-life practical level all the way up to crazytown spiritual, this much is true: you get to create who you want to be, on this playing field, in this game of life, and there isn't anyone out there who can stop you.   *~ CREATOR*

184

Conversation becomes co-creation

My professional life these days consists of conversations. People call me, or visit me, and we talk.

Someone once asked Steve Hardison just how this coaching thing would work. They expected to hear an answer filled with complexity and depth, but what Steve said was, "You talk and I listen. Then I talk and you listen."

That's the process, for sure. And I admired Steve for giving the answer Lao-Tse might have given. But he (knowingly) left out the best part of what really happens. He had to leave it out because words don't reach it. He left out what gets created.

What gets created is an insightful breakthrough that has us see life differently and then live life differently. This breakthrough arises in the field of creative listening.

When you drop out of the equation and can now listen openly to a person from a wide-open place beyond personal concerns and judgments of them, from beyond the ego, then real understanding shows up. And with more understanding, more compassion.

Soon you're seeing ways to create a relationship based on this wide-open listening. Inspired ideas. They always come from beyond. Beyond the thought-bound ego. Beyond the personal.

The ego never creates anything.

Its job is to worry about lack of creation . . . and to find out how to personalize that lack. So it has a heartless job, the performance of which does us no good whatsoever.

But my own experience is that creativity comes from beyond the ego, even if the ego is what told me to sit down to solve something. Creativity itself comes from beyond the ego, or the contracted "me" made up of personal thoughts, psychic wounds, fears and desperate desires.

So I want to allow all of that to drop out when I'm listening. I want my agenda to disappear.

I've learned a great deal about listening in the past year through my work with Dr. Mark Howard, a psychologist who assisted me in understanding how clients can receive the greatest benefits from a coaching conversation.

The new practice for me was learning to listen without myself being in the picture. So if I took a photo of you and me in our session when we looked at the picture later I wouldn't be in it. Ideally.

You can't photograph true listening.

And without the ego there to obstruct everything, creative impulses, little flashes of light, appear. They appear because they don't have to work their way through the thought-cluster of fear-based judgments.

They just appear.

Maybe that's why when I heard my children playing with other children (when they were young and had under-developed egos) I'd so often hear them yell out excitedly, "Hey! I've got an idea!"

I've spent many hours inside companies and other organizations and I've never heard an adult yell that out.

~ *CREATOR*

185

It's more than making things

Not all creating involves making something. Even though we usually think of it that way. We think things like, "What's the next *thing* I want to create?"

That question is almost always asking what one should produce, or manufacture, or string together so it can be added to a world that didn't have it before.

So we think of creating a new blog, or a sand castle on the beach, or a big meal with experimental recipes or a quilt or a painting or a new business or a rap musical based on the life of one of the founding fathers. Things created that weren't here before. Things added to life.

But creativity is more versatile and powerful than just that.

Because it can take away as well as add.

When I remove clutter from my room and clean the desk and windows I have *created* a freshly re-organized and clean workspace. When I take books and clothing and furniture to the Salvation Army I've *created* space in the home for a better life.

And if I realized I was *creating* during those activities I'd be having a much better time. Instead, I often fall victim to the culture's story that those activities are dull and tedious. Not available for enjoyment. No joy to be taken from something you have to get *through*.

Michelangelo notwithstanding. (Michelangelo created beautiful statues by carving away and taking away marble from a large slab of stone.)

Ralph Waldo Emerson said, "As the gardener, by severe pruning, forces the sap of the tree into one or two vigorous limbs, so should you stop off your miscellaneous activity and concentrate your force on one or a few points."

Why should you do that?

Because more creative light and power is now available for the few points really important to you! So the pruning is a great idea. Look at the dying branches the gardener took away from the tree. Doesn't the tree look healthier and more beautiful?

When you creatively prune your office desk does it not appear to be more clean and beautiful? And the stuff you hauled out of the house to Salvation Army—didn't it open up and beautify your home? You are creating beauty.

We don't glamorize severe pruning. We don't even want to talk much about it. Even though upon further review it's seen to be profoundly creative. So is organizing and cleaning. By doing those creative activities we produce new beauty.

Hall of Fame basketball star Kobe Bryant tells young college players that the path to success in sports lies in being willing to "edit your life!" By *editing* he means to delete and remove all the short-term temptations and distractions pulling you away from your long-term objective—the career you want to create. Editing is his word for pruning.

After two years of working on "Hallelujah," Leonard Cohen still had an unfinished song that had eighty trial verses. Now it was time for the real creativity: editing and pruning.

My friend Dusan Djukich helps small business owners create more productive businesses. When he sits down with a new client to review the current problematic state of their life and business he asks an important question:

"What are you tolerating?"

In that moment, Dusan is his own version of Michelangelo. He's looking for what problematic thing can be cut away from his client's cluttered life. They will work together to edit and prune those things out of existence. That will create the life the client wants.

Most of us miss out on using this vital form of creativity by labeling it incorrectly. It's not drudgery until we say it is. Pruning, editing and deleting are acts of creativity that we can look forward to with as much good feeling as we get when we're "making something."

Average people like you and I can thrill to subtracting as much as we do to adding. We can start doing this ourselves, no matter how "not creative" we think we are. We don't have to leave all this subtractive power in the hands of Michelangelo and Dusan Djukich. We don't have to believe that they have "access" to powers we don't have access to. They don't.

Society has a condescending view of this form of creative expression because of its narrow belief of what is creative. It has blinders to creativity. There aren't great media tributes to people whose very job titles have become terms of disparagement, like "cleaning ladies," "garbage men" or "exterminators." They just take stuff away!

We don't see that they create beauty by what they know to take away. But when we do, it can open many aspects of our own lives to acts of creativity.

~ CREATOR

186

I can always just breathe in

If people create best when they are inspired, then I want to breathe in, which is what inspiration actually means, and feel how inspired I feel when I hear a song whose lyrics delight me, like Leonard Cohen's when he sings (or Judy Collins sings or Roberta Flack sings) his song, "Hey, That's No Way to Say Goodbye":

> I loved you in the morning,
> our kisses deep and warm
> Your hair upon the pillow,
> like a sleepy golden storm

As I'm breathing in the first two lines of that song, I want to read them again. And then listen to them again.

But were you to ask me to carefully analyze why or how the song delights me (because maybe you want to be able to write like that, and so you want to understand the underlying process behind it) my words would just be, after a long silence, "Your hair upon the pillow, like a sleepy golden storm."

Because what else could I say?

Fortunately for me, as I look to inspiration to wake me up to the creativity I already am, I *can* find something else to say to your question about that song lyric, and where the poetry might come from. The clue would be from Cohen himself in his novel

Beautiful Losers. Because in there I find this: "God is alive. Magic is afoot."

I'm not following you.

Okay, I'm saying maybe that's *how* he wrote it. You're looking for a "how," right? A process to learn? What if his process was simply knowing that "God is alive. Magic is afoot."

Can you say more about that?

Cohen can say more about that, not I. In the book he goes on. After he writes "God is alive. Magic is afoot." He follows it with, "Alive is afoot. Magic never died."

Oh.

He goes on like that. It's spellbinding actually. He goes on and on. Read the full chapter, the full passage. You can find it online. You can read it to yourself as an incantation. Buffy Sainte Marie turned it into a song, a strange, native-people's mystical drone of a song. A spell. It will take you places. Leave you spellbound. The whole passage is the closest thing I've ever seen to a poetic confirmation of creativity's source. And such an inspiration:

God is alive; Magic is afoot
God is afoot; Magic is alive
Alive is afoot . . . Magic never died . . .
This I mean to whisper to my mind
This I mean to laugh with in my mind
This I mean my mind to serve 'til
Service is but Magic, moving through the world
And mind itself is Magic coursing through the flesh
And flesh itself is Magic dancing on a clock
And time itself, the Magic length of God

~ Leonard Cohen

Is this the kind of inspiration you have to get hooked by before you before you create something?

No. It's not a requirement. I used to think it was—that you have to be inspired in order to create. But that turns out to be untrue. You can create any time. And why would that be? I'm just guessing it's because whether you're feeling inspired or not, God is alive and magic is always afoot.

So you don't need inspiration to begin creating what you want to create. You can just get to work. But that doesn't mean you can't also be a big fan of inspiration and enjoy finding it.

I'm inspired by acts of creation that are amazingly beautiful and moving. And I keep noticing that they are timeless. They don't have to be trendy or up to date. Brenda Ueland's inspiring book was written in 1938, and the poet who most inspired her, William Blake, was born in 1757! He famously wrote:

To see a World in a Grain of Sand
And a Heaven in a Wild Flower,
Hold *Infinity* in the palm of your hand
And Eternity in an hour.

Wow. And if I can risk being crude in the face of such beautiful writing, he nails it. Right there. That's what it is to fully know you are Creator. It's to see what the poem sees and to hold what the poet holds . . . to hold infinity in the palm of your hand and eternity in an hour. That's it. He knew. He saw.

~ CREATOR

Courage

187

Death is like the rose

I was sitting in Byron Katie's nine-day school and we were about to go on a field trip to conduct some very brave experiments. Many of us, including me, were scared. As we were about to board the buses Katie said to all three hundred of us, "Remember, the worst thing that could happen to you is a thought."

I burst out laughing! It wasn't the first time I laughed or cried in that school. But the laughs were always joyful and the crying was sweet and grateful. Like crying at a wedding. Finally experiencing the marriage of mind and spirit.

Of life and death.

I'd been listening to Katie for a few years prior to the school on audio recordings played in my car as I drove around or in my headphones as I drifted off to sleep at night. She said one night, as I was falling into a dream state, that if she were to throw me out of an airplane without a parachute the worst thing that could happen to me all the way down was a thought. I slept well that night.

Our fear of death is staggering. Sometimes I think if we could simply erase *that* fear, everything would be okay.

Death even causes us to fear how our bodies change as they get older. We judge the body's changes to be a bad thing. Yet the rose I bought you fades and dies beautifully. You save it, even. You thumbtack it above our bed. It is dry now, and even what some might call dead. But it looks so beautiful and natural.

All form changes. All pain comes from fear of that. Fearless is the rose that fades and dries and falls from the wall, beautiful all the way down.

Some say that *all* fear is fear of death. But why do we fear death? Do we fear sleep? Deep, peaceful dreamless sleep? Where does the world go when I disappear into dreamless sleep? Why am I not anxious about going to sleep and losing everything there? After all, a day is ending . . . a day that is always my life in microcosm. Asleep now, I am happily "dead to the world," and feeling no hint of trouble as I lie fearless beneath the faded red rose pinned above the head of the bed.

You have done a good thing by putting the rose up to die so beautifully right before our eyes.

~ Fearless

188

Our life will never end

To understand the elimination of fear from my life, I must appreciate the role of thought. Because every feeling—especially fear—begins with a thought. And every thought causes a feeling. Nothing else can cause a feeling. Let me give you a very gentle example to begin with. Then we'll crank it up later.

In most of the world, and in Michigan where I grew up, rain was a metaphor for sadness and pain. Our whole society seemed to regard it this way. Into every life a little rain must fall. George and Martha have a "stormy" relationship. Rain is sorrow.

But sunshine! Sunshine is good . . . rain bad, sun good . . . you are the sunshine of my life. Things going badly? Don't worry. Here comes the sun! And it's all right.

The secret to bad and good and love and fear is reflected in our views of rain. How we interpret the rain. In Arizona, for example, we don't think the rain is so bad because weather itself is not a concept that we are overly familiar with. When clouds appear, we start feeling romantic. When we watch a movie mystery set in rainy, foggy London town, we wish we were there.

Driving to Tucson recently the romance of the rain did not let us down. The winds blew across the desert, and as we looked out toward the Catalina Mountains black clouds crackled with thunder and lightning. Rain fell. We smiled and walked slowly from our car to go meet our friends Fred and Lynette.

Fred is Fred Knipe—someone I met in Tucson at college in 1964. Later the two of us wrote songs together for a living for a number of years. Three of our songs had the word "rain" in the title. ("Rain on Me," "Rain Forest" and "Melinda Rain.") In each of those songs, the element of rain was a positive *romantic* element. Most songwriters write songs wherein the rain is a negative thing: "Stormy Weather," "Baby, The Rain Must Fall" and "I Made It Through the Rain" are examples.

But it's all perception. Every feeling in life is! Perceive something one way and you are terrified. Perceive it another way, and you are happy. You yourself get to write the perception. Always in life, *you* get to compose the song.

Consider the eerie power of Jim Morrison singing "Riders on the Storm." ("The world on you depends / Our life will never end.") You hear rain behind the opening cascading keyboards as Morrison sings of the storm and how it brings out the dark side of humanity, a killer on the road; his brain is "squirming like a toad."

But without his interpretation, the rain means nothing.

I actually saw a little toad come out of the desert last night. I wasn't thinking like Morrison at the time, so I decided it was good. The toad hopped across my path and enjoyed moving along the rain-slick patio tiles at the resort. He had suction-cups for feet. I smiled at the sight of him. Rain is a thought that is welcome here. All sad things can be beautiful when the mind is right. Fear is washed away in the blink of an eye. In the turning of a thought, fear is washed away.

~ Fearless

189

Be proud of your days as a junkie

A man we'll say is named Duke raised his hand in a seminar and said, "I've been a self-help junkie most of my life—Napoleon Hill, Tony Robbins, Wayne Dyer, the works. My friends and family mocked me. When is it going to be enough? I am doing well in my life now, but I wonder if they have a point."

I'd gotten to know Duke quite well prior to this seminar, and I could identify with him. Ever since a friend of mine showed me Napoleon Hill's *The Master Key to Riches* in 1984, I myself have been hooked.

But why do I say hooked? And why did Duke use the word junkie? And why are motivational speakers and self-help authors sometimes distastefully mocked by the media, Hollywood and the arts?

Why does anyone do anything distasteful? Fear. Fear is at the bottom of all dysfunctional, unfriendly behavior. If you were not afraid you would not behave that way. If you didn't feel threatened, you'd be relaxed and kind. But only always.

Fear of self-help is like the fear felt by the out-of-shape person, threatened by the condition of his own body. The out-of-shape person asking his in-shape friend, "Why do you have to work out so much?"

We only fear what we don't understand.

If you, too, are a "self-help" junkie, I do understand you. And please do not think poorly of yourself. You are an unusually brave and self-responsible person. Should you be mocked for constantly exploring your own potential? Is that really a negative thing? Or just something another person doesn't understand.

Most devoted readers of personal growth material are far better off because of it. Ask yourself what your life would be like today if you had *not* delved into self-exploration and self-improvement.

How would your body be today if you had never, ever exercised? It's the same question.

Because your mind benefits from exercise and stretching just as your body does. How many people do it with their minds, though? Not many. It's a powerful, creative thing to do, but not many do it. Most people don't realize how powerful it is. They went to school, and they think that should be enough.

What did they really learn at school about their minds? At best, they learned to deploy their brains as recording devices, playing back information at exam time.

But the best personal growth books and audio programs ask more than that. They ask you to consider changing everything! They ask that you attempt rigorous self-honesty and learn to grow. Personally. On your own time. In the face of your deepest fears. For no reason other than it will grow you. Not to please or manipulate anyone else.

It's not easy.

But this I know is true: self-help saved my life.

I mean that literally and truly. I was just self-destructively *lost* before I found it. I found Napoleon Hill, Earl Nightingale and Norman Vincent Peale ... all those old guys who said you could take back your mind and rise above conditioning and create a positive, fearless career in the face of negative mobs of people who are begging you to join them as victims of circumstance. The Fraternal Order of the Disappointed.

I had just gotten sober, and I thought, what now? Yes it's wonderful to be clean and sober, but what about all these debts and no good employment history and no visible skills? And who am I to turn to? I had no idea how to be a self-responsible, successful . . . much less prosperous . . . adult.

And then self-help appeared. To save the day. To save my life.

Duke (my seminar attendee) said that prior to first reading *The Road Less Traveled* his own life was about pleasing his boss for eight hours then fearing he wouldn't please his family when he got home, an endless cycle of nervous anticipation. Always wondering what would win their approval. Anticipating their moods. Putting his head on their laps like a golden retriever would, looking up with sad doggy eyes to see if everything was okay. There, there, Duke, good dog. Good boy.

But sometimes, of course, it would be, "Bad dog!" and Duke's heart would race and he would jump back, and his spine would curve in anticipation of a good swat. That swat didn't hurt so much physically as it was just heartbreaking. All that trying-to-please out the window with one good verbal swat. That's the fate of those whose mission is to impress others.

The seeker in you seeks higher ground than that.

~ *Fearless*

190

It's time to break my mind

I went to a 12-step meeting the other day to spiritualize my mind. In the meeting, a man with fifteen years of sobriety said that life still sometimes gave him problems. He said, "Even though the monkey's off my back, the circus is still in town." I looked at him and smiled. I thought about the song "Paper Moon" after he said that. In that song there's a line about this circus of a world we live in that says, "It's a Barnum and Bailey world, just as phony as it can be."

I'll be doing a lot of business traveling throughout this Barnum and Bailey world in the coming weeks. The circus is definitely in town. Because look how fear shows up unexpectedly, riding in on the back of the elephant. Look how fear causes me to lie.

First the fear, then the lie. Because I feel a little like I'm doing a Tour de France, I think about a bike race I read about called the Vuelta a Espana. The American cyclist Tyler Hamilton tried so hard to explain how someone else's blood had found its way into his veins during that bike race in 2004. (He was apparently cheating with transfusions.) First fear, then the lie: Hamilton argued that he was a chimera—someone with two types of blood, the result of having shared his mother's womb with a vanished twin.

Wow. I compare that one to all the lies I've told and I really feel dull and unimaginative. So I'm saying it isn't the cheating itself that fascinates us so much as do the amazing stories and explanations. Fear results from the belief that you're going to lose something. That you might even lose the Vuelta a Espana!

To stop that mental two-step—first the fear, then the lie—I had to learn to break the pattern. In a way, to break my mind.

George Hamilton IV had a song back in the 50s that I always liked, called "Break My Mind". It was also later sung by Linda Ronstadt and more than twenty other recording artists. I love it because it captures the image of how we freeze ourselves with our scary beliefs. Those beliefs crystallize and the mind becomes like a sheet of ice.

I remember growing up in Michigan and after a freezing rain you could lift sheets of ice, about the size of record album covers, up from the sidewalk. They were translucent and crystalline. You would hold them in wonder, then fling them against a Maple tree and shatter them. That's how our minds get! Our minds are like ice when we freeze with fear. Like a picture frame full of ice. Frozen. I can feel it.

That's when I know I need to break my mind.

Music can break my mind because the vibrations are so powerful. They shake my nerves and they rattle my brain. How marvelous to get untracked this way. What a glorious wake-up call to clarity. Break my mind! Soon I'm thinking of this lyric by the Grateful Dead: "The bus came by and I got on, that's when it all began. There was Cowboy Neal at the wheel of the bus to Never-ever-land."

The song was called "The Other One," and that Neal at the wheel was Neal Cassady, whom Allen Ginsburg called the secret hero of his poems and who inspired *On The Road* by Jack

Kerouac. Kerouac and Cassady were drunks who had "Creative Writers" as their cover stories. Because writing takes such discipline (to access the subconscious, creative mind), most writers would rather drink than write because it seems to work faster. Have a few drinks and you feel creative. Now they can hang out with other "writers" who drink and hope they are *living* their unwritten novels.

I tried that approach myself! Why not just get drunk and LIVE your novel?!? Seemed easier. But it never delivered. Laziness turns out to be hell itself. The lazy mind must be broken.

My best mind break occurred when I went into a recovery program and found out there were three things in life, not just two. I found out that there was more to life than just the mind and the body. There was also spirit. Beautiful, fearless spirit.

~ Fearless

191

All our fears are optical illusions

A *fata morgana* (Italian translation of Morgan Le Fay, the fairy shape-shifting half sister of King Arthur) is a mirage. It's an optical illusion that results from temperature inversion.

Objects on the horizon (follow this, please, as it relates to everything out there on the horizon known as your future, your fear) . . . objects like ships, cliffs, islands and icebergs look distorted, elongated and elevated.

The mind does that, too. It inverts itself, making life's circumstances look distorted, elongated and elevated. Because all my fears are optical illusions. Therefore, all my trials will soon be over.

Follow this: warm air drifts in over cold air close to the cold ground. The interface of warm and cold creates a kind of refracting lens that inverts images and displays these shimmering fata morgana. Shifting shapes! Fears!

Fata morgana are usually seen in the morning after a cold night. After a cold dark night of the soul. Soon heat has radiated into a cold space and for men at sea it's as if they had taken acid.

Just as hot tempers flow over the cold ground of fear. Anxiety for the morrow sets into your day. And the next thing you know you think you are being tormented by the shape-shifting half sister of King Arthur. You think she is against you.

But in truth? In absolute reality? She loves you more than you know. And more than you *can* know.

~ Fearless

192

The secret is that you are a sculptor

Sometimes the secret of life comes down to bold, creative moves. In the mind and in the world. And maybe a truly fearless life doesn't take a lot of accumulated wisdom.

It might simply be reflected in what Southwest Airlines' brilliant founder Herb Kelleher used to say: "Yes, we have a 'strategic plan.' It's called 'doing things.'"

I loved what the famous sculptor Henry Moore said about this subject to the poet Donald Hall in Hall's book, *Life Work*. Hall had asked Moore—now that Moore had just turned 80—what the secret of life was.

Moore said, "The secret of life is to have a task, something you devote your entire life to, something you bring everything to, every minute of the day for your whole life. And the most important thing is—it must be something you cannot possibly do!"

Moore's task was to be the greatest sculptor who ever lived, and to know it.

Most people would think that was a bit obsessive. Most people would scoff at that kind of goal. But I must be different than most people. Because when I came to that part of Hall's book, I was lit up for days! I loved it! Because whenever I read something bold like that I suddenly know what I want to do with my life, too.

Courage inspires . . . even the courage of a fearless, impossible vision.

I'm not going to say what my task is, because, for me, talking about it takes energy away from the actual doing of it. Suffice it to say that I am doing it right now.

~ Fearless

Afterword

It's now or never!

People often ask, after they've found out I've written or co-written more than thirty books, "How did you become so prolific?" and my answer is always slow in coming, because I certainly don't see myself that way.

That might be because the books don't just flow out as fast as I can write them down. In fact, there have been many times when I've decided at the end of a book that "That's my last book. I don't have much more to say."

And then, as I'm working with my coaching clients and new ideas pop up about how people can change even faster and in even more long-lasting ways, I'll wake up with a new idea for a book, and I'm off to the races writing it. That all seems to be happening on its own, with no over-arching master plan or goal to be an author of many books.

Also, I learned long ago not to think of a whole book while writing. Most of my chapters are short and self-contained, so I'm only really just doing my next short chapter each day I'm writing, not trying to "write a book." What stops so many people I work with who think they have a book in them that they'll "someday write" is that they are always thinking about the whole book, and that becomes intimidating.

Early in my journey as a seminar leader and coach I learned to follow the great basketball coach John Wooden's motto to "Make each day your masterpiece" and stay centered in the day I'm living.

In the past, when I was struggling, I was always straining to get into my own future. I always thought happiness and success must exist in the future somewhere, once I'd achieved enough. Therefore my days (and my self-concept!) were experienced as "not enough." My idea of *now* was always negative. It was a place I had to get out of.

Books, like those by Eckhart Tolle, and being coached by great, enlightened and centered coaches led me back to the beauty and eternal possibility of the now, this present moment right here. It's where every good thing in life gets created.

This came to be true for everything, not just books. Relationships, careers, mental, physical and spiritual well-being all find their origin in the now. It's now or never. Like Elvis used to sing, "It's now or never, come hold me tight."

If I stay here in the here and now, I will be held by the same inner wisdom and creativity we are given at birth. As Yogananda says, "The wave is the same as the ocean, though it is not the whole ocean. So each wave of creation is a part of the eternal Ocean of Spirit." And he also says, "Live quietly in the moment and see the beauty of all before you. The future will take care of itself . . ."

This book you've just finished is meant to be the writing that reflects the best of the coaching I have received, and the concepts in my work that have been most useful to others over the years.

That's where all the writing comes from.

But when people ask me what my best book has been, in my opinion it is one that is not included at all here. Because it was pure fiction . . . a detective mystery called *The Woman Who Attracted Money*. I decided to write it one day just for fun, and just to see if I could do it. It turned out to be my best book, and that says very little about me, but it says a lot about the creative function of having fun.

It was good to experience that, because it's something I try to teach. When we are having fun we are accessing our best energy and the most innovative use of the brain. And fun can only occur in the now.

I've learned so much from reading books. A lot of people have told me, "You won't find it in books," but I have found it in books, so I don't know what they are talking about. However! Books only get me halfway there. What I do with what I got, and how I apply and use and practice what I got, is what gets me all the way there.

My favorite observation by Werner Erhard is this one: "Power doesn't come from knowledge. What people know doesn't make them powerful. It's being present to what you're dealing with that gives you power."

My experience is that the biggest obstacle to being fully present is my ego, my personality and the illusion of being an isolated separate self "lost and afraid in a world I never made." That ego is what wants to get into the future. It talks to me this way: "You haven't made it yet" and "One day you'll arrive to where you want to be" and "Be careful, because if you rest into present moment awareness you'll be falling behind."

In my spiritual recovery program from alcohol, we learned to be serene and relax into the present moment in the meetings.

Some of us learned, for the first time, to really listen to other people, and experience the expanded sense of connection to everyone in the room. We left our egos at the door. When I am singing in church with all the other parishioners I wonder at the rarity of this uplifted feeling of spirit. Why is it so uplifting?

We left our egos at the door. We're not singing a hymn called "How Great I Am."

We are in harmony with being itself. So it was hard for me to write an introduction and an afterword to my own writing without seeming to have it be about how great I am.

So I'll end with an observation that often gets labeled as my personality's so admirable "humility." I insist on assuring you it's not that. It's not a personality trait of mine, it's truth: there's nothing I do that you can't do, and there's nothing I write that you can't write.

Also, there's nothing you have read in this book that originates with me. Everything has been passed down through me from people who have mentored, taught and coached me. Even those beings whose physical bodies are long since gone, through their books and the books about them, they have mentored, taught and coached me. They are the ones we should be thanking right now. I am merely the instrument through which their music plays on these pages.

Acknowledgments

To the many people who have made all these writings possible:

Steve Hardison
Kathy Eimers Chandler
Maurice Bassett
Chris Nelson
Fred Knipe
Dr. Nathaniel Branden
Tom Rompel
Jinendra Jain
Dicken Bettinger
Mark Howard
Francis Lucille
Michael Neill

and

The wonderful grads from the
Coaching Prosperity School (ACS)

About the Author

Steve Chandler is the author of more than thirty books including the bestsellers *Time Warrior*, *How to Get Clients*, *Reinventing Yourself*, *The Prosperous Coach* (with Rich Litvin) and *100 Ways to Motivate Yourself*.

He is the founder and primary teacher at the internationally celebrated Coaching Prosperity School. He has degrees from The University of Arizona in English and Political Science, a degree in Russian from the Defense Language Institute, and an honorary degree from The University of Santa Monica in Spiritual Psychology.

He currently lives in Michigan with his wife Kathy and two canine companions, Jimmy and Hastings. He can be reached at SteveChandler.com.

Selections for
The Very Best of Steve Chandler
were drawn from the following titles:

Additional titles by Steve Chandler include:

Steve Chandler Coaching Prosperity School

Steve's world-acclaimed ACS (Advanced Client Systems) is now available as an online masterclass at a tenth of the cost of the original program.

Check out all the features and content of the *Steve Chandler Coaching Prosperity School* on Steve's website, www.stevechandler.com

- Learn to convert your coaching skills into prosperity.
- Hear our powerful guest teachers share their insights and secrets to getting clients and creating a financially thriving practice.
- You'll learn from Steve Chandler and great coaches like Rich Litvin, Carolyn Freyer-Jones, Michael Neill, Karen Davis, Ron Wilder and many more . . . all graduates of the Coaching Prosperity School.

- Over 30 full video lessons and more than 50 short video tips, plus bonus audio programs to build your coaching practice.

"This man has changed—and continues to change—my life! One of the reasons that I am the coach I am today is because of his wisdom and leadership.

"Seeing him model masterful coaching and transformational living and practice building through the Coaching Prosperity School program was one of the most insightful and empowering experiences of my life.

"If you are a coach who is committed to greatness in building your practice without internet marketing tactics or having to have a huge mailing list or Twitter followers, AND get the results from yourself that are required to truly be prosperous, being a part of Steve Chandler's new program may be the greatest investment you ever make in yourself."

~ **Jason Goldberg,** master coach and author of *Prison Break*

GO HERE to learn more:

www.stevechandler.com

A handsome, tall, thin fellow approached me.

He was dressed in a tweed jacket, khaki trousers, wore brown loafers and carried a cane.

"You look pretty depressed, pal," he said with a smile as he sat down beside me. "Anything I can do for you?" he asked.

Then he introduced himself.

"I'm Jack Kennedy. What is your name?"

This fortunate encounter sparked almost two decades of friendship between John F. Kennedy and the author, John G. W. Mahanna.

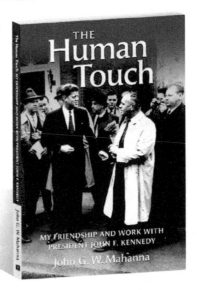

Available from Amazon, Barnes & Noble and other bookstores.

The Human Touch is Mahanna's unique memoir, which shows Kennedy as a genuine friend, and which also reveals the savvy inner workings of JFK's political campaigns. Readers will gain a fresh perspective of JFK by seeing him through a friend's eyes, and experiencing his "human touch" — his unbounded charisma, humor, and warmth.

A full-color, coffee-table style photo album of 67 previously unpublished and seldom-seen photos of Jackie Kennedy from her childhood and teen years.

There must be hundreds of thousands of photos of Jackie Kennedy (1929-1994), our much-loved First Lady, either with or without President John F. Kennedy, but what you are about to experience in *Early Jackie* is strikingly different from the well-known and classic Jackie photos. These are the "lost" photos of Jackie from when she was known—prior to marriage—by the name of "Jackie Bouvier."

Jackie Kennedy lovers everywhere will delight in owning this remarkable, full-color photo album!

MAURICE BASSETT

Publisher's Catalogue

The Mahatma Gandhi Library

#1 Towards Non-Violent Politics

* * *

The Prosperous Series

#1 The Prosperous Coach: Increase Income and Impact for You and Your Clients (Steve Chandler and Rich Litvin)

#2 The Prosperous Hip Hop Producer: My Beat-Making Journey from My Grandma's Patio to a Six-Figure Business (Curtiss King)

#3 The Prosperous Hotelier (David Lund)

* * *

Devon Bandison

Fatherhood Is Leadership: Your Playbook for Success, Self-Leadership, and a Richer Life

Michael Bassoff

RelationShift: Revolutionary Fundraising (Steve Chandler and Michael Bassoff)

Roy G. Biv

1921: A Celebration of Toned 1921 Peace Dollars as Numismatic Art

Dancing on Antique Toning: A Further Celebration of Numismatic Art

Dancing on Rainbows: A Celebration of Numismatic Art

Early Jack: The "Lost" Photos of John F. Kennedy

Early Jackie: The "Lost" Photos of Jackie Bouvier

Sir Fairfax L. Cartwright

The Mystic Rose from the Garden of the King

Steve Chandler

37 Ways to BOOST Your Coaching Practice: PLUS: the 17 Lies That Hold Coaches Back and the Truth That Sets Them Free

50 Ways to Create Great Relationships

Crazy Good: A Book of CHOICES

CREATOR

Death Wish: The Path through Addiction to a Glorious Life

Fearless: Creating the Courage to Change the Things You Can

How to Get Clients: New Pathways to Coaching Prosperity

The Prosperous Coach: Increase Income and Impact for You and Your Clients (The Prosperous Series #1) (Steve Chandler and Rich Litvin)

RelationShift: Revolutionary Fundraising (Steve Chandler and Michael Bassoff)

RIGHT NOW: Mastering the Beauty of the Present Moment

Shift Your Mind Shift The World (Revised Edition)

Time Warrior: How to defeat procrastination, people-pleasing, self-doubt, over-commitment, broken promises and chaos

The Very Best of Steve Chandler

Wealth Warrior: The Personal Prosperity Revolution

Kazimierz Dąbrowski

Positive Disintegration

Dale Dauten

Experiments Never Fail: A Guide for the Bored, Unappreciated or Underpaid

Charles Dickens

A Christmas Carol: A Special Full-Color, Fully-Illustrated Edition

Anthony Drago

Go Prove Something!

Melissa Ford

Living Service: The Journey of a Prosperous Coach

M. K. Gandhi

Towards Non-Violent Politics (The Mahatma Gandhi Library #1)

James F. Gesualdi

Excellence Beyond Compliance: Enhancing Animal Welfare through the Constructive Use of the Animal Welfare Act

Janice Goldman

Let's Talk About Money: The Girlfriends' Guide to Protecting Her ASSets

Sylvia Hall

This Is Real Life: Love Notes to Wake You Up

Christy Harden

Guided by Your Own Stars: Connect with the Inner Voice and Discover Your Dreams

I ♥ Raw: A How-To Guide for Reconnecting to Yourself and the

Earth through Plant-Based Living

Curtiss King

The Prosperous Hip Hop Producer: My Beat-Making Journey from My Grandma's Patio to a Six-Figure Business (The Prosperous Series #2)

David Lindsay

A Blade for Sale: The Adventures of Monsieur de Mailly

Rich Litvin

The Prosperous Coach: Increase Income and Impact for You and Your Clients (The Prosperous Series #1) (Steve Chandler and Rich Litvin)

David Lund

The Prosperous Hotelier (The Prosperous Series #3)

John G. W. Mahanna

The Human Touch: My Friendship and Work with President John F. Kennedy

Abraham H. Maslow

Abraham H. Maslow: A Comprehensive Bibliography

The Aims of Education (audio)

The B-language Workshop (audio)

Being Abraham Maslow (DVD)

The Eupsychian Ethic (audio)

The Farther Reaches of Human Nature (audio)

Maslow and Self-Actualization (DVD)

Maslow on Management (audiobook)

Personality and Growth: A Humanistic Psychologist in the

Notes

Notes

Notes

Notes

Notes

Notes

Notes

Notes

Notes

Made in the USA
Middletown, DE
17 July 2022

69572912R00285